"Neil Ducoff is one of the 'good guys' in business. He helps people understand business and leadership all over the world. He shares his experiences and he puts his practices to work in his books, speeches, his company and his life. *No-Compromise Leadership* is more than a great read, it's what true leadership is all about."
— Jack Stack, CEO, SRC Holding Corp; author, *The Great Game of Business* and *A Stake in the Outcome*; Springfield, MO

"Don't blame the competition, the economy or your employees for holding your business back. The real culprit is compromise at the leadership level. *No-Compromise Leadership* is a wake-up call for leaders of companies large and small, and an antidote to the mediocrity that afflicts so many of them. Neil Ducoff provides a step-by-step road map to becoming a leader capable of building the kind of organization that everyone dreams of having. Once you absorb the lessons in this extraordinary book, 'no compromise' will become your watchword and your company's battle cry."
— Bo Burlingham, editor at large, *INC.* magazine; author, *Small Giants: Companies that Choose to be Great Instead of Big*; Berkeley, CA.

"In the multitude of business books available through the years, *No-Compromise Leadership* stands out for its clarity and usefulness. If I could only have five business books on my shelf, this would be one of them. After 15 years at Southwest Airlines and 35 years of working with other high-performance teams, I have seen Neil's four business outcomes and BIG 8 drivers at work among the highest achievers. No-compromise leadership is the difference between high performance and mediocrity. And, you get a smattering of Neilisms as a bonus. You will want all your people to read, execute and live the no-compromise mantra."
— Terry "Moose" Millard, former Southwest Airlines pilot and expert on corporate culture; Henderson, NV.

"Having collaborated with Neil for over a decade, I know him to be a man of rare integrity, visionary leadership and in-the-trenches practice. His *No-Compromise Leadership* book is the game-changing business manifesto for our times — and nothing less than a paradigm reset. If you're ready to take your business to the next level, buy and apply the genius principles within this book."

– **Matthew Cross,** president, LeadershipAlliance.com; author, *The Hoshin Success Compass*; Stamford, CT

"Neil Ducoff has a special gift that allows him to analyze a business's needs, then communicate the necessary business knowledge to entrepreneurs effortlessly in order to solve their challenges with manageable systems and solutions. *No-Compromise Leadership* truly makes the difference between success and failure for entrepreneurs. *NCL* is a non-negotiable must-read."

– **Paula Kent Meehan,** founder, Redken Laboratories and Kenquest; Beverly Hills, CA

"Complacency is the true killer of business growth and opportunities for its employees. Neil has written a blueprint on exactly how not to accept 'good enough.' *No-Compromise Leadership* is not a book about what you want to hear, but what you need to hear."

– **John R. DiJulius III,** author, *What's The Secret: To Providing a World-Class Customer Experience*; Cleveland, OH

"Finally, a book that puts the leader on notice that he or she has to stop looking the other way. Leadership is taking action and no compromise is the key to success in today's high-speed, high-change environment. Neil masterfully breaks down the key areas of business that demand no compromise and then describes, only as Neil can, how to make *No-Compromise Leadership* a part of your lifestyle and culture."

– **John Harms,** president/founder, Harms Software Inc.; Boonton, NJ

"Imagine yourself on a mountain trail coming to two paths — one leading you higher to the pinnacle, the other taking you back to where you started. The easy decline offers you excuses, compromises and the psychological pain of not seeing a higher view of yourself and your team. The other path looks up to places you've only dreamed of, the trip and the treasures unknown. Where is the map that will help you go higher? It's in your hands. You're holding Neil Ducoff's higher standards of leadership and thinking map. *No-Compromise Leadership* shows you each step up this challenging mountain; more importantly, it offers you the alternative to excuses and the psychological pride in refusing to compromise again. Read this book today, rather than tomorrow, and you'll be at the peak a day earlier."
– **Dr. Lewis Losoncy,** author, *The Motivating Team Leader*; Melbourne, FL

"Are your influence and leadership on compromised and shaky ground? Do people know where you stand? You can't just hang out somewhere in the middle with your standards, your morals, or your approach. Let Neil's *No-Compromise Leadership* book and his message help you determine the role you play as a leader in your world today."
– **Winn Claybaugh,** dean and co-founder, Paul Mitchell Schools; author, *Be Nice (or Else!)*; Laguna Beach, CA

"If your sales and profitability are not where you want them, if your customers are not raving fans, if your employees are not fully engaged and highly evangelistic about you and your company… you are seeing the effects of your compromise. And Neil's book is going to give you a no-compromise wake-up call. Here's the good news. After Neil gets you to see how your compromising is the source of the majority of your critical problems, he shows you how to clean up your act with a set of simple, clear processes that will change how you think about your business — and will change your leadership thinking and behavior forever."
– **Jim Horan,** president, The One Page Business Plan Company; author, *The One Page Business Plan*; Berkeley, CA

"Once again, Neil Ducoff gets it right with *No-Compromise Leadership*. One can only wonder if there is any effective leadership style besides no compromise. Every leader should ask themselves how often are they are confronted with these artificial trade-offs that only have the appearance of logic and end up taking away the space that is needed for leaders to exercise initiative. These compromises come in many forms, the most frequent being, 'we can achieve the sales target but price needs to come down,' or its opposite, 'we can achieve this profit target but sales will take a hit.' The list is endless. There is no truth to this appearance of compromised logic; we must fight complacency within our organizations and perform better than our competitors. We must promote creative thinking; get everyone to think outside of the box and get out of their comfort zones to the place where innovation happens. Enjoy the reading!"
– **Dominique Conseil,** president, Aveda Corporation; Blaine, MN.

"At a time when nothing less than breakthrough business activities will do, *No-Compromise Leadership* comes as a gift from the torch carrier of no-compromise leadership practices for entrepreneurs everywhere. Balance sheets may deliver vital signs, but people are the true measure of leadership, and here Neil leads without fault."
– **Sam Brocato,** founder, Brocato Products; owner, Sam Brocato Salon NYC; author, *Beautiful Business;* New York, NY

"Thank you for bringing no-compromise leadership to Taiwan. Your teaching and profound insights are universally applicable. And now you wrote the book on it. *No-Compromise Leadership* is the future for entrepreneurial leaders to create the right no-compromise cultures, not just in the United States, but around the world."
– **Ping Chu,** president, Canmeng International; Taipei, Taiwan

"If your values demand excellence of yourself and you want the best for your company and team, read, learn and live this book. If you are satisfied with status quo — buy a different book."
– **Peter J. Wright,** FACHE, COO, Littleton Regional Hospital; Littleton, NH

"In *No-Compromise Leadership*, Neil has culled the best of business principles, fundamental human philosophy, and his own insights into an inspiring and useful blend of principles. Leaders will read this book and emerge with renewed vitality and a deeper understanding of what's important in business and in their own lives."
– **Kenneth M. Lankin,** MD, MBA, MPH, president, Dr. Lankin's Specialty Foods, LLC; Groton, CT

"As a business owner and leader in my company, I often think of Neil and his approach to leadership. His time spent over the last 12 years inspiring and lifting me up to be a no-compromise business owner has allowed my company to be launched, grow and soar. Read Neil's book for the compelling philosophies and how-tos contained within."
– **Jill Kohler,** president, Kohler Academy; Scottsdale, AZ

"Whenever Neil puts pen to paper, he stirs up the fire in my thinking. I have to stop and re-examine my beliefs, decisions and directions for my business. *No-Compromise Leadership* sheds a fresh, new perspective on how businesses, small and large, need to operate in today's challenging environments. And it's written by a guy who has been in the trenches, made his share of mistakes, but learned from all of them to come up with this book. It's more than just another business philosophy — it's a practical, 'this is what you gotta do!' plan to move your business forward, because status quo means failure!"
– **Brian Mulcahy,** owner/innkeeper, Rabbit Hill Inn; Lower Waterford, VT

"Leadership lies not only in knowing what is right, but why — then having the courage to instruct, inspire and reinforce the behaviors that create a powerful and successful adventure. In every way, Neil Ducoff lives the *No-Compromise Leadership* business model that he teaches with such unrelenting passion. And now, he delivers his experience and strong guidance in one powerful book, a leadership model to which all great business minds aspire."
– **Douglas A. Cox,** director, Team Member Communications, Seminole Gaming of Florida; Hollywood, FL

"At first I thought, who needs another book on leadership? Just a few pages in and I knew this book was miles above the rest. Neil makes becoming a no-compromise leader easy. So much so, I have adopted the no-compromise concept into all I do. This book clarifies leadership thinking and raises the bar — while maintaining compassion for those we lead. Hats off to you, Neil. I want the first case of books for my family."
– **Geno Stampora,** Stampora Consulting, Inc.; Purcellville, VA

"Neil Ducoff is a genuine original thinker. His highly creative and effective approach to *No-Compromise Leadership* soars over the best-of-the-best and is a must-read for every executive and those who aspire to become one."
– **James K. Ahlquist,** managing director, SRI Inc.; Danville, CA

"Business leaders are created not born! Neil's concept of no-compromise leadership is a must know. His *No-Compromise Leadership* book provides you with the step-by-step guide to cultivate your own leadership skills, to stop being in control and start taking control."
– **Maria Keiser,** president, The Entrepreneur Circle; Manchester, CT

"Neil long ago attuned to what the world of business was calling for and has stayed true to his calling with no compromise. He has responded to the opportunities business has presented by remaining mindful of the obligation to give back. The opportunity/obligation cycle is sourced in Neil's depth of caring. In *No-Compromise Leadership*, Neil is masterful in creating the distinctions that create the clarity of thinking that is core to the success and sustainability of business today."
– **Debra Neill Baker,** CEO (aka Chief Energy Officer), Neill Corp.; Hammond, LA

"This book defines *No-Compromise Leadership* as only Neil Ducoff can. After reading this book, you'll understand just how much higher the leadership bar goes and how to get there."
– **Daryl Jenkins,** business coach and trainer, Queen Creek, AZ

"Neil gave literal meaning to the inspiring message 'break a leg' when lecturing, fell off the stage and did exactly that! Despite this, in his 'no-compromise leadership' style and in excruciating pain, finished the lecture and dazzled the audience. Well, he's done it again — this time in print! *No-Compromise Leadership* is a sure roadmap how to avoid bad breaks by inspiring and leading your team. With this book, those who haven't had the pleasure of hearing Neil speak can finally learn his message."
– **Howard Hafetz,** CEO, Raylon Corporation; Reading, PA

"Neil Ducoff's *No-Compromise Leadership* is a must-read for every business owner/manager who cares deeply and passionately about the success and well-being of their enterprise. More than just a book, *No-Compromise Leadership* is the Bible of 'business being.' Read it, use it and keep it by your side always."
– **Andrew Finkelstein,** salon/spa marketing guru and founder, The Beauty Resource; New York, NY

"Truly inspiring… the right questions with the right answers and, more importantly, fun to read. Neil's *No-Compromise Leadership* book is truly a must-read for anyone in business."
– **Sergi Moiset,** founder and CEO, I-Tasc; Girona, Spain

"Neil Ducoff's concept of no-compromise leadership places emphasis on the responsibilities of leadership, and does so at a time when the norm is for leaders to focus too much on their rights and privileges. If you are a leader who is truly looking to leave the world a better place than you found it, and understand the time-honored phrase, 'From those much has been given, much will be expected,' you will find Neil's book confirming and powerful in its simplicity. And for the leader who clings to the rights and privileges of his leadership position, you may find just the jolt you need. The great news is that the improved business results and improved lives of your employees who drive those results will confirm your efforts."
– **Bill Fotsch,** head coach, The Great Game of Business; Springfield, MO

NO-COMPROMISE LEADERSHIP®

A HIGHER STANDARD OF LEADERSHIP THINKING AND BEHAVIOR

Published by Strategies

40 Main Street, Suite 7

Centerbrook, Connecticut 06409

www.strategies.com

For orders other than individual consumers, Strategies grants discounts on purchases of 10 or more copies of single titles for bulk use, special markets or premium use. For further details, contact:
Strategies
40 Main Street, Suite 7, Centerbrook, CT 06409
tel (800) 417-4848

Cover design and page layout by Cameron Taylor

Cover photograph by Mitchell Funk/The Image Bank

Book set in Adobe Jenson Pro

Library of Congress Control Number: 2013949961
Ducoff, Neil.
No-Compromise Leadership: A Higher Standard of Leadership
Thinking and Behavior / Neil Ducoff. – 1st ed.
316p. | 23.5cm.
ISBN 978-0-9848620-3-0
1. Business Management.   2. Leadership.   3. Entrepreneurship.
4. Creative Thinking.   I. Title.
First Strategies Press Edition
10 9 8 7 6 5 4 3 2
Printed in the United States of America

NO-COMPROMISE LEADERSHIP®

A HIGHER STANDARD OF LEADERSHIP THINKING AND BEHAVIOR

BY NEIL DUCOFF

neil@strategies.com
strategies.com

CENTERBROOK • CONNECTICUT

For my wife, Joanne. Through all the years, all the ups and downs, you always believed in me. To my son, Eric, the joy of my life who plays the guitar blues like no one else; his wife, Krista; and the two most amazing grandchildren in the world, Lillian and Wesley.

Acknowledgements

As with any book on leadership and business, there are individuals who influenced and played a role in the development, the content and eventual publishing of *No-Compromise Leadership*. First and foremost, I thank Dr. Lew Losoncy for not only being a friend, but for being on that flight from Edmonton to Chicago. You instantly got what this book was about and introduced me to your publisher. For my new publisher and friend at DC Press, Dennis McClellan, thank you for believing in me and *No-Compromise Leadership*. To Mara Dresner, the only true no-compromise editor I've ever worked with. You helped set the bar for this book and I'll be forever grateful. To my trusted and valued graphic designer, Cameron Taylor, together we created a cover worthy of the title of this book. To my wife, Joanne, for supporting me through the rough spots. To my son, Eric, for believing in me when I needed it most. To Laura Crandall for reviewing, editing and offering inspiration. To John Harms for your incredible feedback, recommendations and exuberance for the book. John, I loved those 3:00 am emails. To Jack Stack for being a friend and mentor. To Bo Burlingham, who kept asking where the book was. To Matthew Cross for taking me through that initial Hoshin Mind Map for the book. To my most trusted and dearest friend, Andrew Finkelstein. You helped me more than you'll ever know. I'm eternally grateful. To John DiJulius for sharing his authoring and publishing experience. To Jayne Morehouse for your enthusiasm and embracing of no compromise. To Rozanne Schoell, who took the first book order and takes amazing care of our customers. To Terry McKee, who gets what being "a director" is all about. Most of all, I want to thank my team: Lorinda Warner, Daryl Jenkins, Michael Yost, Heath Smith, Leslie Rice Winterrowd and Roseanne Klementisz. You never stopped believing in me. I am honored to work with each and every one of you.

Contents

When leaders compromise, or look the other way when compromise occurs, it's the equivalent of a captain drilling holes in the bottom of a ship. A business can sink just as quickly as a ship.

Becoming a no-compromise leader is truly a road less traveled. Not because it's necessarily long or difficult, but because of the unwavering commitment and perseverance to be such a leader.

Making the shift to no-compromise leadership is far more complex than the flip of a mental switch. You must change at a deeper level.

The productivity business outcome is all about doing the work of the business — and executing that work in the most efficient and timely manner possible to the highest no-compromise standards.

The profitability business outcome is all about achieving predictable cash flow and bottom line profitability — and doing so with the highest level of no-compromise financial accountability at all levels of the company.

Foreword by John Harms

I love to read management and business literature to continuously "sharpen my saw." *No-Compromise Leadership* is simply one of the most significant books I've read. It resets the leadership bar for anyone in business from the start-up entrepreneur to the CEO of a Fortune 500 company. In my 20+ years building a successful software and education company, I've stayed true to my principles and led my company from being unknown and in debt to the #1 software company in the $80 billion Beauty and Wellness industries. How did I accomplish that? By being a doer and creating a culture of action and execution. Sounds simple, right? You'd be surprised how many companies just don't react fast enough and charge forward. Internal compromise and fear to act can paralyze a leader, causing drag, drama, lost money and missed opportunities.

Neil Ducoff has been a mentor to me since the late 90s. His straight-talking, honest approach to coaching has made him a legend in the beauty industry. Neil's company, Strategies, is known as an innovative company that turned compensation and commission-based pay upside down long before others realized the value of their Team-Based Pay system. It was Neil's foresight that helped me realize the importance of building cash-flow forecasting into my software and the importance of growth indicators — not just revenue. I owe him many other credits as to how I run my business and how I educate my clients. We have large annual user group conferences all over the United States that draw clients from around the world. There is only one educator who I bring back year after year — Neil Ducoff. If you want to roll up your sleeves and take off your business blinders, Neil is the person to deliver the wake-up call and guide you through the process.

When Neil first sent me the draft of *No-Compromise Leadership*, the title alone resonated with me. I couldn't wait to dive in and see what literary journey it would take me on. What a journey it was. By the time I finished the introduction and first chapter, I knew Neil hit a home run. I didn't stop reading until 3:00 am — and I had a company to run in just a few hours. No compromise is exactly what the culmination of my career and experience has taught me. It's what the great leaders in history from Martin Luther King, Jr. (political/social perspective) to Jack Welch (management/business perspective) have all understood.

No-Compromise Leadership means:
  + Everything matters.
  + You can no longer look the other way.
  + Inaction is compromise.
  + Compromise leads to stress — it's a passion killer.
  + No-compromise leadership leads to...
    + peace of mind;
    + increased ownership of processes and accountability at all levels of the organization;
    + ability to consistently compete and win;
    + no-compromise employees who understand core values — a true no-compromise culture.

> *"Anxiety is caused by a lack of control, organization, preparation and action." – David Kekich*

Action is the essence of no-compromise leadership. Strategies, planning and creativity are all important aspects of visionary leadership. However, the leader who can execute and lead through constant action is a leader who understands no-compromise leadership. Basically, inaction or the tendency to look the other way is "compromise." Why would anyone want to compromise principles, passion, employee development, product development or even cash-flow concerns? No leader wants to compromise but many do it, albeit unknowingly, everyday. Here are two examples of leadership compromise:

1. Bill's performance continues to slide every month and his attitude is affecting the rest of the sales department. Every day you look the other way; you compromise.

2. Your product is known as the best-in-class, but competition is increasing, larger companies are entering your market and technology is changing fast. You ignore these outside factors and they chip away as you continue to blow your best-in-class trumpet. You're compromising everything — including the future of your company.

Let me give you a simple example from my own company, Harms Software Inc. The first software system we designed, called Salon Solutions™, was at the peak of its popularity in 1998 with thousands of systems installed and sales increasing by the day. Sounds good so far, right? Around the same time, I started hearing more and more about spas and day spas — salons that were adding spa treatment rooms and opening businesses to offer these new body services and wellness experiences. I knew I had a decision to make. Salon Solutions in name and in functionality would not excel in this new, high-end, more complex business environment. We had two choices. First, continue to focus solely on salons and leverage the million-plus lines of code we had written. Second, start from scratch with a complete, expensive, time-consuming rewrite in the midst of our increasing popularity and high sales. With the help and push (maybe even a shove) from my no-compromise wife, Rosana, I hired new developers and, over the next two years, entirely rewrote the software. I chose a generic name, Millennium™, so it would work for salons, spas, medical spas and fitness centers. Then, I abandoned the Salon Solutions brand name we had fought for years to establish. That decision to rewrite and start over while on top proved to be the tipping point for Harms Software. Today, only eight years later, the company is 10 times the size with revenues up 10,000%. The companies I once competed with that didn't change fell victim to their own compromise — they're no longer around.

You must lead by example. Never look the other way. Everything matters. No-compromise leadership means making informed decisions that are followed by ACTION. Execution is the difference between a good planner and a great leader.

Open your mind and your heart for what you are about to read. *No-Compromise Leadership* takes you from understanding no compromise, to living no compromise, and finally to creating a no-compromise culture that shapes the collective thinking and behavior of your entire company.

I'm excited for you! No-compromise leadership begins today and is a never-ending journey both professionally and personally.

John T. Harms
President & CEO
Harms Software Inc.

ACCOLADES:
Winner "Top Entrepreneurs Under 40"- *NJBiz Magazine* 2004
Inc. 5000 Fastest-Growing Companies 2008
New Jersey Top 5 Businesses – *NJBiz Magazine* 2008
American Salon Favorite Software 2008
American Spa Favorite Software 2006, 2007, 2008
Salon Today Top 200 Salons #1 Software

Introduction

A number of years ago, I began using the term "no compromise" in my lectures, consulting work and writing. I used it to communicate, without question or misinterpretation, a leadership style that is resolute in its commitment to consistency, accountability and integrity. It seemed the more I used "no compromise," the more it seemed to strike a deep and resonating chord in business leaders. I heard stories about leadership team and staff meetings targeting key issues with "no compromise" as the non-negotiable outcome. Business owners and managers would tell me how no-compromise thinking helped them decisively deal with difficult situations, problem employees or tasks they previously avoided. Today, barely a day passes without receiving a no-compromise story or reference to how it impacted a leader's personal thinking and business.

Joined together, these two simple words immediately establish a higher standard of leadership

No-compromise leadership is all about the thinking, behavior and accountability that support all leadership results and business outcomes.

thinking and behavior. Think of no compromise as a powerful internal compass that keeps you and your company steadfastly on course. In his latest book, *The Success Principles: How To Get From Where You Are to Where You Want to Be*, Jack Canfield talks about a concept he calls, "99 percent is a bitch, 100 percent is a breeze." In an interview with Strategies, Canfield explained, "I brush my teeth every day; I have a 100 percent commitment to dental health. I don't have to think about it. It's a done deal. … If I commit 99 percent, almost every day I have to re-decide. If you commit to answering your phone calls within 24 hours, don't go to bed without doing it." 100 percent commitment, that's the essence of no-compromise leadership.

No-compromise leadership is all about the thinking, behavior and accountability that support all leadership results and business outcomes. By design, no compromise cuts through the myriad excuses, emotional blockages and procrastination that silently infect leadership performance. If "no compromise" becomes the mandate — the guiding principle upon which all other leadership behavior emanates — the resulting business outcomes will be nothing short of breakthrough.

If no compromise is all about the thinking, behavior and accountability of business leaders, the gap between "what's being done" and "what needs to be done" can be alarmingly wide and deep. Take a walk through your company and grade everything you see and experience it as either compromise or no compromise. How does your company measure up in the following?

- Customer greetings and customer service
- Customers with a demeanor and body language reflective of the service experience your company promises to give
- How managers and leaders communicate with employees
- Work environment, attitude and team spirit of staff
- Cleanliness and organization of workspaces
- Quality and delivery of the service or product
- Extra touches that make doing business with your company a delight
- Balance sheet, profit and loss statement and statement of cash flow
- Accounts payable and receivable reports

How much compromise or no compromise do you see?

With no compromise as the mandate, even the best and most respected companies reveal the need for improvement. Business size truly doesn't matter. The more compromise that seeps in, the more drag it places on growth, momentum and energy of the company. Allow it to go unchecked, even for a nanosecond, and the most achievable goals instantly turn into pipe dreams... yet another collection of missed opportunities. *No compromise means no missed opportunities.*

To understand the concept of no compromise, you must first understand what compromise is. In its simplest terms, compromise is the acceptance of a situation or outcome that varies from what was originally intended. Call it settling for something less, lowering expectations or making unnecessary concessions — there is no place for compromise in business. True, goals and objectives may need to be revised as business and market realities change, but lowering expectations or settling for less, with the knowledge that compromise was embedded in the decision, is unacceptable. Reality certainly cannot be ignored. However, allowing compromise to knowingly become part of your reality represents the intentional degrading of the integrity of the company. And the more compromise takes hold, the more energy it takes to flush it out.

But the definition of compromise also has a darker meaning. It also means a breach in security, structural integrity or a failure to obey, keep, or preserve something — like a law, a trust or a promise. If the darker side of compromise infects the culture and behavior of an entire company, its shear weight can force it to implode, taking with it the trust of its customers, stockholders — not to mention the pensions and retirement dreams of its employees.

Just as no compromise is a mode of thinking and a discipline, so is compromise. Both are choices and both require discipline. Compromise offers the path of least resistance. It's easier to avoid a leadership responsibility than to do it. It's easier to avoid financial accountability than to do it. It's easier to avoid addressing a difficult employee's behavior issues than to do it. It's easier to deliver mediocre customer service than world-class service. Even in our personal lives, it's easier to be a couch potato than adhere to an exercise routine. It's all a choice in our personal thinking and behavior.

Is there a good side to compromise? Of course there is. The basic tenet of negotiation is to reach a compromise that is satisfactory to all parties. You're not compromising in a negative way when you "negotiate" a work schedule that helps an employee manage family responsibilities while still fulfilling his or her duties. You're not compromising if you deviate from your financial budget to take advantage of a great opportunity that will add value or cost savings to the company.

That being said, there is compromise that is good, compromise that is bad — and then there is no-compromise leadership. No-compromise leadership is a commitment to a higher standard that guides and nurtures a business culture capable of extraordinary achievement. No compromise defines the type of leader you are. It defines the DNA of the business you lead and whose success you are charged to achieve.

This is not about the pursuit of an elusive state of perfection, but rather the pursuit of consistency, accountability and predictability.

I have been an entrepreneur almost my entire working career. I've devoted myself to teaching, consulting and writing about business and the kind of issues that keep leaders up at night. You know, the tough stuff like growth challenges, cash-flow nightmares, lethargic productivity, partnership conflicts, employee turnover, behavioral and toxic business culture issues. I've met countless business owners and leaders who unknowingly *strive to struggle* because of the compromise they create and spread in the very companies they want to grow. I've listened intently to employees tell their side of the story, and I must say, this is often the most enlightening source for identifying where and how much compromise has infected a business. (Yes, there are two sides to every story.) I've met burnt-out leaders who just want to quit. Through it all, I have seen firsthand the anguish, financial devastation and the remnants of great dreams that were all contaminated by compromise. In every case, the compromise emanated from the leader's own behavior and failure to be "accountable." In striking contrast, I've certainly had the honor of meeting many forward-thinking individuals who lead dynamic companies, divisions or departments. Without exception, all have no-compromise leadership embedded in their thinking, behavior and culture.

Countless books have been written on leadership, accountability, systems, and self-improvement. With the multitude of "How to master this" or "The ten secrets to …" books and courses available, there is no shortage of guidance. But when your operating system — your behavior — your company's DNA — is missing key components, no amount of learning, new ideas or motivation is going to create lasting change in your behavior as a leader. Try as you might, your compromising thinking and behavior — your internal operating system — will pull you and your company back to its old behavior. Until you shift to and embrace no-compromise leadership, compromise will continue.

The decision to write this book was a simple one, because I have seen the damage that compromise can inflict not just on a business, but on its leaders, employees, families, vendors and all those who depend on it. And like it or not, believe it or not, compromise is choice. And because it is a choice, any individual can also choose to be a no-compromise leader. Becoming a no-compromise leader is a commitment to take a higher road that is sadly less traveled. It requires tenacity and a deep understanding of yourself. This is not about the pursuit of an elusive state of perfection, but rather the pursuit of consistency, accountability and predictability. It's a voyage of continuous improvement that will never end; you'll just move closer to being a no-compromise leader — because even the best have room for improvement.

Business is more than an exciting game. Leadership is more than getting things done through others. I have always viewed a business as a living entity to which entrepreneurs and leaders give life. I have the utmost respect for that life, even though its vital signs are read on balance sheets and income statements. In the end, when you guide a business through its many stages of life, it can give so much back to all who were responsible for making it strong and vibrant. This goes so far beyond financial rewards. It's not about the money — the money is only one of many measurements of success. Who could ever put a monetary value on fulfillment, sense of accomplishment, pride, respect, loyalty, gratitude and achieving your full potential?

I know firsthand what no-compromise leadership can do to bring vitality to a business. My company, Strategies, is a no-compromise company.

No, we're not huge and we don't have thousands of employees. We simply run a small, dynamic and highly efficient company that adheres to a no-compromise mandate. We make money and we have fun. As the founder and CEO, I have the freedom to do the work I enjoy, because my team is empowered to make decisions. We measure our performance and efficiency through our balance sheet, income statements and cash flow. Most of all, we built a company based on relationships with our customers — and no compromise is the hallmark of successful relationship building.

So, am I a no-compromise leader? The only way to answer that question is that I'm much closer today than I've ever been. I know where I need to improve and I'm sure I'll discover other things, as well, as I move forward. As I wrote earlier, it's a commitment to continuous improvement — and I'm 100 percent committed.

This book had to be written to give every business leader, manager and entrepreneur a no-compromise operating system that will allow dynamic companies to emerge. A business is a life form and it must be cared for and respected in order for it to grow, prosper and endure. That is the true role of the no-compromise leader.

Three steps to no-compromise leadership: The thinking, the application and the shift

Part I of this book is all about understanding, preparing and the thinking of no-compromise leadership. Throughout the years of teaching, consulting and referencing no-compromise leadership, it's amazing how many in leadership roles at all levels almost instantly embrace the concept. It's like hearing a collective, "There is no option, I'm going to be a no-compromise leader from this moment forward." And just as quickly as they throw that switch to the NCL position, they are vulnerable to flipping back into their compromise-as-usual mode faster than an overloaded circuit breaker. Time and time again I've seen leaders make wonderful progress, only to have their old compromising behaviors rise to the surface and take over. This is why Part One of this book is so critical to understand and digest before we can move forward into the disciplines.

In Part II, I'll take you through a series of business disciplines I call The *Four Business Outcomes*. These four outcomes will create the optimum balance your business will require to achieve quantum leap growth. ***No-compromise leadership is all about driving and creating balance across The Four Business Outcomes.***

In Part III, I'll give you strategies to make your shift to no compromise not only stick, but endure. For now, you need to be centered on what it truly takes to become a no-compromise leader.

PART I

Discovering the No-Compromise Leader Within

PART I

Introduction

B ecoming a no-compromise leader takes more than the flick of a switch. It takes an understanding of what no-compromise leadership is at the deepest level of human behavior. It will require a 100 percent commitment from you. You must be open to recognizing how your own approach and style of leadership may slow or stall your transition to no compromise. You must understand and meet every qualifier.

No-compromise leadership cannot be faked. Most certainly, you cannot be a part-time, no-compromise leader. If you're not prepared to go all the way, why start the voyage at all? No compromise isn't about big starts and getting within sight of the finish line. *It's doing whatever it takes to cross that finish line and keep going — to keep getting better.*

Your transition to no-compromise leadership will not happen overnight. It's going to be an ongoing process of personal leadership discovery and skill development. Yes, there will be setbacks. You will slip at times and you'll have to push yourself to get back in the no-compromise groove. You will get better at it the longer and harder you work at it. Simply put, you learn to be a no-compromise leader.

You will sense that something is different. It's like installing a new operating system in your computer where functionality is familiar but new capabilities are now available to you. In essence, you begin transitioning to a *no-compromise operating system* that now governs your leadership thinking and behavior. Here's a sampling of what you can expect to see:

+ Your sense of purpose is focused and sharp.
+ You know what needs to be done — and do it.
+ You tackle pressing issues that you would ordinarily keep on the back burner where they fester and grow.
+ You are more decisive with your communication and how you relate to those you lead.
+ Your demeanor is focused and determined.
+ Those around you can sense that you are engaged and leading — not dictating.
+ You listen with a heightened sense of interest and intent.
+ You make better decisions, because no compromise demands a thorough attention to detail.

What's really cool is that all this no-compromise stuff is going to produce measurable results in your company's performance. Look for results like these:

+ Sales are consistently hitting or surpassing goals.
+ Costs are down.
+ Consistency is evident throughout the company.
+ Customer loyalty and retention are at an all-time high.
+ Your leaders and employees are engaged in growing the company. They feel empowered because you have empowered them.
+ Employee job satisfaction and staff retention are excellent.
+ Your company is conducting business better, faster and more cost efficiently. It's like everything is just easier.
+ Change initiatives move smoothly, without the once-common internal resistance.
+ Profits are best described as impressive.

Your personal mandate to become a no-compromise leader will thrust you out of your comfort zone. It will challenge you to engage when, in your previous thinking and behavior mode, you would take a detour to avoid that tough conversation, decision or task that's outside of your comfort zone. *No-compromise leaders stand on the higher ground of discipline and accountability.* This is one transition that will require your leadership muscles to stretch and burn.

Throughout the chapters in Part One, you will learn the inner workings of no-compromise leadership and how to begin your transition. Part I is all about YOU and how to install a no-compromise operating system into your thinking and behavior.

CHAPTER 1

THE TITANIC COST OF COMPROMISE

When leaders compromise, or look the other way when compromise occurs, it's the equivalent of a captain drilling holes in the bottom of a ship. A business can sink just as quickly as a ship.

Compromise can occur in every nook and cranny of your business. It can be as simple as employees taking personal calls while servicing customers, wasting company supplies or circumventing procedures. Even the most basic forms of compromise can derail productivity, sap profits and destroy vital customer relationships. Leaders are ultimately accountable for these seemingly minor breaches, as most all business malfunctions can be traced back to those who lead. Further, think about the financial impact on a company when compromise exists in the core behavior and thinking of the leaders themselves. When a leader avoids making a vital decision of any kind, the cost of compromise can truly be colossal.

Every aspect of a company's performance is a reflection of its leaders' thinking, behavior and ability to execute. Consider the following three stories, classic examples of the cost of compromise.

Story One:
Hates numbers — big ego

Bob's architectural business was in dire financial straights and bleeding cash badly. Bob was on vacation. The bookkeeper faxed him a current set of financials and the accounts-payable aging report. She also included three options and asked him to get back to her on which one to execute. Option one was to find $80,000 immediately so she could run payroll checks. There was an addendum to option one; find more money so she could pay the rent and the bank loan. Option two was to tell the employees to go home and shut the business down. Option three suggested that Bob file for bankruptcy.

Got the picture? It was ugly. Like a two-by-four hitting Bob in the head, his business finally got his undivided attention because it was not only in pain, it was on life support and fading quickly. Bob was looking for a cure, or at least a sign of hope, that his business could be saved.

Bob's business didn't get in that shape overnight or while he was on vacation. The condition of Bob's business was fueled by his compromising behavior and thinking. He totally ignored his numbers. He was tough to work for and often allowed his ego to get in the way of making the right decisions for the company. And when it did, it demoralized staff. The business culture was contaminated. Productivity was dismal and client dissatisfaction was obvious. Under Bob's leadership, compromise was everywhere.

STORY TWO:
Avoids difficult conversations — Avoids tough decisions

Rick just hired a new general manager for his distribution company. He had done business with this individual before when she was the general manager of a major product supplier. She had an impressive resume that included sales management, project planning and goal achievements. As this was his company's first general manager, hopes were high for remarkable results.

Their new GM got right to work in her office. She was one of the first to arrive every day and the last to leave. Piles of detailed reports quickly grew in her office, where the GM spent most of her time. She would come out to lead a few meetings and occasionally talked about some projects. But as the months went by, the piles grew and talk about those exciting projects continued, but nothing seemed to be implemented.

In a small company without all the corporate camouflage to mask it, the GM's deficiencies were glaringly obvious. Rick now realized that he hired a report-generating, wheel-spinning, nothing-ever-crosses-the-finish-line, general manager who just could not execute. Rick attempted to pull in the reins by giving specific timelines to all of the GM's projects. Still, nothing got done. No progress on anything. Nada. Zilch.

The general manager's inability to implement became obvious to employees. The failure to engage on the part of the owner was compromising the company's culture. The trickle effect of not holding the GM accountable, while acknowledging the negative behavior and failing to address it, is compromise of the highest order.

Rick was suffering from a common leadership blockage where emotions interfere with one's ability to see and confront reality. He knew the GM needed the job and the money. However, the owner chose to compromise by avoiding what he perceived as a difficult and confrontational conversation. Only after great expense, distraction and prodding did the owner engage in a long overdue crucial conversation. He quickly discovered that the GM was frustrated, too, and knew she was ineffective and costing the company precious money. It was mutually agreed to part company. Rick wondered why he waited so long.

STORY THREE:
Lacks vision alignment — entitlement behavior

Susan and Jessica decided to merge their graphic design firms and create a new company with broader, more competitive offerings. A year into the merger, the business has grown but is beginning to sputter, as challenges grew within the partnership. Whenever the partners met, there were constant references to "at my old business" and "my employees" (meaning those employees who worked for each owner prior to the merger). The turf battles between the partners created similar divisions in the employee ranks.

Although a partnership existed on paper, the partners never merged their thinking and their business cultures into a larger and more dynamic entity. Despite the fact that they were under one roof, each partner was fiercely territorial. It was dysfunctional leadership at its best.

For example, Jessica was a master of leadership entitlement. She would rearrange project assignments, buy new equipment or adjust prices without the thought of consulting her partner, Susan. She was chronically late for work. She regularly missed appointments with customers, partnership meetings, staff meetings and vendor meetings. Whenever Susan broached the subject, Jessica would justify her tardiness with, "I'm the owner and I can do what I want." You could almost see the compromise freight train barreling through this business.

It's there — find it

Those three stories might appear as extreme examples of compromise at the leadership level. However, while it might not be as obvious in your company, compromise in some form is alive, thriving and doing damage. It's your responsibility to identify and eliminate it — especially if you're the one compromising.

In a no-compromise company, compromise is easy to identify. It's the elephant in the living room.

Compromise spreads through a company like a virus. The compromising behaviors of the leaders in the preceding stories demonstrate the damage they can inflict on a business in terms of lost productivity and increased costs, as well as decreased levels of customer and employee retention. The impact is not merely subjective, because it can be measured in extreme detail in a host of performance and operating reports, and most definitely, in financial reports. Compromise is real and it's costly. It infects and degrades everything, everywhere. It burrows in fast and deep and hunkers down for the long haul. It can kill change initiatives and be resistant to efforts to weed it out.

Still not convinced that compromise exists in your business? Well, think again. Perhaps the compromise isn't as severe as the examples just shared, but rest assured, compromise is lurking in your company. And you don't have to look very far to find it. So buckle your seat belt and get ready for a reality check. Here is a hit list of compromising behavior that is as common as employees surfing the Internet and sending personal e-mails on company time.

Have you ever experienced any of these common compromising behaviors?

+ Creating a double standard for you versus your employees.
+ Creating separate standards for different employees.
+ Not maintaining and following ethical standards.
+ Procrastinating.
+ Agreeing to do something and not delivering what was promised when it was promised.
+ Being late for work or meetings.
+ Not following the budget.
+ Failing to address obvious problems and issues.
+ Not responding to employee suggestions.
+ Believing that "it" cannot be done.
+ Talking "empowerment" but never letting go of control.
+ Giving up too easily.
+ Not creating opportunities to listen to what employees have to say and their insights to make things better.
+ Focusing on the negative.
+ Failing or a personal resistance to disclose and share key information that employees need to do their jobs.
+ Withholding positive feedback.
+ Not rolling up your sleeves and pitching in.
+ Reprimanding in public.
+ Talking about, gossiping or degrading an employee with others.

+ Stereotyping and making assumptions about people.
+ Not listening to customers.
+ Accepting inferior performance or quality service.
+ Playing the "blame game."

As you can see, the compromise list is extensive, but it's only the tip of the iceberg. Yes, we're all guilty as charged when it comes to compromise. *You cannot condone, tolerate or ignore compromise.* The more we, as leaders, practice and adhere to a no-compromise mandate for ourselves and the companies we lead, the more difficult it is for compromise to surface.

In a no-compromise company, compromise is easy to identify. It's the elephant in the living room.

Running through minefields

Ever wonder why it's so difficult to change behavior or implement new systems in your business? The answer becomes clear when you understand how deeply rooted compromise is in your culture. Getting change initiatives to stick when compromise is present can be agonizingly slow and painful. It's like trying to run a race through a minefield. It doesn't take long for the change initiative to hit a few mines before it's either blown up or retreats to status quo. Old compromising behaviors will return in an instant if an opportunity presents itself.

Even when change initiatives appear to have finally taken hold and it's full speed ahead, compromise can derail it. In his book, *Leading Change*, change guru John Kotter details how behavior and thinking associated with the old culture continue to lurk below the surface just waiting for the slightest crack to occur. Even years after a seemingly successful change initiative, compromise at the leadership level

> For me, more than anything, I wanted a company that would allow me to do work I enjoy and not get bogged down with the traditional employee productivity issues.

can create a crack sufficient enough to create a new set of minefields, as compromise surfaces and regains a foothold.

A no-compromise culture is a formidable deterrent that can prevent cracks in your culture from occurring. And when a crack does occur, no compromise quickly stops it from expanding, then seals it with focused attention and accountability.

And just because a leader identifies compromise, it doesn't necessarily translate that front-line employees see it the same way. You may have to get creative to convey the concept of compromise to your staff. Here's an interesting story that John Kotter shared with Strategies about how one leader communicated a major compromise sighting to his staff:

> *He was new in his job and was meeting with one of his biggest customers for dinner. He knew that the plant was going to have to change to be able to become more competitive. He knew that the people in the plant*

had been there forever. They had their own "pride" in their workmanship, but they also had a great deal of complacency.

So, he meets with this large customer. My guess is after a drink or two, the guy started to leak out more of his dissatisfaction. The customer had to take their products and redo them. When the factory people were confronted with that, they had nodded their heads but hadn't done anything about it. The costs of switching [to another factory] were high or difficult; it's not like buying butter.

Instead of getting defensive, the guy drew the customer out and let him get more explicit and let his frustration out. He said, "My people need to see just what I've seen."

This guy was interested in videotape, and asked, "Would you mind if I send someone around tomorrow with a video camera and would you say what you said tonight?"

And he talked him into it. The next day, he sent over a guy with a video camera and he got the customer talking. He filmed maybe 30 minutes and edited it to 15 minutes. Then, he started calling work groups into a conference room in the factory to view the video. Afterwards, he said, "What do you think?" He got some defensiveness, of course. Any number of people almost had their jaws on the floor. They simply didn't realize. That shook things up enough and got rid of enough of the complacency to get things rolling.

Confronting your leadership blockages

Compromise thinking and behavior emanate from bad habits, procrastination and insufficient leadership skills. Collectively, it's like all that annoying stuff you or employees do. It's when you avoid or knowingly ignore something, while that voice inside you is screaming, "Hey, you gotta do this." It's when you know that you should engage and be accountable, but something inside you compels you to turn away and disengage. This is where the real damage to leadership careers, employees and business cultures is done. Be assured, it's lethal enough to derail any company.

I use the term *"leadership blockages"* to describe this avoidance behavior.

Leadership blockages defined

Leadership blockages are quite common. Even the best leaders have their quirks that trip them up and result in compromise. Here are a few examples of leadership blockages to get you started:

- You need to address an employee's behavior or performance but avoid it because you view it as confrontation and not a coaching opportunity.

- You never liked numbers, so you avoid your responsibilities to plan and monitor your company's financial performance. You know getting a handle on the numbers is vital — you just don't do it.

- You avoid making tough decisions out of fear or how they will impact others. The entire company pays the price for your failure to act.

- You have a friend or relative in a key position and he or she is not performing. It's having a negative impact on the company, but you refuse to act. Problem is, everyone else sees this, too.

- You see problems, even acknowledge them, but fail to act. And when you do act, you turn to quick fixes rather than long-term solutions that might require some tough decisions or sacrifices.

- You don't like structure and systems, so you lead like a shoot-from-the-hip cowboy. You give excuses and the problems continue.

- You want employees to think and act like owners, but you refuse to let go of the controls. You override decisions. You violate levels of authority. You meddle in everything. As a result, you stifle employee growth — and frustrate the heck out of those you seemingly empower to lead.

- You overflow your plate with projects, tasks and responsibilities like some superhero, because you can't or won't say "no." Your perpetual state of being overwhelmed or overworked is affecting your ability to lead. You can't lead when you're fighting fires and trying to keep things from falling off your plate.

When you avoid or fail to act on an issue or problem, you are dealing with a leadership blockage. Like the fear of flying or public speaking, these behavior patterns are embedded into one's core thinking and take time, practice and determination to overcome. In business, especially at the leadership level, leadership blockages create drag. When blockages cause essential leadership accountabilities to shut down, the drag can stall forward momentum. In acute cases, blockages can create so much drag that it can cause a business to wobble, crash and burn. If you did a forensic analysis on the problems you are currently experiencing in your business, at some level of your organization, leadership blockages would be identified as the root cause. You, or someone in your company, failed to be accountable to step in and engage an issue or challenge, demanding attention and action.

Neilism
Giving into a leadership blockage today gives you a bigger problem tomorrow.

This is a good time to give you the first Neilism of the book: "Giving into a leadership blockage today gives you a bigger problem tomorrow."

Leadership blockages create an interesting concoction of compromise that can do all sorts of damage to a company's performance and culture. And just like having a fear of flying or public speaking, the causes for such leadership blockages can be varied and deeply rooted in one's behavior.

The good news is that any leader can choose to overcome and work through his or her blockages. You can learn to improve communication skills and control the flow and outcome of crucial conversations. You can learn and master numbers, strategic planning, decision-making, system design, delegation and time management. It begins by making a no-compromise decision to overcome your blockages. *Remember, 100% is a breeze, 99% is a bitch.*

Begin by acknowledging what your leadership blockages are and how they are creating drag in the company. To create no-compromise results, you need to develop new behaviors and productive habits. What are the blockages that keep you from getting the results you want? Get them down on paper. Once you identify them, start replacing them with behaviors and habits that will get the results you want. *A no-compromise business culture cannot be achieved with leadership blockages getting in the way.*

No room for compromise

When I started Strategies in 1993, my goal was to build a highly efficient company driven by a small and dedicated team. Although my "no-compromise" battle cry didn't emerge until a few years later, it was clearly the mandate and the most sacred of our governing values. Yes, we have had encounters with compromise, but they were rare and always short-lived, like failing to thoroughly plan for an important meeting or not following up on a hot customer lead. It's easy to use the "we didn't have time" excuse when the real reason is not planning our time. How we addressed those compromises is a testament to our culture and behavior. No, we are not perfect, but we work hard at living no compromise every day.

I wanted a company with a high sense of urgency. Urgency is no-compromise energy. Focus a sense of urgency at a crisis, challenge or behavior, and it's like channeling an army of antibodies at an infection. It surrounds it, stops it from spreading — then kills it. I can't remember one compromise or crisis at Strategies that we didn't work through in short order.

When creating my vision, I knew precisely what I wanted and the type of culture it would require. More than anything, I wanted a company that would allow me to do the work I enjoy and not get bogged down by the traditional employee productivity issues. I wanted an open company with free-flowing information. I wanted a high sense of urgency to grow revenues and control costs. Open-book management was a given (*a system of sharing financials with employees so everyone can make better profit-driving decisions*). I wanted mutual responsibility and accountability. Integrity and trust would be the foundation of our core values. Customer responsiveness and building enduring relationships

Neilism
If I can't sleep at night, no one sleeps at night.

with clients and vendors were non-negotiable. I wanted us to work hard, have fun and balance it all with personal and family growth. And at the end of the day, every team member at Strategies should feel fulfilled and rewarded for our individual and collective accomplishments. If work isn't fulfilling and enriching, then it truly is work — and that makes getting out of bed each day a task unto itself.

Focus a sense of urgency at a crisis, challenge or behavior, and it's like channeling an army of antibodies at an infection. It surrounds it, stops it from spreading — then kills it.

Looking back at the first 15 years of Strategies and all we have accomplished is proof that no compromise is a powerful mode of thinking. Our small but focused team manages three highly profitable revenue divisions. Visitors to our corporate offices and Business Academy are quite surprised when they don't find rows of cubicles. No compromise drives efficiency. *I'll take it one step further and label "no compromise" as a new and powerful business design and structure.*

For example, Thursday is numbers day at Strategies. That's when the weekly balance sheets, profit and loss statements, statement of cash flows, accounts receivable and payable reports are run. I get a warm glow inside when I hear my staff ask if the reports are ready yet and then watch as they dissect them. No one hesitates to ask tough questions. It's really cool when someone spots something that needs to be fixed, reclassified or given immediate attention. It's truly inspiring when employees fight for both top- and bottom-line growth while seeking ways to build our cash reserves. *By the way, I hate referring to those I work with every day as "employees." The reason is simple. We are all accountable for the success or failure of Strategies. Our company is totally open and we measure our performance by our financials. We have a culture where everyone thinks and acts like an owner.*

A Neilism: "If I can't sleep at night, no one sleeps at night." From a leadership perspective, there is a ton of no-compromise thinking in this Neilism. Over the years, I've seen too many leaders and entrepreneurs who, during tough times, can't sleep at night. Out of fear, they elect not to share the severity of the crisis with employees — not even key employees.

They rationalize that sharing bad news, even dismal news, could be the signal to "abandon ship." Well, there's nothing like a good business crisis to inspire and bring out the best in a leader to rally the troops, get them focused and fix what needs to be fixed.

It's about choices

It is important to understand that leaders make choices on how they want to lead and behave. I'll let the psychologists of the world offer up their scientific explanations on why people behave like they do and make the decisions they make. In business, in leadership and in life, there are only two choices. You can choose to lead to the best of your ability or you can choose to do it at a level of something less. *To do your best is no compromise.* Something less is a compromise. If you choose to do it (anything) to the best of your ability, then you are also committing to improving and honing your abilities. That's no compromise. It's beyond continuous improvement. It's striving for the highest levels of performance and achievement. It's a sacred commitment to be your best in the game you're playing.

> **Neilism**
> If you're not striving for no compromise — you're striving for mediocrity.

Here's another Neilism. "If you're not striving for no compromise — you're striving for mediocrity." That is a choice many leaders make. Those who do pay a terrible price in terms of stress, lost opportunity, employee turnover, inefficiency and financial loss, all of which spill over into their personal lives. That's not why anyone ever goes into business, but sadly, it is the outcome that results from compromising decisions and behavior.

It is so much more fulfilling to go no compromise. Is it more work? You could argue that it is. But here's my take. There are non-negotiable rules in business. There is work that must be done. So from my vantage point, no compromise simply means doing what needs to be done, working through your leadership blockages and following the rules. *No compromise.*

By design, no-compromise leadership requires accountability at all levels of your company. But, it can only begin with you and your commitment to a higher standard of leadership thinking and behavior. Just as a new coach can dramatically raise the focus, intensity and consistency of a losing team into one capable of winning a championship, so can the leader of a company. First you must look inward at how you allow compromise to influence your thinking and behavior. *You'll be setting your company up for failure if you attempt to create a no-compromise culture if you don't change first.*

Neilism
Success is an outcome. No compromise is the true essence of success.

I'll end this chapter with a Neilism: "Success is an outcome. No compromise is the true essence of success."

Action steps before reading on...

1. Set aside 30 undisturbed minutes to identify compromise in your leadership behavior. The telltale signs to look for are:
   + Procrastination. Is there is a pattern you can identify, such as not doing reports, making sales calls or starting projects?
   + Leadership blockages, such as avoiding thorough reviews of your financial reports, avoiding difficult conversations or making necessary but unpopular decisions. Leadership blockages stall progress through avoidance behavior.
   + A bread crumb trail of failed projects, programs, procedures and change initiatives. If so, compromise is alive and well, and breeding in your company.

2. Of all the compromising behaviors you just identified, which one do you believe is most crucial for you to address? You'll learn how in the coming chapters.

3. Take a slow walk around your company to identify and record every sighting of compromise you see. Look for behavior issues, inappropriate language, customer-service deficiencies, safety issues, wasteful practices and sanitation problems. Bring a fresh note pad. You're going to need it.

4. Effectively communicate your compromise sightings to employees and decide on a plan to remedy the compromise.

CHAPTER **2**

YOUR JOURNEY TO NO-COMPROMISE LEADERSHIP BEGINS

Becoming a no-compromise leader is truly a road less traveled. Not because it's necessarily long or difficult, but because of the unwavering commitment and perseverance to be such a leader.

No compromise is not a leadership style you can conveniently slip in and out of. There is no room for dabbling, middle-ground or fence-sitting. You cannot fake it, nor can you put it on like some power suit to appear as an authoritative commander in chief. It's certainly not something you morph into only when your company needs fixing or is in trouble. To become a no-compromise leader is an all-or-nothing proposition. You want it or you don't. Anything less is a compromise.

Your personal road to no compromise will vary based on where you are right now as a leader. For example, those with more leadership blockages will have to work harder than those with only a few. Like diet and exercise programs, commitment and perseverance are essential to making new leadership behaviors stick. Yes, you will slip. We all do. But learning to identify and acknowledge those slips is key to getting yourself back on course. No-compromise leadership is not an absolute state of being. It's a process and discipline to refine your thinking and behavior to become the most effective leader you can possibly be. It's working to achieve a higher standard of leadership performance for you, your company or area of responsibility.

To better understand your journey, I assembled a list of 10 requirements that you must understand and agree to before you can begin the journey to becoming a no-compromise leader. Each requirement raises the bar higher to make you stretch. Collectively, they provide the thinking and behavioral foundation to support what you will learn in the chapters that follow.

Let's begin.

REQUIREMENT NUMBER 1:
Clarity: Have absolute clarity on where you're taking your company.

OK, I need to do a little rant on *vision* and *mission* before continuing. I could have used company "vision" (where are you going) or "mission" (how will you get there) in Requirement Number 1, but they just don't evoke the no-compromise thinking at the level we need here. Now I must admit, having said that vision and mission don't make the grade may sound like blasphemy to management purists. But think about it. In more than 38 years of studying, teaching and coaching business, I've seen an endless parade of companies with some of the finest and meticulously crafted vision and mission statements you could ever see. I'm talking top shelf "meet and exceed — relentless pursuit of quality" statements that make you want to stand up and salute the company flag. I've seen these grand statements on everything from etched on the granite walls of the company lobby to laminated pocket-sized versions for employees to carry around for daily inspiration.

Vision and mission statements are absolutely essential. Together they point the way and offer insight into the desired culture of the company. But vision and mission do that on a grand scale with broad brush strokes. Within the words, there is ambiguity and room for individual interpretation. And that means a company can wander off course while the leader perceives that it's still moving toward its vision. After all, it is the leader who interprets the vision and determines the way. Also, factor in that reality can and will dictate that course changes be made. If the leader fails to identify new threats or opportunities and adjust course as needed, a price will be paid for such a compromise. Given that, the no-compromise leader needs to do more.

Having absolute clarity on where you're taking your company is what distinguishes the no-compromise leader from other leaders. Having absolute clarity of objectives, direction and action plans brings the vision and mission of the company into the highest level of alignment. Here's a Neilism to lock in my point on absolute clarity: "Absolute clarity is like business GPS. It sets the where and the how."

In a Strategies interview with Ken Blanchard; he shared the following insights on the importance for a company to know where it's going.

They're really clear on what they're trying to accomplish. All good behavior starts with clear goals. If you don't know where you're going, what you're doing doesn't matter. We wrote a book called Full Steam Ahead!™ *about the power of visioning.*

> **Neilism**
> Absolute clarity is like business GPS. It sets the where and the how.

Great companies have a clear vision, no matter what business they're in. I see mission statements all the time. I ask if they mind if I put them by my bed in case I can't sleep! I'm working with a bank. … I told them I would hope they're in the peace of mind business. If I gave them money, they would take care of it and grow it. Walt Disney said, "We're in the happiness business not the theme park business."

Secondly, you have to know what your picture of the future is. For Walt Disney, it was to have every guest leaving the park with the same smile they had when they entered.

No-compromise leaders must be grounded in their understanding of where they are taking the company. Absolute clarity ensures that the company doesn't wander off course or make decisions that are not in alignment with its vision, such as expanding too fast or entering unknown markets. Decisions or course changes remain true to the vision and mission. I must drive this point home because entrepreneurial leaders are notorious for justifying whatever it is they want to do. *Compromise resides within that justifying behavior. Absolute clarity deters this behavior.* If it's not taking the company toward its intended vision, it doesn't happen.

REQUIREMENT NUMBER 2:
Values: If you want them, live them.

Syndicated columnist, Bruce Weinstein, Ph.D. is The Ethics Guy and author of *Life Principles: Feeling Good by Doing Good*. In a *Strategies* interview, he defined how vital it is for a company to maintain its values and ethical center.

"When we take the low road, we not only cheat our customers, our company, and the company's shareholders — we cheat ourselves. At the end of the day, all we really have is our integrity. Once we give others a reason not to trust us, it is often hard, if not impossible, to regain that trust. Only by taking the high road consistently can we prosper in the long run."

When you admire a business for its uncompromising quality, relentless customer service and delivering what was promised when it was promised, what you're actually admiring is the culture created and governed by its values. That level of refined values-based behavior doesn't just happen; it's designed and meticulously cared for. Most importantly, it begins at the top. The structure, discipline, values and guiding principles are the granite blocks that a company's culture is built upon. That doesn't mean a company is so rigid that it is incapable of changing, just that the core behaviors that allow it to be consistent are deeply rooted. In contrast, the entrepreneurial dark side is much like a cowboy wandering from one shoot-from-the-hip gunfight to the next with the dream of riding off into the sunset on a successful business.

Tampering with the values of a business is much like tampering with the forces of nature. Compromise values anywhere in your company and minute changes, often called the butterfly effect, can cause a tidal wave of otherwise avoidable issues, problems and drama.

Here are some common examples of compromising behavior that will degrade the values of your company:

Stealing or embezzling from your own company: You would fire an employee for stealing. Just because you're the owner or leader, it doesn't give you a license to steal. Double standards compromise the values of a company. Taking cash, fudging expense reports, taking supplies or running personal expenses through the company are willful values and ethics breaches. *Oh, one more thing: Tax evasion is against the law.*

Making up the rules as you go: Nothing does more damage to a business culture, staff morale and performance than assuming that everyone knows the rules of the game, and then suddenly announcing, via a new rule, policy or procedure, that they didn't. Making up new rules when things go wrong immediately places the company's values on the hot seat. All of the issues, frustrations, lost productivity, lost respect and lost trust in leadership can be avoided by mapping out processes and outcomes before hitting the launch button.

Not keeping your word or outright lying: A leader earns the trust of others one day at a time. You can't build a dynamic company around a compromising leader who breaks his word, lies or says whatever is convenient at the time.

Overriding the authority of others without their knowledge: Why empower others or share accountability if you see nothing wrong with going behind their backs to get things your way? The wish of every leader is for employees to think, act and make decisions like an owner. That cannot occur if the leader is meddling, overriding and "snoopervising" all over the place.

"Do as I say, not as I do." Leaders lead by example. Demanding one set of standards for everyone else and a lower set for leaders is the cardinal sin of leadership. So much so, that many in leadership roles would be better placed among the rank and file. Failure to live the company's culture is a values compromise.

A well-defined set of values should handle the occasional dart with ease. But when it's the leader who is hurling the darts, the governing values will fail taking with it the vitality, productivity and profitability of the entire company.

If it's your entrepreneurial dark side that is hurling darts at the values and ethics of your company, you must address your own leadership and communication styles without delay. Changing your leadership style takes time and discipline. The services of a qualified leadership coach can be a worthwhile investment to ensure that your new leadership style is a worthy, appropriate and permanent fix. If compromise is coming from a leader below you, address it without hesitation. Preventing the degrading of governing values is so much easier than fixing the damage done to a company's culture.

REQUIREMENT NUMBER 3:
Accountability: If it needs to be done, get it done.

I received a call from Jacque to let me know that she could not attend the Strategies' seminar series she was registered for. When I inquired why, Jacque began describing cash-flow problems and other seemingly insurmountable business challenges. There was no mistaking her frustration over the state of her business. This seminar series was just what she needed, so I offered this struggling entrepreneur a seat and that we would figure out a payment plan that would make attending possible.

We had a long discussion about her business and how her leadership behavior, attention to detail and follow-through needed to dramatically improve. Jacque had to become a no-compromise leader if she wanted to turn her business around. There was a positive air in her voice and a reassuring determination to get to work on re-building her business.

At the first of the four sessions, she was totally engaged. However, as she returned for each succeeding session, I could see compromise creeping back into her behavior. Together, we addressed her fading sense of urgency and backsliding. Although there were some gains, many of her most pressing challenges remained. Not because they weren't identified, but because she failed to commit and be accountable to execute the clearly defined solutions she now had in her possession. Compromise was alive and well. Nothing really changed, because Jacque, the leader, didn't change.

Jacque's story is a simple lesson that it takes more than "showing up" and talk of change to be a no-compromise leader. It takes resolve, tenacity and courage to begin and stay the course. Jacque did the talk but not the walk. She wasn't ready to commit and failed requirement number three: If it needs to be done, get it done. When the seminar series concluded nine months later, Jacque's business was still aimlessly wandering around the starting gate. She eventually sold the business but at a price far short to clear up the debt. Had Jacque embraced no compromise, you could have been reading a nice success story here instead of this obituary.

Call it procrastinating, leadership blockages, lack of knowledge or whatever — failure to be accountable and do what needs to be done is the ultimate compromise for a business leader. It contaminates the very fabric of the business culture, because the leader's propensity to compromise, and sets the behavior standard for the entire company.

> **Procrastination, or simply avoiding difficult decisions or actions, are behavior traits that breed compromise.**

Procrastination, or simply avoiding difficult decisions or actions, is behavior that breeds compromise. Living by requirement number three is non-negotiable for the no-compromise leader. A leader is defined by his or her resolve, tenacity and courage to get things done.

REQUIREMENT NUMBER 4:
Transparent: No excuses when you compromise. Own it.

You would have to be living under a rock not to understand that doing business today demands focused leadership, teamwork at its highest level, the ability to rapidly adapt to change, relentless innovation, uncompromising customer service and fiscal accountability. Business today is an unforgiving and high-risk game. And if you're an entrepreneur, it's likely that your home and personal guarantee all hinge on the decisions and actions you take. Given this, being a leader in business is about getting things done, working through challenges and dealing with those raise-your-blood-pressure issues that are all part of the game. That's doing business that no-compromise way.

But what happens when excuses enter the mix? In my work as a business trainer and coach, I encounter a steady stream of excuse makers. I started calling them "excuse manufacturers," as they always appear to be in full production mode. From "I don't like to look at the numbers" and "I think the performance problem will go away if I give it more time," to "The economy is not good — everyone is feeling the pain." And just as the sun always rises, you can count on excuses being backed up with concocted reasons why goals were not achieved, why expenses are so high or why a project wasn't completed. Here's a Neilism: "Excuses will never explain away compromise."

Growing a business is like raising a child. If the diaper needs changing, you change it. If the baby needs to eat, you feed it. When it misbehaves, you coach it. As it matures, you lead the child by showing growth paths and to master the disciplines to achieve his or her full potential. As a parent, there is no option. It must be done. Then why is it that otherwise responsible people compromise their businesses, and the livelihoods of all those who depend on it, by manufacturing excuses rather than taking action — even when their personal assets are at risk? True, business can be difficult and challenging at times, but wearing blinders to shield you from reality is not an option.

Neilism
Excuses will never explain away compromise.

Excuses are an easy way to justify and explain away compromising behavior. The true no-compromise leader rises above the masses to openly acknowledge and take responsibility for his or her compromises. They own it. "I screwed up. It was a bad decision. I was wrong." Owning their compromises creates a level of transparency that reveals their human side, that they are not infallible — that they have no hidden agenda. Owning it ends the drama and related stress, much like hitting a huge pressure release valve. More than anything, it builds trust.

REQUIREMENT NUMBER 5:
Culture: Don't destroy from within.

"Don't destroy from within" is the first of a two-line mission statement at SRC Holdings Corp. of Springfield, Missouri. (The second line is, "Don't run out of cash.") When I heard Jack Stack, SRC's CEO and author of *The Great Game of Business*, utter these words, their simplicity and profoundness stuck with me. Why? Because time and again I see leaders who refuse to confront the reality of what's happening in their own companies, as negative behaviors contaminate their cultures. Even worse is when leaders see the problem and fail to act. It doesn't matter how successful your business is or how wonderful you believe your culture to be, it is vulnerable. As a leader, it's your responsibility to protect its culture and to do so at all costs. *Leaders cannot allow the company to be held hostage by an individual's talents and abilities versus his or her behavior.*

> To be a no-compromise leader, you must strengthen, nurture and protect your business culture from contamination.

If you trace the origin of most business challenges, crises and missed opportunities, you will discover they were created internally. Someone wasn't paying attention or being accountable and the blame game begins. Destroying from within has everything to do with behavior and how negative behavior contaminates a business culture. To be a no-compromise leader, you must strengthen, nurture and protect your business culture from contamination.

Your business culture is…

- a truly dynamic entity that embodies the heart and soul of your company.
- the energy source that not only powers your business, but links all behaviors and thinking to a common purpose.
- what attracts and retains the best employees.
- what rallies the collective energy of the business to achieve breakthrough goals and to drive growth.
- what carries the business through those inevitable tough times.
- what touches customers in that special way that keeps them coming back for more.
- what communicates the who, what and why of your business to every employee and the world around it.

Just as computers are vulnerable to virus attacks, so are business cultures.

Culture contamination can be devastating to a business. Consider it a toxic poison that can seep in at any time from any direction — internally or externally. Contamination reveals itself in the form of negative behavior, meaningless drama and decreased productivity. However, unlike computers in which you can install firewalls and virus protection, your business culture is always exposed. *Always.* Economic downturns, fierce competition, headhunters preying on your best talent, even the weather, can seed contamination in your culture. But those external attacks on your culture are nothing compared to attacks that destroy from within.

Protecting the culture is hard work and must always be done with integrity. I am by no means suggesting that leaders walk around with pink slips at the ready. I am suggesting that leaders keep the lines of communication open at all levels and invest the time and energy to protect and maintain their business cultures. Great leaders aren't great because they're innovative, understand numbers or have good communication skills. They're great because they design, build and fiercely protect the cultures they are empowered to lead. They identify, coach, and, when necessary, cut loose the anchors creating drag and impeding forward progress before their behaviors contaminate the culture. *That is the work of leadership. Failure to do so, no matter how difficult, is a compromise.*

REQUIREMENT NUMBER 6:
Unity: Don't be dictatorial and inflexible.

No compromise *is not* a leadership style void of compassion. When I do a presentation on no compromise, someone always seems to say something like, "No compromise sounds like I have to become a Marine drill sergeant." The discussion conjures up images of dictating leaders who hone their ability to shout commands and to say "no" to just about every request. Becoming a no-compromise leader doesn't mean that you must become an imposing messenger of darkness who demands unquestioned, unrelenting and absolute obedience. Frankly, anyone flipping to the drill sergeant style of leadership would likely find stacks of resignations on his or her desk. *Count on my resignation to be the first.*

If you think about the bulk of performance issues that plague business today, compromise has a hand in it. Often, it's due to lack of structure, poor information flow or just plain laziness. The personality of the leader also comes into play. Many leaders believe that saying "Yes" to everything makes them popular and well-liked by employees. Others are perfectly fine being dictatorial and inflexible and have little concern for how well liked or popular they are — just as long as the job gets done.

> **When integrity, trust, compassion, ethics, tenacity, and courage merge, they form the framework for no-compromise leadership.**

If your first reaction to no compromise is hesitation for fear of shifting to a leadership style that is too dictatorial and inflexible, ponder this. When integrity, trust, compassion, ethics, tenacity and courage merge, they form the framework for no-compromise leadership. That framework would be torn apart by the dynamics and warp-speed pace of change in business if it was incapable of flexing. Everything changes. One set of behaviors might work fine today but not tomorrow. The no-compromise leader must be open to and ready to embrace change, no matter how fast it comes.

REQUIREMENT NUMBER 7:
Focus: Avoid *office-itis*.

Office-itis is simply a term I use to describe what happens to leaders at any level who lose their focus on their company's vision and objectives. It's when they get bogged down in day-to-day minutia or other projects that tend to keep them busy but disconnected from the current reality and performance of the business.

Dennis, the owner of a construction company, had just made a major change in his role at his company. For years, in addition to managing the business, he spent much of his time at construction sites overseeing progress and working alongside employees. He recognized that his company was growing, and decided it was time to channel his efforts on managing that growth from the office. He hired a general field manager and completely removed himself from construction site work. Three months into his "lead from the office" transition, Dennis became afflicted with a full-blown case of office-itis.

This otherwise bright and energetic business leader admitted that he was frustrated in his new role and often found himself bored and looking for things to do. Dennis spent most of his time making calls, paying bills, placing orders and some systems development. At the same time, he expressed concern that his employees were getting lethargic and that teamwork performance was just not at the level it once was when he was out there with them. I asked Dennis a question to help him see how his office-itis was compromising his company: "If you got out of your office and asked each of your employees what the vision of your company is, how many would be able to answer?" I could sense by the silence that my question hit its mark. Like a kid caught with his hand in the cookie jar, Dennis answered, "I don't think any would be able to get our vision right." His office-itis was exposed. He thought he was working on his business when, in reality, he was disconnected and unplugged from the real work of leadership. And his business was responding accordingly. While Dennis was in his office counting ceiling tiles, the sense of urgency that drives team performance was compromised. *No business can run on autopilot.*

Neilism

Give your company a break — manage what's on your plate.

It is essential to not only identify office-itis but to create a business culture that makes it difficult for office-itis to creep in. If you feel bored, unproductive, disconnected or find that you're spending your day majoring in minor tasks just to keep busy, you've got a case of office-itis.

Think you're immune to office-itis because you don't work in an office? Think again. Whenever your daily work routine disconnects you from the action and dynamics of the business to the point where your leadership effectiveness is compromised — you've got a case of office-itis. Leaders who are also doctors, engineers, hair stylists, consultants, programmers and similar types of hands-on occupations, can all suffer from office-itis.

If you have a case of office-itis, you need to give yourself a huge wake-up call and get back in the action. Likewise, leaders need to look for signs of office-itis in others. Believe me, I've seen productive and responsible employees fall into office-itis work modes that could have been avoided if leadership was paying attention. *Office-itis is a compromise.*

The best prevention for office-itis is to consistently maintain the sense of urgency of the business. Communication, information flow and accountability must never be compromised.

REQUIREMENT NUMBER 8:
Strategic: Manage what's on your plate.

If you had to pick one word to describe your leadership work style, would it be *superhero*? Do you just love to pile on the work and the projects? Is so much crammed into your daily schedule that it's a challenge to give your focused attention to conversations and tasks? Are you juggling a dozen balls at a time — and begging for more? If you answered "yes" to any or all of those questions, this is your superhero mantra, "Bring it on; I can handle it all." Unfortunately, the truth is you can't handle it all. Before you say, "Oh, yeah?" take a reality check on how well you've been executing all that work.

In reality, superheroes resemble an overloaded speedboat. Rather than gaining speed until it planes over the water, an overburdened speedboat leaves nothing but an impressive wake in its path, as it struggles to push through the water. That impressive wake then becomes an obstacle that others are forced to deal with every time their superhero passes by.

> **When you try to do it all, you create that impressive wake that throws everyone in your company off balance.**

Many individuals confuse no-compromise leadership with "I must do it all." Well, you can't do it all — and when you try, you create that impressive wake that throws everyone in your company off balance. Simply put, the superhero leader becomes the disturbance that creates drag rather than lift.

I always enjoy the first consulting session with a new client because, it's like the beginning of a great mystery novel. I say this because the initial issue for hiring a consultant isn't always the issue that is causing the client's pain. The client might think the issue we need to work on is that dead elephant in the living room and how to get rid of it. Actually, the dead elephant is just a symptom of a host of potential problems. It's my job to discover how it got there, what was the murder weapon and who actually did the nasty deed. That's what makes each consulting assignment an intriguing mystery to uncover the compromise.

Neilism

The dead elephant in your living room is a symptom of a bigger problem.

One such mystery began with a call from Shelly. Her company was suffering from stalled growth and spiraling from one cash crisis to another. The call was like a desperate plea for relief from her chronic business stress. Shelly took on every project and task that came her way. And if a morsel of space on her plate cleared, she'd fill it in a nanosecond. Shelly made all the decisions in her company, and when she empowered others to make decisions, she corrected those she didn't like. Shelly complained incessantly that her managers never displayed initiative or took accountability. (She never gave them a chance to perform.) She was so overburdened that the only impressive outcome was the massive wake she created in her company. As Shelly's coach, my challenge was to help her see that wake she was creating.

It was a struggle for Shelly to look objectively at her plate and to comprehend that the inefficiencies that were stifling her company's growth were emanating from her. *Shelly's effort to do it all was actually a major source of compromise.* After months of coaching, Shelly was making progress. Morsel by morsel, her plate became more manageable. Shelly's newfound focus on the business accelerated growth and the perpetual cash crisis eventually faded away. By managing what she allowed on her plate, Shelly became an extremely effective leader — a no-compromise leader.

I understand that it's just the nature of some leaders to take on anything and everything — that they're just not "happy" unless they're running flat out. *If you're one of these pile-it-high leaders, you are compromising.* The frenzy you build around yourself makes you unapproachable, irritable, short-tempered and quite unpleasant to associate with. And if you think your superhero antics create urgency in your company, how wrong you are! Just remember how that overloaded speedboat casts out a huge wake that creates turmoil for everyone else to deal with. Time for a Neilism: "Give your company a break — manage what's on your plate."

REQUIREMENT NUMBER 9:
Resolute: Be tenacious and courageous.

In 1991, I had the opportunity to buy a small commercial printing company. Having been involved in business magazine publishing since the early 80s, I enjoyed the whole process of creating a printed piece. From writing and design, to film, plates, ink and paper, to see a print job go from idea to finished product was a fun and fulfilling experience. It still is.

So, touched by an entrepreneurial seizure, an old high school friend and I bought a local printing company. I had done business with the former owner for many years and knew that the business was generally stable and had a good customer base. The big customer was a local company that had about 80,000 subscribers for its monthly collection of five crossword puzzles. That's five times 80,000 crossword puzzles every month — a dream job for a commercial printer. This one account represented 25 percent of the printing company's annual revenues. *Translation: This account was key to making the acquisition work.*

> **Neilism**
> A healthy cash reserve is "sleep good at night" money.

So we bought this company and got to work. Since the printing equipment was old and basic, we immediately went out and purchased a big, shiny new press and computerized the graphics department with the latest Macs, color scanners and imaging units. These upgrades were essential in order to go after larger clients and more lucrative jobs. I must say, we had a blast buying all this new stuff. (*Hey, it was a big entrepreneurial seizure.*)

Remember that one big customer? You know, the one who for years paid the previous owner the day it received the invoice? Well, two and half months into our new venture, that one big customer ran up almost six figures on its account. It kept sending us work and we kept printing — it just never sent a check. Finally, I had to make my first accounts receivable collection call. The owner asked for a private meeting.

My mind flashed to the moment I signed that collateral mortgage on my home to secure the bank loan. It was a surreal moment I will never forget.

Instantly, the mother of all knots formed in the pit of my stomach.

Well, we had that private meeting in which I was informed that they had bet the ranch on their last major holiday mailing — and it bombed. They were broke. To make matters worse, I was told that 80 percent of their annual sales came from their holiday promotions. Then, the owner of the company asked if we could float them for nine months until their next holiday selling season. My mind flashed to the moment I signed that collateral mortgage on my home to secure the bank loan. It was a surreal moment I will never forget.

Needless to say, our fun little acquisition turned into our worst nightmare. Our biggest customer was going under — and owed us a ton of money. We made a major investment in new equipment. We had a huge monthly loan payment. Oh, I guess I might as well tell you that we really didn't know enough about running a commercial printing company. We were seriously in over our heads. *And this, my fellow entrepreneurs, became the bleakest and most desperate business situation I had ever been in.*

I wish I could tell an incredible story of how I pulled the company out of this mess and went on to become the greatest printer of all time. Unfortunately, with the combination of losing a major customer, the cost of new equipment (all of which was financed) and the loan payment, we just couldn't find a spec of daylight at the end of the tunnel. After two very ugly and stressful years, we worked out a deal to return the company to the previous owner. Financially devastating as it was, it was time to move on.

Personally, I had never been through anything so stressful and draining than those two ugly years as what I now describe as being "a pretty bad commercial printer." Yes, I was drained mentally and physically and my sense of pride had taken some serious body blows, but I was ready to get back in the game. *I needed to get back in the game.*

The one positive thing to come out of the printing debacle was the initial concept for *Strategies* magazine, including cover and page design. (For me, part of the reason to buy the printing company was to print *Strategies* and all of the promotional pieces on my own presses.) So, on September 13, 1993, I moved my office furniture and computers from the printing company four miles away to a small office on the first floor of 40 Main Street in Centerbrook, Connecticut.

For the first few months, I worked by myself writing *Strategies*, doing all the graphics, promotional mailings and taking subscription orders over the phone. For me, it was the best and only way to purge the printing company fiasco from my system. Yes, it was long days, but I enjoyed it and looked forward to going to work again. I was having fun. I was feeling that wonderful sense of fulfillment and accomplishment. More importantly, my pride and confidence returned. *Little by little, the nightmare of the printing company faded into a collection of leadership lessons that remain permanently part of my thinking.*

Fast-forward to today and Strategies occupies the entire second floor of 40 Main Street. Since year one, we've had double-digit growth on both the top and bottom lines. We fiercely maintain and protect a healthy cash reserve. So much so, it deserves a simple yet profound Neilism: "A healthy cash reserve is 'sleep-good-at-night' money."

By design, the no-compromise leader must be tenacious and courageous. As much as I wanted that printing company to succeed — for me to lead it into daylight — it was not to be. I was tenacious until the end. I refused to give up. However, after 24 months of business hell, reality posed that dreaded question no entrepreneur ever wants to hear, *"Is there a reason for this business to continue on?"* Personally, I was on the verge of losing everything I had. There was only one decision and that was to muster the courage to confront reality and admit it was over. That was one of the toughest decisions I ever had to make. I ached not only for myself, but also for all of the employees who depended on the company for their livelihoods. Although it was the darkest period of my business life, I had resolved to begin my quest back to success. I yearned to look forward to going to work and for work to be fun again. *No compromise.*

I learned a lot of business lessons in those 24 months. I also learned a lot about myself. Looking back, if it were not for my tenaciousness, the printing company would not have lasted as long as it did. I learned how tenacity and courage take you through the tough times. More importantly, how these qualities are a requirement to be a no-compromise leader.

REQUIREMENT NUMBER 10:
Inspiring: Lead with passion.

There is a dividing line that separates leaders from no-compromise leaders. On one side, "leader" is something that describes a title or job. It's simply the work you do. This leader says, "I lead." On the other side of the dividing line is an inherent and unmistakable *emotional intensity* radiating from the no-compromise leader. It's like a gravitational pull to higher calling that converges on the vision and greater purpose of the company. It's intense passion and it's impossible to be a no-compromise leader without

Passion fuels a higher calling and a natural enthusiasm to all that you do. So much so that others can sense and capture that same passion.

it. Why? If you don't have passion for what you do, it's just too easy to give up — to compromise. The no-compromise leader says, "We're going to make the world a better place for all," and believes this with every fiber of his or her being. Here's a Neilism for leading with passion: "Without passion, work is work. Who wants to follow a leader with no passion?"

Passion fuels a higher calling and a natural enthusiasm to all that you do. So much so that others can sense and capture that same passion. The no-compromise leader's passion attracts and engages others in the most positive way. That shared passion then lifts the performance of the entire company.

Consider any great leader in history, business or otherwise, and you will find an innate passion as the driving force behind his accomplishments.

In his book, *Small Giants: Companies That Choose to Be Great Instead of Big*, Bo Burlingham talks about that special "mojo" that's present in all great businesses. It's that special something you feel as a customer, employee or vendor. As Bo explained it to me, while researching the 14 companies he wrote about in *Small Giants*, he began to understand the true meaning of mojo and the role it plays in the success of a business. When a company has mojo, it has something uniquely and distinctly special. Likewise, if it loses its mojo, it's just another business that's indistinguishable from the competition.

> **Neilism**
> Without passion, work is work. Who wants to follow a leader with no passion?

My take is that the mojo that makes a company unique and great begins with the passion of its leader. I believe Strategies has a special mojo and it began forming the day my passion for writing and training others about business inspired me to sign a lease and start my company. And I knew the success of Strategies would depend on finding others who shared my passion and vision.

Passion is rightfully the 10th and perhaps most important requirement to be a no-compromise leader. If you have the fire in your gut to achieve your dreams against all odds, you have passion. If you get excited and light up when you tell others about your work, you have passion. When you hear your employees talking about their work and the company with the same passion as you — your company has mojo.

As you can see by the 10 requirements, there is a higher level of behavior and thinking that is woven into the DNA of no-compromise leadership. Rather than rigid, no-compromise leaders are compassionate and flexible with an unwavering sense of purpose to be the best, inspire the best and to win the game. They earn respect through consistency, integrity and trust. They create unflappable and dynamic cultures. They are certainly tenacious and courageous. They get things done because they expect nothing less than the best from themselves and those they lead.

One last additional requirement

For the no-compromise leader, having fun is essential. Fun puts bounce in your step. Fun gives you energy. And when you're having fun, it's infectious in the most positive way possible to everyone you come in contact with. The leader's mood and demeanor set the tone for the company. A moody, crotchety and miserable leader will create a moody, crotchety and miserable culture to work in. That's compromise.

Of course, not every day will be full of blue sky and popcorn clouds. Business can change like the weather and sooner or later, you'll have to deal with a storm or two. I'm always saddened when I meet a business owner or leader who just isn't having fun. Their energy is sapped and the company's performance pays the price. *Their perpetual funk is spinning off compromise in every direction.* In such cases, only a major wake-up call or change of job will snap them out of it. Interestingly, when I've coached business owners through an exit strategy, I often see them brighten up and have fun. For some, the best strategy for burned-out leaders is to move on and seek out work that will reignite their passion and bring fulfillment and fun. Here's a Neilism: "Life is too short to work hard at something you hate. Find your calling."

Neilism

Life is too short to work hard at something you hate. Find your calling.

Many entrepreneurs discover that the business they built thrust them into a leadership role they're totally unprepared for. Others find themselves in leadership roles that they never truly aspired to, such as having to take over the family-owned company after the passing of a parent. Making peace with your role as leader can be a difficult transition. For those reluctant leaders who never made peace with their role, shifting to the no-compromise leadership style can be a challenge. Reluctant leaders tend to resist, and sometimes fight, the transition. Only through a deeper understanding will they allow the leader inside them to emerge. A personal leadership coach is invaluable in such situations — if the desire to change is authentic.

Herb created no-compromise fun

Herb Kelleher, co-founder of Southwest Airlines, is one leader who totally embraced the fun part of leadership. Starting a commercial airline was a daunting task and the odds of success were stacked against them. A lot of what made Southwest successful was its "have fun" culture. They ran advertisements for employees saying things like, "If you like coloring outside the lines, Southwest is for you." The picture in the ad was a dinosaur from a coloring book. Southwest celebrates damn near everything, often with balloons and balloon arches that are works of art.

Kelleher became known for his high publicity antics, like settling a trademark lawsuit by arm wrestling the president of the other company. He did it again when he announced that Southwest won the "Triple Crown Award" for on-time departures, baggage handling and the fewest customer complaints. The president of a major airline called to find out what the heck the Triple Crown Award is. Kelleher simply took an FAA report and turned it into a PR winner. He made up the "Triple Crown Award." Kelleher just knows how to have fun. Plain and simple, a fun culture will show up on your bottom line. No compromise.

Action steps before reading on...

Take this fast little quiz to see how you match up against the 10 no-compromise requirements. Circle the number that best reflects you. Number 1 is least like you. Number 10 is most like you.

REQUIREMENT NUMBER 1:
Clarity: You have absolute clarity on where you're taking your company.

Least like you					Most like you				
1	2	3	4	5	6	7	8	9	10

REQUIREMENT NUMBER 2:
Values: You want them and you live them.

Least like you					Most like you				
1	2	3	4	5	6	7	8	9	10

REQUIREMENT NUMBER 3:
Accountability: If it needs to be done, you get it done.

Least like you					Most like you				
1	2	3	4	5	6	7	8	9	10

REQUIREMENT NUMBER 4:
Transparent: You don't make excuses. You own it.

Least like you					Most like you				
1	2	3	4	5	6	7	8	9	10

REQUIREMENT NUMBER 5:
Culture: You never engage in behaviors that will destroy from within.

Least like you					Most like you				
1	2	3	4	5	6	7	8	9	10

Requirement Number 6:
Unity: Your leadership style is not dictatorial and inflexible.

Least like you					Most like you				
1	2	3	4	5	6	7	8	9	10

Requirement Number 7:
Focus: You avoid office-itis.

Least like you					Most like you				
1	2	3	4	5	6	7	8	9	10

Requirement Number 8:
Strategic: You manage what's on your plate.

Least like you					Most like you				
1	2	3	4	5	6	7	8	9	10

Requirement Number 9:
Resolute: You are tenacious and courageous.

Least like you					Most like you				
1	2	3	4	5	6	7	8	9	10

Requirement Number 10:
Inspiring: You lead with passion.

Least like you					Most like you				
1	2	3	4	5	6	7	8	9	10

Scoring and Recommendations:

Add each of the circled numbers and enter the total here _____ .

If you scored 10 – 30: Not qualified to be a no-compromise leader.

You are going to find your transition to no-compromise leadership a serious challenge, because your current behaviors will be working against you. *Simply put, you compromise too much.*

RECOMMENDATION: Review the requirements with the lowest scores and select one or two to work on. Practice behaviors that will move your score to the "most like you" range. Be tenacious and courageous, and you will see positive results.

If you scored 31 – 55: You must truly want it to qualify.

It's time to look in the mirror and make the most important career decision of your life. You must be committed and willing to go the distance by adjusting your behaviors and locking them in for the long haul. You have a tendency to compromise, especially when it really counts. *You must change, or your desire to become a no-compromise leader will elude you.*

RECOMMENDATION: This is the time to decide what kind of leader you want to be. It's time to get off the fence and take action. You have a lot of leadership disciplines to master and catching up do to. *So what will it be, become a no-compromise leader or get comfortable on those lower rungs of the leadership ladder?*

If you scored 56 – 70: You show promise and may have what it takes to be a no-compromise leader — if you commit yourself.

Your score shows that you might have the potential to transition into a no-compromise leader. However, scores in this range indicate that you have a tendency to display inconsistent leadership behavior and that you have issues with accountability. *Becoming a no-compromise leader is your decision if you choose to step up to the plate.*

RECOMMENDATION: It's time to work on your follow through and commit to strict a regimen of no-compromise accountability. When you feel that urge to quit, compromise or drop the ball, trigger your no-compromise commitment to cross the finish line. And remember, just crossing the finish line doesn't cut it. Whatever you do now, do it to the best of your ability. Most of all, you must confront your leadership blockages. *The more you work through your blockages, the more you become a no-compromise leader.*

If you scored 71 – 90: You have what it takes.

Your score indicates that no-compromise leadership is within your grasp and it's yours for the taking. You are generally consistent, accountable and determined. You govern yourself well and try to set a good example for those you lead. *What stands in the way is your tendency to become complacent, which allows compromise to derail consistency, momentum and progress.*

RECOMMENDATION: Closing that gap between where you are now and no-compromise leadership all comes down to your desire, commitment and personal discipline to adhere to a higher standard of leadership thinking and behavior. *No compromise must become your personal mandate and guide all that you do.*

If you scored 91 – 100: You can be a no-compromise leader.

You definitely have all the characteristics of a no-compromise leader. It is largely a case of you mastering the disciplines, behaviors and systems of no-compromise leadership. *Go for it!*

RECOMMENDATION: No-compromise leadership is not something to wear or tout to others. It doesn't automatically make you a super-leader. *Allow it to evolve and you will begin to notice your effectiveness improve — as will others. Don't flaunt it. Just focus on it and enjoy the process.*

If you scored 100 – I wish I had met you while writing this book.

CHAPTER 3

SHIELDS DOWN: NEW BELIEFS AND THINKING

Making the shift to no-compromise leadership is far more complex than the flip of a mental switch. You must change at a deeper level.

I n this chapter, I present a range of developmental lessons critical to becoming an authentic no-compromise leader. The key word here is "authentic," because the no-compromise leader cannot be anything less. To be perceived as a leader with moral integrity who is just and trustworthy, authenticity is non-negotiable. The no-compromise leader must steadfastly adhere to the highest principles of self-discipline, accountability and professional standards. Master the lessons in this chapter and you will begin to understand why no-compromise leadership truly is a higher standard of leadership thinking and behavior.

> **Neilism**
> To be a no-compromise leader, you must be 100 percent authentic. Trust, commitment and loyalty flow both ways.

Let's start this chapter off with a Neilism: "To be a no-compromise leader, you must be 100 percent authentic. Trust, commitment and loyalty flow both ways."

Consider this, we are all governed by our personal set of beliefs of how the world around us works. It's what gives uniqueness to each individual. Our personal set of beliefs is a reflection of our upbringing, family culture, education and life experiences in the world in which we interact. We shape and mold our beliefs through mentors and those we choose to interact with personally and professionally. When you enter the realm of leadership, your personal beliefs regarding people, business, communication and how people need to be led will define your leadership style, behavior and thinking. *More specifically, your beliefs will shape the vision and culture of your company.*

Leadership behavior is an outcome of what you believe, and what you believe is what drives your thinking. If a leader believes that people will only produce if strictly supervised, his or her thinking is both governed and limited by these beliefs. The leader's behavior will reflect a rigid, inflexible and controlling "my way or the highway" mode of leadership. Imagine the difficulty persuading this leader that employees can think and make decisions like an owner if given the knowledge, tools and opportunity to do so. Deep-seated personal beliefs function like *mental shields* that prevent other points of view and opposing beliefs from getting in. *Essentially, your thinking is locked in its present operating mode because your shields deflect anything that fails to conform to your current beliefs.*

> **Deep-seated personal beliefs function like mental shields that prevent other points of view and opposing beliefs from getting in.**

Taking command of your mental shields

Every leader has a unique collection of beliefs and behaviors. There is no one-size-fits-all strategy for upgrading who you are as a leader to no-compromise status. Some leaders are open to new ideas, systems and concepts. There are leaders who acknowledge or recognize that their skills and abilities need improvement and seek out the best education, mentor or coach. In contrast, there are leaders who are extremely closed to new ideas and reject any attempts to change their thinking. Their minds and thinking are locked and inaccessible and, intentionally or not, they prefer to keep it that way.

The ability for a leader to change his or her beliefs and thinking requires the highest level of openness and contemplation to achieve breakthroughs. But, I caution you that no matter how open you perceive yourself to be, your beliefs will continue to filter and reject conflicting input and data — unless you allow your mental shields to lower.

In Chapter 1, I wrote about the dark side of compromise. Within the dark side, there are shields that can block you from truly seeing how your personal behavior could be the root cause of problems in your company or area of responsibility. Over time, your shields can become hardened and locked in the up or closed position, causing you to be highly resistant to change or other points of view. *In extreme cases, perpetually closed shields can cause a leader to become cynical, derisive and distrusting.* New ideas, innovative strategies and effective solutions are blocked from further consideration. Any leader who knowingly or unknowingly locks his or her shields in the up position is just plain difficult to work and communicate with. *With shields up, productive dialog is impossible.*

Neilism
Are you open to new ideas and points of view — as long as they match yours? Time to lower your shields and grow.

The first step is to resist the temptation to raise your mental shields, thus allowing yourself to be open to new ideas and different points of view. Only when your mental shields are down can you objectively explore new opportunities. Are there elements that could work for you and your company? If so, how can you implement those elements to produce optimum results?

A Neilism: "Are you open to new ideas and points of view — as long as they match yours? Time to lower your shields and grow."

When your shields are down, you gain a unique perspective of how your thinking can positively or negatively influence business outcomes. You become more self-aware and accountable for your own behavior, actions and decisions. You rise above the pettiness of blaming others for situations — especially when you might have been the original source of compromise. *Only when your shields are down is there an opportunity for true leadership thinking breakthrough.*

Sometimes it might require a major crisis to get your shields to lower. There's nothing like a massive dose of business pain to convince a leader that it's time to hit the emergency "shields-down" switch. Interestingly, when the pain gets bad enough, that's when shields-up leaders often seek out the cure. They're suddenly open to all sorts of new ideas, solutions or points of view that they never would have accepted without lowering their shields — or when they were able to tolerate the pain.

The challenge in such situations is getting leaders to stay the course long enough for new behaviors to become entrenched in their leadership thinking. It's common to see leaders respond to marginal gains or small wins by proclaiming, "The crisis is over — all clear." Up pop the shields and the compromising behavior that seeded the problem returns and the cycle begins all over again. That's when employees, as if on cue, say, "I knew this change wouldn't last."

Shields up — thinking locked

You can study, train and be coached to become a better leader. But that's just the beginning. Here's a non-negotiable Neilism: "Without a personal mandate to change your thinking, no-compromise leadership will elude you." All of that newfound knowledge might allow you to impress others with your ability to recite all of the latest buzz-words and concepts, but if you fail to change your thinking and behavior at the core level, you're merely cloaking compromise. Leaders are measured by deed and performance.

> **Neilism**
> Without a personal mandate to change your thinking, NCL will elude you.

It if has to be done, it gets done. That's no-compromise thinking.

Many leaders selectively decide to lower their shields or not, based on how willing they are to understand their own thinking. It's no different than an obese person lowering his shields to see that he must change his thinking that governs his eating behaviors. My father was obese his entire life. I'm talking a cruising weight of 350 pounds. His name was Harry, but everyone called him "Duke" — it just fit him better.

Being obese, and the eating behaviors that drive it, can be humiliating and embarrassing. When my father would buy a new car, he had to have the seat tracks moved back just so he could fit behind the wheel. At one point he was so heavy, the doctor's scale didn't go high enough to weigh him. The only scale the doctor could find to weigh him was at the meat market. Humiliated, Duke hung on the meat scale like a side of beef.

My mother and father owned a dry cleaning and tuxedo rental business. I remember my mother going ballistic when she found his secret stash of Mars candy bars under the bow ties in the file cabinet. (To this day, I believe there were many more secret stashes never discovered.)

Yes, there was a suicide attempt. We found him passed out in the car with the engine running and garage door shut. *How bad does it need to get for someone to change his operating system?* My father certainly knew he needed to change his thinking and behavior, he just couldn't lower his shields long enough to let the new thinking in.

Throughout his life, my father tried every diet imaginable. A couple of heart attacks later, worsening diabetes, being hospitalized regularly and a diagnosis of inoperable heart disease, finally got him to lower his shields so he could change his thinking and self-destructive eating behavior. In that last year, my father got down to a trim 240. He died of a heart attack a month before his 60th birthday. *Duke's willingness to change his thinking and behavior came too late to repair a lifetime of self-inflicted damage.*

Make no mistake; business leaders routinely do the same destructive damage to their companies as my father did to his body. The change begins by allowing your shields to lower. That's the willingness part. Keeping your shields down and your mind objectively open to new ideas is the commitment part. Going the distance to change your thinking is the accountability part. Lowering your shields is the easy part and merely creates opportunities to learn and grow. Only the no-compromise leader will turn those precious opportunities into a higher level of personal leadership thinking.

Unlearning past practices

Many of today's most powerful strategies and systems were derived from leadership thinking that challenged conventional wisdom at the time. But empowerment, systemization, process management, open-book management, Team-Based Pay and other contemporary approaches to achieving breakthrough results will surely fail if the leader's beliefs and thinking conflict in any way. Here's a Neilism to drive that point home: "Leadership beliefs and thinking must align with strategies for measurable results to occur."

> **Beliefs act like an internal guidance system. It doesn't matter if you're headed in the right or wrong direction, beliefs keep you on course.**

For leaders, few challenges eclipse the need to objectively examine their basic beliefs about leading people in order to harness and organize their collective efforts to achieve the right outcomes. Beliefs act like an internal guidance system. It doesn't matter if you're headed in the right or wrong direction; beliefs keep you on course.

To become a no-compromise leader, you must unlearn many of your past practices.

- You must find new ways of challenging your beliefs, so you can be open to new ideas and opportunities.
- You must create your own compelling value proposition for change. Begin by answering two simple questions. (1.) If you continue your current leadership thinking and behavior, will you ever achieve the results you seek? (2.) If you change and adopt new leadership thinking and behavior, what would the possibilities look like?
- You must avoid resisting new ideas, concepts and points of view that differ from those that supported your past successes. *What got you here could be obsolete tomorrow.*
- You must adopt a mindset that helps foster more fulfilling relationships in your organization. *Lead to serve. Lead to win.*

+ You must believe that it's not only possible to find a more enlightened path as a no-compromise leader — it's your responsibility to your company, your employees, your customers and yourself.

Knowledge can be defined as information organized in a framework that renders that information useful. Simply put, it might be that your context for viewing information about leadership might significantly reduce or even prevent its effective use. Very often, your mindset stands as an invisible shield to innovation and learning and renders you informed but not knowledgeable. *To become more knowledgeable, you will have to accelerate a process of self-examination and resist the temptation to seek simple answers.* To accomplish that, the no-compromise leader must keep his ego in check or it will render any attempt at self-examination pointless.

This process is a difficult one. Even for the leader who is willing to challenge his or her mindset, the task can be daunting. *We simply don't have good methods for challenging the way we think.* Without good methods, many leaders simply don't explore their own assumptions and have, instead, chosen to experiment with behavioral models that are easy to understand, easy to apply, and often give a leader a greater sense of predictability and control. For many, these approaches represent a pragmatic solution to the question of how to continually upgrade their leadership skills. Predictably, these methods rarely stimulate meaningful improvement beyond a quick but fleeting jolt in productivity. *No-compromise leadership is not achieved via quick jolts or instant upgrades. It's achieved via a profound shift at the core of a leader's thinking.*

Neilism
Leadership beliefs and thinking must align with strategies for measureable results to occur.

At times in the last half-century, the arguments for re-examining our leadership thinking have been compelling. Douglas McGregor made it his life-long work to help leaders down a path of self-examination and discovery. And even though he was recognized as the foremost thinker of his time, much of his message has been misinterpreted or ignored.

McGregor realized the complexities involved in challenging one's own context for viewing leadership information and suggested a number of methods to begin the process. He believed that leaders might find it easier to examine their thinking if they had a model that could provide a comparison. So McGregor suggested Theory X and Theory Y, two very different sets of assumptions about the nature of people. He asked leaders to compare their beliefs to the fictitious beliefs outlined in X and Y. His theory remains highly relevant today:

Are people naturally motivated to work? Or must people be given incentives to get them to give their best?

Is it natural for people to seek rewards for the least amount of effort? Or are de-motivated workers a symptom of stifling organizational and leadership practices?

Can we realistically expect people to act unemotionally on the job? Or are emotional reactions part of the human spirit that can be suppressed but never left behind?

Theory X and Theory Y are still recognizable terms for most. However, McGregor's hopes for this theory were quickly frustrated decades ago. Discussions of X and Y degraded into conversations of leadership style shortly after their publication. In fact, most people in 1960, as well as most today, think that a Theory X leader has *authoritative tendencies* and that a Theory Y leader has a more *democratic style*. This gross misinterpretation of his ideas frustrated McGregor who, before he died in 1962, called his desire to have leaders challenge their basic assumptions about people a "pious hope, and little else." He was hopeful, however, that a time would come when it would become necessary for leaders to challenge what they are by following these simple, yet powerful, four steps:

1. Begin a process of self-examination and self-discovery.
2. Resist the temptation to seek simple answers. *You must seek clarity, not simplicity.*
3. Examine the decisions and choices you make in order to better understand how your accepted values differ from the values you currently adhere to as a leader.

4. Choose a different set of beliefs — one that is more consistent
   with building inspired teams.

The good news is that today, for the first time, leaders may find that no-
compromise leadership and inspired teams are prerequisites to business
survival. A rapidly changing world demands speed, flexibility and responsiveness. *Past systems of command and control, strict hierarchical structures
and dictated actions are as outdated at the buggy whip and most certainly
inadequate for the task.*

We have all seen leaders with diverse leadership styles who are successful at inspiring and creating dynamic team cultures. Some have
charisma; some do not. Some seek consensus; some do not. Some have
quick tempers, while others have
great patience. However, what they
all have in common are similar
beliefs about people and what they
can achieve in the right environment
and culture. They recognize that the
difference between ordinary people doing ordinary work and ordinary
people doing extraordinary work is contingent on their leadership. They
have a genuine commitment to the success and wellbeing of those they
lead. Most important of all, people trust that the behavior they see in
their leader is truly authentic because everything he does is consistent
with his beliefs.

> **People trust that the behavior they see in their leader is truly authentic because everything they do is consistent with their beliefs.**

So how do you go about choosing a different set of beliefs or determine
if some of your beliefs just need upgrading? To get you pointed in the right
direction, I offer you a set of 13 no-compromise beliefs. Study them one
by one and benchmark them against your current beliefs. Which ones do
you agree with and why? Which ones challenge your current beliefs and
why? *And now the most difficult question, which ones do you agree with but
your current thinking and behavior indicate otherwise?* For example, a leader
might believe that he is not gender biased, but selects a male with lesser
qualifications for a key position over a female who has both the qualifications and experience to excel in the job.

BELIEF ONE: Trust is given, not earned. People don't trust people who do not trust them. If we want people to trust us, we must trust them first. If we can't trust them, why should they trust us? Why do we expect others to earn our trust, while they are supposed to trust us because of our position? *When people truly trust each other, team dynamics flow so much more easily and openly.*

BELIEF TWO: People want to do the right thing. People want to live values that are consistent with their aspirations. *Values are a common ground by which dialogue flows, decisions are made, and people have an implicit understanding of lines not to be crossed.*

Neilism
The no-compromise leader envisions opportunity — not mediocrity.

BELIEF THREE: Freedom is the essence of motivation. The freedom to choose is a fundamental human need. The more that need is restricted unnecessarily, the more frustrated a person will become. *Only when we create environments based on self-direction and mutual accountability will we capture the potential of people.*

BELIEF FOUR: People are naturally driven to make things better and seek meaning in their work. Just challenge a group to make a contribution and watch the level of energy. There is a yearning for meaning in life and in work. People will do things for a cause that they will not do for money. *Watch how people work when they are proud to tell people where they work and how they contribute.*

BELIEF FIVE: People have great capacity and need to learn and grow. The need to learn and grow is as natural as the need to eat. Abraham Maslow noted after one of his first days working in a company that, "Any job not worth doing is not worth doing well." Work must be designed so that every person, regardless of pay level, can learn, grow and make a substantial contribution. *Higher expectations will lead to higher performance in the right environment, but not if the leader's expectations of a group communicates a vision of mediocrity.* A Neilism: "The no-compromise leader envisions opportunity — not mediocrity."

Belief Six: People prefer responsibility to dependency. In the right conditions, work is as natural as play. We need to be engaged and responsible. Too many management practices rob people of the ability to be responsible. Empowerment often means, "I have the power and if I trust you, I'll share power with you." It is not about getting people to change in order to conform. It's about getting people to take responsibility for creating a different future. *People want to be engaged. People want to be passionate. It is the leader's responsibility to create that environment and the opportunity.*

Belief Seven: People seek to be led, not managed. People don't want to be managed. No one wants to be planned, organized and controlled. *People want to be part of a team. They want to participate. They want to be a partner in the process of business growth.*

Belief Eight: Teamwork is not a tactic. It is the way people work best. However, there is power in a leader who drives with passion, integrity, and has the courage to make decisions and provide direction as needed. *As much as people can be frustrated by micro-management, they can be equally as frustrated when there does not appear to be any leadership or direction.*

Belief Nine: People want to work cooperatively toward a shared goal. People have a need to be part of a group and to help others. That natural tendency is often lost when people are given incentives to compete against other members of the team. That can do more to degrade teamwork than inspire it. We need to overcome our belief that internal competition leads to better performance. *The moment a company consists of two or more people, it must be a team-based organization.*

Belief Ten: Clarify expectations as much as possible — to as many people as possible. Can you remember the last time you were asked to do something and had no idea why you were doing it? Can you remember how excited you were? We simply cannot commit to what we don't understand. *Widely distributed information and a shared understanding of that information and expectations should be the right of every employee.* As Jack Stack told me in an interview, "The more information you give people, the better decisions and forecasts they can make."

BELIEF ELEVEN: People want to belong and feel a sense of pride in their work and the company they work for. People come to work hoping the opportunities will allow them to make a maximum contribution to the company. Initial experiences are compelling and people need to see that the company is worthy of their commitment. *At times people will turn down promotions, transfers or new jobs, based on a desire to stay a part of something they are proud of, or to avoid moving to a place where the opposite is true.*

BELIEF TWELVE: People desire to be treated as unique individuals in the workplace. People crave to be recognized and appreciated for the individual strengths and talents that they bring to the team. Too often, organizations look at people to see who most closely fits the "organizational mold." *Harnessing the energy that comes from individual strengths can make a formidable team more capable of delivering results at a phenomenal level.*

> No-compromise leadership not only changes how you accept and process information, it gives you permission to lead based on the highest and most worthy beliefs about people.

BELIEF THIRTEEN: People seek fulfillment in the workplace. *They want to feel important, needed, useful, confident, successful, proud and respected, rather than unimportant, useless, anonymous or expendable.*

How did the preceding set of beliefs resonate with your current beliefs about people and those you lead? Did you feel inspired and aligned with them or did you feel the ache of conflicting beliefs or behavior? If you agreed with the above set of beliefs but your leadership behavior indicates otherwise, you might be talking a better game than you're playing. The good news is that you can change your thinking by lowering your shields and adopting a new set of beliefs. No-compromise leadership not only changes how you accept and process information, it gives you permission to lead based on the highest and most worthy beliefs about people.

What mode is your leadership thinking in?

I don't believe that it's too much of a leap to compare leadership thinking to a computer operating system. Each leader operates on his or her own operating system to process information, make decisions and to execute tasks. And just like a computer, each individual's operating system has capabilities and limitations. Most definitely, all have glitches and bugs that can cause erratic behavior, often times when you least expect it.

Here are some questions to help you evaluate how your own operating system guides your thinking:

+ Why is it that some individuals are natural-born leaders, while others flounder in a leadership role?
+ Why is it that some leaders consistently make good decisions, while others, with the same resources, just can't get a win?
+ Why is it some leaders excel at empowering individuals and teams, while others can't let go of their command and control style?
+ Why is it that some leaders are fast and others are slow?
+ Why is it that some leaders command great respect and loyalty, while others deal with excessive turnover?
+ Why is it that some leaders can execute and get things done, while others struggle to get anything across the finish line?
+ Why is that some leaders approach tough issues head-on, while others get bogged down by their leadership blockages, hoping it all just goes away?
+ Why is it that one business can operate with great consistency and high productivity, while others are consistently inconsistent?
+ Why is it that one company can build cash reserves, while other companies seemingly function in a perpetual cash-flow crisis?

I could go, on but I think you get where this line of questioning is going. Just like the operating system installed in a computer, the answers to all of the above can be found in the operating system that guides your thinking. *The good news is that your operating system is upgradable.* In fact, it can be dramatically upgraded, but only if you choose to do so.

You can talk no compromise to your heart's content, but until your thinking shifts into no-compromise mode, you will never walk it and your company will never live it. Get the thinking right and you immediately establish a standard for company-wide performance and behavior. Most importantly, it will be your no-compromise thinking that will shape and refine your company's culture. *The change in thinking must begin with you.*

There is no better way to describe how important leadership thinking is than my favorite phrase, "The fish stinks from the head down." This book is about no-compromise leadership. It's about business performance at its highest and most enlightened level. If the leadership thinking is "stinky" at the top, the performance of the company will be equally stinky all the way down the line. Enron is perhaps the most painful example of what happens when leaders at the top allow their thinking to become compromised. The trickle-down effect of Enron's tainted leadership thinking brought down the entire company — and the hopes, dreams and fortunes of all who believed in its vision.

Action steps before reading on...

1. Practice lowering your shields by heightening your awareness of whether they're open or closed. When you sense that initial resistance to a new idea or concept and feel your shields closing, or slamming shut, take a deep breath and allow the other point of view in for consideration. Even though you're uncomfortable with it, try arguing the case for the new idea. That alone, will give you a better understanding to make the best decision.

2. I provided you with a new set of beliefs to consider. Try writing your own beliefs about people. Take what you like from the 13 offered and make them fit you. *Make your new set of beliefs your personal mandate to being a no-compromise leader.*

3. Slow down your leadership pace for at least one week to allow you to practice listening and maintaining your objectivity before making decisions. Take on fewer tasks or fewer appointments. Take time to wander around your company and talk to people. Smile and listen to what they have to say with your shields down. When presented with new ideas, listen with your shields down. Practice. Practice. Practice.

4. Try living these "I musts" of no-compromise leadership:

+ I must be consistent.

+ I must be tenacious.

+ I must know my numbers.

+ I must execute.

+ I must never avoid problems or issues.

+ I must do daily meetings and/or huddles.

- I must create and maintain a sense of urgency.

- I must create and relentlessly protect the right company culture.

- I must sincerely demonstrate respect to all team members.

- I must respect myself.

- I must create a plan and work my plan.

- I must be open to change.

- I must never hesitate to admit when I'm wrong.

- I must listen and really hear.

- I must not make excuses.

PART II

No-Compromise
Leadership and
The Four Business
Outcomes

PART II
Introduction

I need to begin Part II with this Neilism; "Most leaders talk a better game than they play." I'm not attempting to be derogatory; I'm just stating the obvious.

Entering the "coordinates" for no-compromise leadership

At this point in the book, you're ready to move beyond the conceptual thinking behind no-compromise leadership and on to practical application. In Part II, I will take you into the nuts and bolts of no-compromise leadership. Consider Part I like gazing at the stars on a crystal-clear night. You see all the wonders of the universe above you in one grand tapestry. You observe and learn how to find the North Star and how to identify the constellations. You become familiar with all the night sky has to offer. You are also grounded in the reality that in order to reach those stars, your thinking and behavior must shift into no-compromise leadership mode.

Neilism
Most leaders talk a better game than they play.

Consider Part II the equivalent of entering coordinates into the Hubble Space Telescope to maneuver it to a point at a specific region of deep space. Without the haze and smog of the atmosphere to distort your view, you will be able to see with extreme clarity the infinite wonders that were invisible to your naked eye. When you master the disciplines of no-compromise leadership, you will have the clarity to see opportunities you never knew existed. It's just a matter of setting the right coordinates.

The four business outcomes:
Productivity, profitability, staff retention, customer loyalty

In the chapters ahead, we will set the coordinates to aim your newfound no-compromise leadership thinking at four specific business outcomes. I call them The *Four Business Outcomes*. A *business outcome* is the end result of leadership thinking and behavior, except in this case, I'm referring to the thinking and behavior that a no-compromise leader drives throughout every nook and cranny of the company.

Each of The Four Business Outcomes is uniquely and inherently bound to one another. If one weakens or falters, it will have an instantaneous and profound impact on the other three. As a no-compromise leader, you are ultimately accountable for driving The Four Business Outcomes in your company. Consider it a non-negotiable.

Take a moment to review the chart on the next page. This chart illustrates The Four Business Outcomes in the form of a wheel comprised of segments and zones. There are four equal segments, one for each business outcome. There are five zones, each zone representing a *no-compromise effectiveness rating* from a perfect 100 percent to dismal zero percent. The wheel is in perfect balance as long as each outcome is at 100 percent. As your rating falls below 100 percent in each business outcome, the wheel becomes distorted and out of balance, creating vibration and drag.

The Four Business Outcomes Wheel

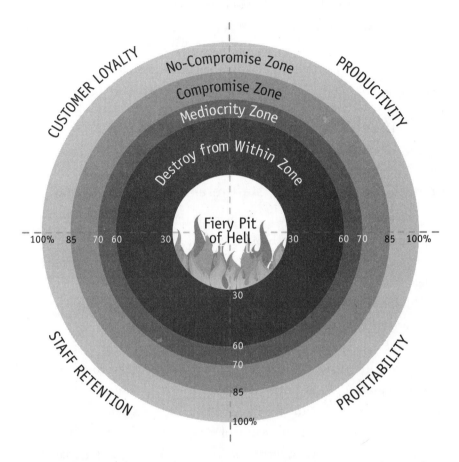

Using the effectiveness rating key below, plot your company's no-compromise performance in each of The Four Business Outcomes on the wheel above. Then, connect the dots to see how out of balance the wheel is and to identify which outcome(s) you need to head back into the no-compromise zone.

| The no-compromise rating key for each business outcome ||
How does your company rate?	Your company is in this NCL zone:
85% – 100%	No-Compromise Zone
70% – 85%	Compromise Zone
60% – 70%	Mediocrity Zone
30% – 60%	Destroy from Within Zone
0% – 30%	Fiery Pit of Hell Zone

How does your company rate?

Study The Four Business Outcomes chart. Beginning with the productivity business outcome, place a dot in one of the zones that best represents the effectiveness rating of your company or department — under your present leadership. Obviously, this is highly subjective. However, if your company is demonstrating less than stellar performance in the productivity outcome, it should be a rather simple process to mark the point that best describes what your best guess is.

Continue around the wheel until a dot is placed in a zone for the remaining business outcomes.

Next, connect the dots for each outcome and study the shape. If you scored a perfect 100 percent, your wheel is per-

> **The Four Business Outcomes, that's it. Drive these four outcomes — laser focus on these four — and your company will grow in quantum leaps.**

fectly balanced and capable of turning at high speed. Imagine putting your perfectly balanced wheel on a high-performance race car and achieving record-breaking speeds. If one outcome scores less than 100 percent, your wheel is out of balance. Now, imagine putting that imperfect wheel on that race car. Should you attempt to run at high speed, the vibration could cause something to break. The more outcomes you score below 100 percent, the more it can cause an imbalance so great that the wheel could cause our race car to crash.

Using this simple chart and rating your own company in each of The Four Business Outcomes is the perfect way to illustrate why so many companies, try as they might, are incapable of achieving sustainable high-speed growth.

The Four Business Outcomes provide an uncluttered target for leaders to aim toward. Remember, no-compromise leadership is about clarity and focus. *The Four Business Outcomes, that's it.* Drive these four outcomes — laser focus on these four — and your company will grow in quantum leaps. Drive these four business outcomes and you will achieve a high level of consistency in overall business performance. That consistency leads to predictability — *and predictability is the most cherished commodity in business.*

Think about it. The end result of no-compromise leadership is consistency across The Four Business Outcomes. That consistency produces the ability to predict future outcomes with a high degree of accuracy. When combined, consistency and predictability allow you to accurately map your desired course

> **No-compromise leadership =** Consistency in all Four Business Outcomes
>
> **Consistency =** Predictability
>
> **Predictability =** Accurate future mapping of The Four Business Outcomes
>
> **Accurate mapping of future outcomes =** Sustainable quantum-leap growth

in each of The Four Business Outcomes. All this adds up to the equivalent of the Holy Grail in business… sustainable quantum-leap growth.

As the sequence above illustrates, the process from no-compromise leadership to sustainable quantum-leap growth is a continuous cycle. In order for sustainable growth of any measure to occur, no-compromise leadership must be the driving force in the process.

Reading phrases like achieving "sustainable quantum-leap growth" may sound pretty over-reaching, or perhaps like buzzwords in a business book to some. I use these words to empha-

Neilism
Sustainable growth only occurs in the presence of no-compromise leadership.

size that the most basic leadership objectives are to create growth and value for the company. More importantly, I use these words to communicate a level of business momentum that is *highly impervious* to the forces that keep compromising companies stuck in marginal performance and growth. A no-compromise company is not only more resilient and able to recover quicker when problems do surface, it makes it difficult for detrimental issues to escalate at all.

Every business leader will have his or her own interpretation of what sustainable quantum leap growth is. For some, it might be 20 percent a year or 40 percent or more for others. No matter what your interpretation is, when no compromise is focused on driving The Four Business Outcomes and keeping them in balance, the results will be impressive and long lasting.

Urgency IS the energy

Urgency is powerful stuff. Urgency is the energy of business success, whether you're the owner, president, vice president, supervisor, manager or team player. Urgency makes stuff happen and the outcome from that stuff can be extraordinary for you, your company and all points of contact with your customers. However, creating and maintain a sense of urgency depends entirely on your success to become a no-compromise leader. That being said, there is no time or room for compromise.

> Make driving The Four Business Outcomes your new company mandate. Everyone pushes in the same direction. Everyone is accountable.

Of critical importance here is the energy generated by the sense of urgency to maintain balance throughout The Four Business Outcomes. It takes energy to move a business forward. Unfortunately, too many leaders leave the quality and quantity of the energy to chance. They don't pay attention to the source of the energy and what generates it. Urgency is the *energy generator*. It's the leader's responsibility to ensure that generator is cranking all the energy necessary to power the business. If the energy generator begins to lose power and sputter, the business will sputter too.

To create a sense of urgency in your company, you must define and drive your critical numbers in each of The Four Business Outcomes. Once critical numbers are defined, you must relentlessly communicate progress through scoreboards and other information flow systems throughout your company. *If one outcome is weak, find that one critical number that, if moved in the right direction, will bring that outcome back into balance.* Make driving The

Four Business Outcomes your new company mandate. Everyone pushes in the same direction. Everyone is accountable. Most importantly, remember that creating a sense of urgency begins with leadership. It begins with you. *No compromise.*

In the following chapters, you will see how creating a sense of urgency plays a key role in creating balance across The Four Business Outcomes.

Time to bring out The BIG Eight

If the mission of no-compromise leadership is to drive The Four Business Outcomes, then what exactly do you drive them with? To answer that question, I'd like to introduce you to The BIG Eight. *The BIG Eight are simply a collection of drivers that, when combined, create a natural and powerful sequence to achieve maximum performance in each business outcome.* Throughout the chapters in Part II, I take you through each of The Four Business Outcomes and how The BIG Eight drivers are used to ensure no-compromise results.

The BIG Eight drivers

1. **Culture:** The collective behavior of the company

2. **Sense of urgency:** The energy that drives performance and growth

3. **Critical numbers:** Numbers that, if changed, have a profound impact on the company

4. **Information flow:** Top down, bottom up — everyone knows the score

5. **Teamwork:** The heartbeat of the company that gets the job done

6. **Innovation:** Stay out of the box. Do it better, faster, cheaper

7. **Systems:** The procedures and structure to produce the right results

8. **Accountability:** Delivering what was promised — when it is promised

The BIG Eight Driver Wheel

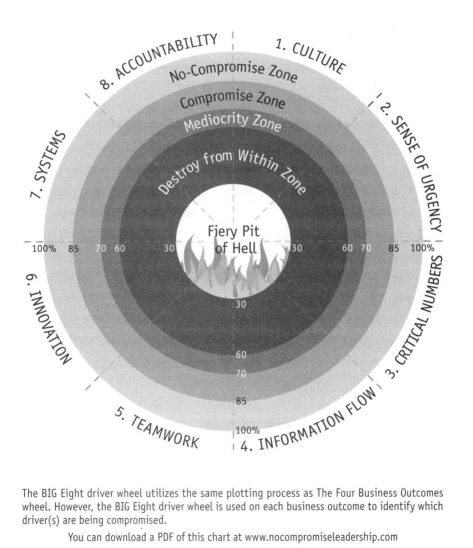

The BIG Eight driver wheel utilizes the same plotting process as The Four Business Outcomes wheel. However, the BIG Eight driver wheel is used on each business outcome to identify which driver(s) are being compromised.

You can download a PDF of this chart at www.nocompromiseleadership.com

ANALYSIS: Aligning The Four Business Outcomes and The BIG Eight Drivers

The chart on the next page has The Four Business Outcomes wheel in the center with a BIG Eight driver wheel assigned to each outcome. Use the following steps to plot and identify where compromise is occurring in your company and doing so under your leadership.

Step 1: Copy your no-compromise effectiveness ratings to The Four Business Outcomes wheel in the center. Connect the dots to create a visual to determine how out of balance your wheel is.

Step 2: Beginning with the productivity business outcome, plot your effectiveness rating for each of The BIG Eight Drivers on the corresponding BIG Eight driver wheel. Think "productivity" and rate how each driver is working to build or degrade productivity. Place one dot for each driver. Complete this process for each of the remaining business outcomes.

Step 3: Connect the dots in each BIG Eight driver wheel to visually see how out of balance your drivers are.

Step 4: When all the wheels are completed, you will be able to see and analyze which drivers are being compromised and require an immediate action plan until all drivers are in the no-compromise zone.

No-compromise thinking for Part II

It is essential that you regard the following chapters as a non-negotiable game plan for implementing no-compromise leadership. Doing so will establish the foundation for building a no-compromise business culture. We'll get to that in Part III of the book.

As I apply The BIG Eight drivers to each of The Four Business Outcomes, you will understand what thinking and behaving as a no-compromise leader is all about.

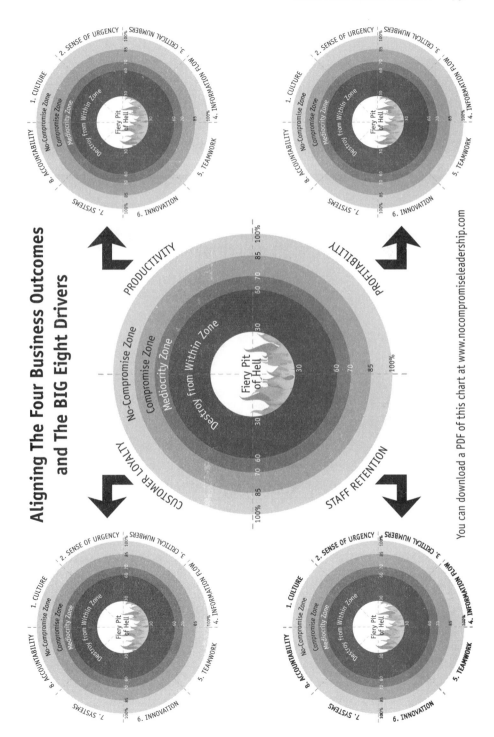

Aligning The Four Business Outcomes and The BIG Eight Drivers

You can download a PDF of this chart at www.nocompromiseleadership.com

CHAPTER 4

BUSINESS OUTCOME #1:
PRODUCTIVITY

The productivity business outcome is all about doing the work of the business — and executing that work in the most efficient and timely manner possible to the highest no-compromise standards.

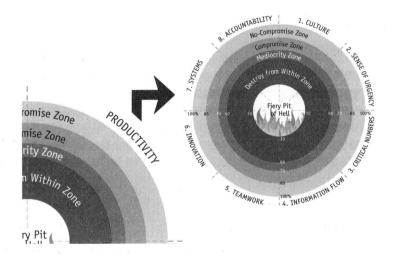

W hat does *productivity* mean to you? If you focus on just this one business outcome called productivity, what would it look like in your business? If there was just one key ratio that you would use to measure the productivity rate of your business, what would that be? Would it be the ratio of hours sold to hours available for sale? Would it be units manufactured per period or perhaps units sold versus shipped? Would it be the ratio of employees to gross revenues or output per hour? Every business has one or a set of key measurements that must be constantly monitored for positive gains or to signal that it's time to sound the alarm.

Brian and Leslie Mulcahy, owners of Rabbit Hill Inn, a 21-room luxury inn in Lower Waterford, Vermont, track occupancy rate. Due to the recent trend of offering themed packaged stays for skiing, hiking and canoeing, they are now tracking occupancy rate versus revenues and average revenue per room night.

Banks track teller productivity by average checks processed per day or period. A retail store might track revenue per salesperson. A call center will track calls per hour. Spas track both room occupancy and the percentage of technician hours sold versus available.

Gabrielle's, a fine dining restaurant I love to frequent right up the street from our office, tracks table turns. The unhurried dining experience inspired the manager to create a unique way of tracking productivity by tracking average tip percentage per check for wait staff. Although this approach is also a measure of customer loyalty, it gives an interesting read on how "productive" her wait staff is. A low tip percentage signals that a waiter may be slow, inefficient, or inattentive to tables in his area.

Good, bad or indifferent, every business has a productivity culture. And whatever that productivity culture is, you created it.

At Strategies, our first measure of productivity is the ratio of employees to gross revenue. Since our consulting, seminar and product divisions each offer up their productivity measures, we found that the employees to gross revenues ratio is a good indicator of the overall productivity, as well as being a key guide to hiring decisions. We also use the ratio of available seminar days and coaching hours against actual bookings.

Productivity is all about doing the work of the business and executing that work in the most efficient and timely manner possible to the highest no-compromise standards. If your company makes jet engines, make those engines the absolute best in the most efficient manner possible. (*I fly a lot, so I hesitate to use "better, faster, cheaper" in reference to jet engines.*) If you own or manage a service business, make the most efficient use of every hour you have available for sale. If you own or manage a retail business, productivity can be measured by inventory turnover. You can't make money in retail if you don't turn inventory. If you lead a research facility, productivity is about the path of failures that lead to incredible break-throughs. If you're not seeing those failures rack up, the breakthroughs aren't getting any closer.

Tiger Woods is all about no compromise in his approach to the game of golf. For Tiger, it's productivity through tenacious practice. The result? At age 32, he's racked up 65 PGA Tour victories, including 14 majors and two Grand Slams. *That's true no-compromise productivity.*

Of The Four Business Outcomes, productivity is the one that has the greatest impact on the other three outcomes. Why? Because productivity encompasses the efficient use of time, people, money and resources, including raw materials, equipment, machinery, products and anything else needed to do the work of the business. Given this, productivity is inherently bound to the other four business outcomes. *If productivity is compromised in any manner whatsoever, there will be an immediate and measurable impact on all of the remaining three business outcomes.* That's why no-compromise leadership's ultimate accountability is to achieve and maintain balance across all four business outcomes.

> **Neilism**
> The spark that ignites the right performance in the productivity business outcome is no-compromise leadership.

As you can see, different businesses and industries have different ways to measure productivity. It may be a straightforward calculation attached to your efficiency of selling hours, turning retail inventory or units shipped. Likewise, your business might dictate the use of a more abstract approach, like tracking average tip percentage like at Gabrielle's, or like Tiger Woods' no-compromise practice regimen that produces championship results when it really counts — like winning the 2008 U.S. Open in a sudden-death match with an excruciating knee injury. *No matter how you look at it, tracking productivity is one of those non-negotiable tasks in business.*

Productivity is the work that produces business results. It's about getting things done. Productivity embodies meticulous execution and follow-through.

But productivity doesn't just happen. All of the goals, objectives, systems, standards and grand vision of the business do not inspire world-class productivity by themselves. A Neilism: "The spark that ignites the right performance in the productivity business outcome is no-compromise leadership." *No-compromise leadership makes things happen.*

Productivity and The BIG Eight Drivers

Let's begin the process of applying no-compromise leadership to The BIG Eight and the productivity business outcome. As I move through The BIG Eight, you will notice how the level of focus and intensity multiplies as no-compromise leadership and thinking take hold.

1. Create a no-compromise culture

What's your business culture like with respect to productivity? Is it fast or slow? Is it streamlined and quick to respond, or complicated, cumbersome and struggles to get things done? Would you describe your business culture as dynamic and focused, or lethargic and a potential candidate to go on life support? Does your business culture invite and easily adapt to change or does it avoid, resist, stall — or even kill — the smallest change initiatives? Does your business culture strive to be the best, or is it best described as striving for mediocrity? Good, bad or indifferent, every business has a productivity culture. And whatever that productivity culture is, you created it.

Think about those times when your team rose to the challenge and pulled off the impossible. You know, when you were seriously short-handed and the work still got done — and got done impressively well. What about those times when you faced a crisis and your team rallied to pull, push and, if necessary, drag the company through to daylight? There is something wonderfully fulfilling when a team puts the everyday bickering aside and rises to the challenge. *The question is, how do you capture and harness that focused determination and what-ever-it-takes energy and make it stick?* Not that a business can operate in "overcome-a-crisis" mode indefinitely, but what would your productivity business outcome look like if you were able to consistently maintain a highly efficient and whatever-it-takes culture? No doubt, the outcome would be nothing short of impressive. It begins with a no-compromise leader who creates a no-compromise business culture whose battle cry is, "If it needs to be done, get it done."

In Part I, I presented the ten requirements to become a no-compromise leader. Number One is to have absolute clarity on where you are taking your company. True, we are talking about vision here, but too often vision statements can be more like broad brushstrokes that paint a picture of where the company is going. Absolute clarity on where you are taking the company is just like having GPS in your car — both excel at delivering the extreme clarity on how to get to a destination.

> **Neilism**
> Never proclaim high standards of behavior today and compromise them tomorrow.

The perfect example of having absolute clarity is Coach Ken Carter, depicted in the 2005 movie release *Coach Carter*. He was coach of Richmond High School's basketball program from 1997-2002. When Carter first met the team, their reputation was for losing games, not winning them. On that first meeting, he handed every player a contract that they had to sign in order to continue playing on the basketball team. The conditions were simple; practice starts at 3:00 pm — you're late if not there by 2:55 pm, attend all of your classes, sit in the front row, maintain a "C" average and wear a tie on game day.

Carter taught the team how to win with no-compromise discipline and had them on the way to an unprecedented undefeated season. When Carter learned that players were compromising the terms of their contracts, he locked out his undefeated Varsity basketball team in order to push them to improve their grades. Carter not only closed the Richmond High School gym, but he banned all basketball-related activities. As a no-compromise leader, he was prepared to cancel the entire season — all because 15 of the 45 players were not living up to the classroom achievements they agreed to meet in contracts they signed earlier in the semester.

Of course winning was the vision, but the absolute clarity on how to win was defined in the contracts the students signed and Coach Carter's no-compromise leadership discipline. A Neilism, "Never proclaim high standards of behavior today and compromise them tomorrow."

I'm not suggesting that you hand employees a contract to sign. What I am suggesting is that you invest the time, energy and resources to define your expectations of what productivity needs to look like in your company and present it with high-definition clarity.

2. Sense of urgency

I keep emphasizing that urgency is the energy that drives business growth. When it comes to driving the productivity business outcome, no other factor rings truer than the need for creating a company-wide sense of urgency. Too often, I meet leaders who are frustrated with productivity in their companies. They complain about the lack of enthusiasm, team-

Productivity culture jump start

To get your no-compromise productivity culture going, add your own high definition to these productivity-based questions:

- Exactly where do you need to be in sales, output, deliveries, inventory turns by _____ date?
- What pace will you have to perform at?
- Who is responsible for what? Define the accountabilities.
- Describe exactly how you will measure productivity. What happens if the team wins? What happens if the team loses?
- What behaviors/skills are required to support the productivity objectives?
- What absolutely has to change in order to reach your productivity objectives?
- What support can the team expect from leadership?

work and entitlement mentalities. I hear leaders complain that employees are only interested in themselves, only doing what needs to be done and punching the clock. "Don't they see the opportunity? What's wrong with them? Why do they think that way?" If any of this fits your company, it is all reflective of the culture you designed and, like it or not, encourage through compromise.

In stark contrast, ponder how you feel when you visit or patronize a business that possesses a high sense of urgency? The service is impeccable. Attention to detail and your needs are expeditiously addressed — they even address stuff you never would have considered. There is an energy level that you can't help but notice. You can "feel" it all around you. You not only see the urgency in how the work is being done, but the sense of pride and high level of engagement of employees. The smiles, the thoroughness, the attention to detail, the on-time delivery — it's all truly inspiring.

> **Neilism**
> There is no auto-pilot setting for creating and maintaining a sense of urgency.

Whether you're the owner of the company or manager of a department, creating and maintaining a sense of urgency is a non-negotiable part of your job. If you don't keep the productivity drumbeat going steady and strong, it will gradually get slower and slower as complacency sets in. Great leaders know when to speed up and when to relax and allow the team to re-energize. Then, it's back in the game.

Through all my years of observing and studying business, I've never seen a business create a sense of urgency without the presence of a fully engaged, no-compromise leader determined to achieve the company's short- and long-term objectives. A Neilism: "There is no auto-pilot setting for creating and maintaining a sense of urgency."

3. Critical numbers

Every business has critical numbers that, when achieved, create profound and lasting results. If you focus solely on driving your productivity business outcome, what are the one, two or three critical numbers that, if moved in the right direction, will push your productivity business outcome on the wheel as close to 100% as possible? (Remember, the goal is to create balance across all four of the business outcomes.)

Critical numbers in the productivity business outcome will be unique to your type of business, industry and current level of business performance. Critical numbers really show their muscle when they target attention on an area of the company that must get better — and get better fast. The beauty of using critical numbers is its pure simplicity to focus attention, resources and energy on a productivity problem or issue. A critical number is like aiming a laser pointer at a piece of the business pain. The key is keeping the focus and energy on fixing the pain until it goes away. In business, that means until new behaviors are locked in.

> Critical numbers really show their muscle when they target attention on an area of the company that must get better — and get better fast.

Be prepared to change your critical numbers for productivity as your business evolves. For example, if your turnaround time for filling orders was a critical number and the new systems are now producing the desired results and behaviors, retire it and focus on a new critical number.

Critical numbers really earn their keep when things get ugly and you need to illuminate the problem for all to see. I'll show you later how other The BIG Eight Drivers add clarity, procedures and discipline to your critical numbers. *You just can't shine a spotlight on a problem and expect it to go away.* You must have objectives, action plans and timelines.

4. Information flow

W. Edwards Deming, the originator of the total quality movement whose philosophies guided post-World War II Japan into an economic superpower, had a very simple approach to quality. Deming said, "If you don't measure it, you can't control it." This simple phrase embodies the importance of information flow as a driver for productivity and overall business performance at the highest level.

Examples of critical numbers for productivity are:

- Turnaround time
- Performing work within time standards
- Ratio of hours sold versus hours available for sale
- Transactions per hour/day/week/month
- Sales calls made versus closes
- Ability to meet deadlines versus deadlines missed
- Work consistency
- Quality ratio (output versus rejects and defects)
- Units made or shipped
- Average sale/ticket/purchase
- New customers per week, month, quarter
- Number of customers serviced
- Waste creation due to inconsistent or shoddy work
- Inventory turnover
- Units per client
- Percent of "up-sell" orders

A great culture, sense of urgency and defining critical numbers to drive productivity are pointless if you do not get information flowing at high speed throughout your company. One of the major causes for lack-luster and mediocre productivity is lack of data and "knowing the score." Expectations and desired outcomes must be unquestionably clear from the leaders requesting the work to everyone who is responsible for getting that work done. The information-flow process continues with the systems, processes and training to do the work in the most efficient manner possible. The measuring and information-flow process kicks in to show how much ground was gained and what it cost to get there. *It's all about getting the data out so everyone knows what's going on.* For the no-compromise leader, having a system for information flow is non-negotiable.

Productivity issues run the gamut from missing goals, deadlines, delivery, time and material waste, to implementation issues, lack of team focus, and no sense of urgency. The culprit is poorly designed, or non-existent, information flow systems. Think about what it would be like to drive your car without a basic instrument panel. First, you wouldn't know how much fuel you have and if it's enough to get to your destination. You wouldn't know how fast you're moving, if your engine is overheating or if your oil level is dangerously low. Just like driving a car, the absence of basic critical operating data can cause a business to stall because it was out of fuel (*a cash-flow crisis*) or to seize up because the oil was low and there was no warning light (*no information flow to lubricate performance*).

Neilism

Teams exist to perform beyond the capabilities of the individual. To do so, teams need data.

An information-flow Neilism: "Teams exist to perform beyond the capabilities of the individual. To do so, teams need data." They need to know how they're doing — they need to know not only the score, but their performance stats as well. *No other system accomplishes this need task easier than scoreboards.* They can be as simple as marker boards showing monthly goals and daily/weekly progress, or fun, colorful charts and graphs strategically located where staff can watch the action unfold. *The key is keeping scoreboards up-to-date.*

Depending on your business and the need to create a sense of urgency, you might want to update your scoreboard daily or even multiple times a day. If the action is less intense, weekly or bi-weekly scoreboard updates might be fine.

Here is a basic scoreboard fact: The less frequently the data on the scoreboard changes, the less meaningful it becomes. Think about it. What's the incentive for anyone to look at a scoreboard with dated information? The answer is a resounding, "none." *If the data isn't critical enough to keep scoreboard data current, don't expect your team members to care either.*

Your scoreboards should broadcast, "Here's where we are today." Remember, information flow is about creating urgency. Last week's or

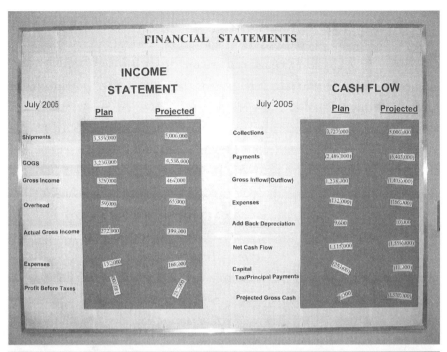

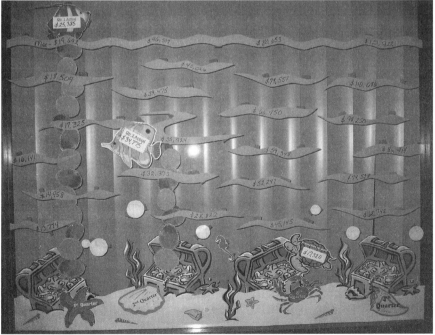

Examples of Scoreboards provided by The Great Game of Business.

last month's data just doesn't resonate the call to action of "Here's where we're at today." Scoreboard updates should match the intensity of your business action. However, what's tracked on the scoreboard should change as the action changes to adjust for seasonal trends, new opportunities or to work through a challenging period.

The no-compromise leader must never allow a scoreboard to die. Yes, scoreboards can die. That happens when compromise sets in and all updating stops. There is nothing worse than a scoreboard hanging prominently for all to see that hasn't been updated in weeks or months. *Even in death, the scoreboard communicates in no uncertain terms, "The game is over."*

> **The no-compromise leader must never allow a scoreboard to die. Yes, scoreboards can die.**

While on a business trip, I decided to visit a customer who I hadn't heard from in some time. As the president took me on a tour of the facility, the conversation revealed (not to mention how quiet the shop floor was) that the business was having challenges. In short, sales were flat and productivity was dismal.

We ended up in the staff break room. And there, hanging on the wall for all to see, was his company's colorful, three-foot-tall and five-foot-wide scoreboard for the month of May. The problem was, it was November and only the first two weeks were filled in. His scoreboard was dead and screaming from the grave that, "The game was over." A full six months had passed with this dead scoreboard serving as a constant reminder that "Productivity doesn't matter here." I stood this troubled business owner right in front of his scoreboard and asked him to tell me what it communicated to his employees. I suggested that it would have been better to take it down than serve as a daily reminder that compromise exists in his business. He got the message loud and clear.

Some companies have taken scoreboarding to the next level by setting up so-called "war rooms" to plot, plan and track company performance and movement toward goals. Walls are covered with charts and graphs all targeting critical numbers and progress, in other words, mission data. *The "war room" approach creates a natural sense of urgency every time anyone enters.*

It's where missions are strategically conceived and relentlessly tracked. It's scoreboarding at its best.

Scoreboard updates and huddles are inseparable. (I'll discuss "huddles" shortly.) Never update a scoreboard without gathering the troops together

Here are some considerations to jump-start or fine-tune scoreboarding in your business:

If you're a beginner to scoreboarding, keep it simple. Begin by scoreboarding two or three critical numbers, such as progress to month sales goal, units sold or hours sold. If your scoreboard is too complicated and hard to follow, no one will pay attention. Too much data also makes it more challenging to update daily or weekly. As you master the scoreboard process, you can gradually add data.

Scoreboard by level of authority or department. If your company has lots of leadership layers or departments, consider designing scoreboards to communicate data based on the degree of accountability. In other words, department heads can have scoreboards that contain more detailed data and critical number tracking that could be overkill for production staff.

Make your scoreboards interesting and exciting. For example, you can color in a thermometer or a swimming pool each day to show progress toward goal. Make your scoreboards really big. Kinko's and other quick-print establishments can blow up, foam-core mount and laminate any color scoreboard you can print off a color printer. (Notice I keep emphasizing the use of color.)

Be strategic where you place your scoreboards. Consider placing them where staff congregate, such as a lunch or break room.

Assign a scoreboard master to post and keep the data current. Be sure to establish the non-negotiable rules of the position — scoreboard updates cannot be late or missed. Rotate scoreboard masters every month or so to keep scoreboard energy levels high.

for a quick huddle. I've seen it time and again where scoreboards become just another piece of wall art that only a few appreciate. However, what's still missing is a system to focus attention on the updated data and what it means. It's an invitation for incorrect assumptions and unclarified expectations.

An information-flow Neilism: "If you're still uncomfortable sharing sales and performance data — get over it." The need for information flow will blow away any excuse you can conjure up for not sharing data. *Get over it. No compromise.*

Neilism
If you're still uncomfortable sharing sales and performance data — get over it.

As stated, scoreboards and huddles go hand-in-hand. Huddles are fast, rapid-fire, meetings or daily briefings. I cannot emphasize enough the impact scheduled daily meetings can have on productivity and company-wide performance. *Five to 15 minutes is all it takes. No small talk, unrelated conversation or sidebars are allowed.* It's all about the scoreboard, the numbers and what has to be done to make goal.

Huddles are also a great time to do an accountability check and ask, "Who's stuck?" to identify who needs help with a project to keep it on task and on schedule. Too often, productivity suffers and projects get bogged down simply because someone was stuck and needed help. It's certainly better to know today that a project is stuck than the day before deadline.

Although they're your front-line tools, huddles and scoreboards are just two tools of the information flow driver. Your department heads, managers and others in leadership positions require productivity data in the form of reports and other documented updates. However, a word of caution regarding the dissemination of data. *Information overload can lead to analysis paralysis.* Technology allows even the smallest company to collect massive amounts of data that can be spewed out in an endless array of reports. Defining and driving your critical numbers is where the power of no-compromise leadership resides, not in mountains of data. I'm not suggesting at all that a lot of data is not good. I'm simply saying that it's easy to miss what's important when it's buried in piles of reports.

Here's a quick huddle checklist:

Daily huddles rule. You can do weekly huddles, but that's only 52 opportunities a year to focus your team on productivity. I'd take 365 huddles a year and the 700% additional focusing power over weekly huddles. It's no contest. Go for daily. No compromise.

Keep them short. Five to 15 minutes is all you need. The shorter the better is the rule.

Make daily huddles work. Don't think about why daily huddles won't work. Those who shift from "why they can't" to "let's make it work" quickly unleash a powerful new information-flow system that produces amazing results.

Everyone huddles. Have staggered work schedules? Do huddles with each shift change. The mandate is that everyone starts their day with a briefing. On the road? If you can check your smart phone every two seconds, you can do a daily huddle, too.

Huddle consistency is everything. Schedule huddles at the same time and location every day. Use an odd start of 8:47am. For some strange reason, it gets everyone there on time. Verne Harnish talked about odd meeting times in his book, *Mastering the Rockefeller Habits*. I tried it — it works. Start huddles on time. Never wait for staff to arrive.

Huddles must be mandatory. Attendance is non-negotiable. Breaking this rule is compromise.

Assign huddle leaders. Rotate them every two to four weeks to keep the energy fresh.

Follow a precise huddle agenda. It can be as simple as review the scoreboard, acknowledge and applaud the gains, identify hot issues for the day, ask "who's stuck," and break. Anything that needs addressing or further attention should be scheduled off line. The intent is to focus on goals and hot issues for the day, not to have a staff meeting.

Technology also gives us the ability to instantly communicate to anyone, anywhere, any time. From tele- and videoconferencing to online training sessions, technology is making it faster and easier to move information throughout a company and its employees. Hey, remember the fax machine? Why use a fax when you can send a proposal, report or a training manual in a PDF format (portable document files) via email — complete with full-color pictures and charts. Today, smart phones are mini-computers in your pocket, capable of email, web access, file viewing and picture viewing. It's all part of the mix that makes up the information flow driver you will need to drive the productivity business outcome.

5. Teamwork

Everyone talks teamwork. It's such a great and powerful word. And teamwork is what every business leader strives for, right? Wrong. "Striving" for teamwork means more than "talking" teamwork. When a leader says, "We are a team and we need to work as a team," what's the result? What is that leader doing to inspire teamwork and team performance other than talking about it? You might think I'm oversimplifying this. I am not. This "talk team" scenario is played out daily in business and the result is nothing remotely close to true teamwork.

No-compromise leadership and teamwork are inherently bound to one another. Teamwork gives life, vitality and urgency to the productivity business outcome. It raises the performance bar to what can be achieved far beyond what an individual can achieve working solo. It was teamwork that gave Lance Armstrong his seventh Tour de France win. Lance gets the glory, but it took a total of 29 Team Discovery members, all

Defining and driving your critical numbers is where the power of no-compromise leadership resides, not in mountains of data.

singularly dedicated to getting Lance across that finish line, to make it happen. A teamwork Neilism: "Teamwork in a no-compromise culture is an imposing and unrelenting force that can turn competition into speed bumps."

Of The Four Business Outcomes, productivity is the key beneficiary of teamwork. Productivity is the end result of teamwork. Without teamwork, driving productivity becomes labored and inefficient. Tasks take longer to accomplish. Goals that a company is capable of achieving morph into pipedreams. Conflicting agendas and personality conflicts all get in the way of productivity. *And this is where frustrated leaders say, "Come on, we need to work as a team," but do little beyond the talk to activate teamwork.*

> **Neilism**
> Teamwork in a no-compromise culture is an imposing and unrelenting force that can turn competition into speed bumps.

Inspiring teamwork requires you to go beyond the broad brushstrokes and get into the details that make the teamwork journey worth the effort. Here's an example for my own company. I want Strategies to be the premier resource for business growth. Strategies will deliver the latest in business thinking and systems to inspire our customers. Strategies' business education will be information rich and hard-hitting but also engaging and uplifting. Strategies Coaching Services will deliver hands-on guidance and training in the most professional, no-compromise manner. There is passion in the work we do at Strategies and it's the quest of achieving that vision that inspires awesome teamwork in our company. We are all energized and committed to the vision that guides our journey.

What great journey are you taking your team on? Teamwork thrives on empowering visions. One of the non-negotiables I wrote about in Part I is the need to have absolute clarity on where you are taking your company. Leaders must have this same clarity in order to inspire teamwork in their area of responsibility. Clarity of vision, clarity of mission, clarity of how goals will be achieved and measured, and clarity on the accountabilities. *High-performance teamwork is all about clarity.*

So much about teamwork is goal driven. Win the race. Hit the sales goal. Beat the deadline. Crush the competition. Close the sale. Delight the customer. Do it better, faster, cheaper. You also need to have the right players (I'll address this in detail in the chapter on the staff retention business outcome). When it comes to teamwork, the no-compromise leader is much like the captain of the ship. It can also be said that it's the captain who serves the crew. The no-compromise leader ensures that the team stays the course — that a singular purpose for work exists. What are the goals that your team is collectively striving for?

You can literally "see" and "feel" teamwork in a business and its impact on driving the productivity outcome. The pace is faster. The workflow appears seamless. There is a sense of determination. Even in times of crisis, the mood is an unrelenting, "We can work through this." There is a tenaciousness that keeps pushing for that next win. What you're actually seeing and feeling is the no-compromise thinking that is embedded in the behavior of each and every team member. Take a walk around your company. Do you see and feel teamwork in action?

What you're actually seeing and feeling is the no-compromise thinking that is embedded in behavior of each and every team member.

The dynamic nature of teamwork seeks out opportunities that improve productivity. You could actually refer to teamwork as being "opportunistic." That means that when opportunities present themselves, a productivity-driven team will take advantage of it. If clients need a recommendation, they get it. If there is a sales lead, they follow it. If there is a better, faster, cheaper way to do something, they design a new system to do it. To understand the significance of that, consider the contrast of a business struggling with productive challenges. Without the initiative of teamwork, opportunities slip through the cracks, customers receive marginal service, waste becomes acceptable and little effort is given to identifying more efficient ways to do the work. Is your team opportunistic or does it watch those opportunities pass by like a parade?

The no-compromise leader excels by inspiring, encouraging, coaching and supporting the highest levels of teamwork. The leader is actively engaged in the teamwork process and ensures that the resources are at hand to do the work. More importantly, the no-compromise leader empowers the team to take ownership of the productivity outcome. That means that a high degree of decision-making authority resides within the team to determine how work is done. This is where the old *command and control* thinking clashes with the no-compromise leader's quest for employees to think, act and make decisions like an owner. This is the precise point in which many leaders talk team but refuse to give up control.

> **Neilism**
> You cannot lead until you give up control.

Try digesting this Neilism: "You cannot lead until you give up control." That doesn't mean that you must surrender leadership accountability; it means that employees have little incentive to play the game at the highest level if the leader controls all decision-making. Jack Stack says it best, "You get a free brain with every pair of hands." I'll add another Neilism to drive this point home: "A leadership dictatorship is the ultimate compromise to creating teamwork." Build your systems right, and you'll be amazed at the growth that can occur when you let off the controls.

As a no-compromise leader, you will be raising the teamwork bar significantly higher. If you've been doing more talk about teamwork than leading teamwork, you must shift from compromise to no compromise. *Teamwork begins with the no-compromise leader.*

6. Innovation

Innovation brings creativity and efficiency to the productivity business outcome. When nurtured by no-compromise leadership, innovation breaks through the "this is the way it's always been done" thinking to reveal previously unseen opportunities. Innovation brings life and lift to the productivity business outcome. Work moves smoother with less drag. Procedural steps are streamlined. Resource and production costs are trimmed. Innovation is a uniquely inspiring force capable of driving company-wide change.

> **Neilism**
> A leadership dictatorship is the ultimate compromise to creating teamwork.

Innovation is typically attached to the creation breakthrough products, concepts or systems. If you're truly grasping the significance of no-compromise leadership, you now recognize how the innovation of such breakthroughs is an integral part of the business culture. To illustrate this, Apple built and sustains its reputation by creating innovative products. So much so that when IBM failed to deliver on their promise of faster PowerPC processors, Apple's CEO Steve Jobs made the bold announcement in Spring 2005 that Apple was switching from the PowerPC that has powered Apple computers since the early 90s to the next generation of Intel processors.

There are two significant innovation lessons in Apple's switch to Intel. First, Steve Jobs is all about no compromise when it comes to innovation. The slow evolution of the PowerPC processor was compromising Apple's future ability to build the kind of innovative computers it was capable of building. Second, during the announcement, Jobs confirmed that Apple's new OS X operating system had been living a double life for five years. He confirmed

When innovation is embedded into the no-compromise thinking and behavior of a company, it can overcome obstacles that would stop other companies dead in their tracks.

that every version of Apple's OS X operating system released to date had been configured to run on both PowerPC and Intel processors. No other computer company possesses the innovative tenacity and ability to pull off not only a switch to an entirely new processor, but to simultaneously create and market its own proprietary operating system — especially one that works on two radically different processors. That's inspiring innovation and true no-compromise leadership.

When innovation is embedded into the no-compromise thinking and behavior of a company, it can overcome obstacles that would stop other companies dead in their tracks. However, just as talking teamwork doesn't make teamwork happen, talking innovation doesn't make innovation happen. The no-compromise leader must create the environment and culture that can nurture innovative thinking. That rules out traditional top-down organization structures, because they tend to restrict free and innovative thinking rather then encourage it. Some great productivity innovations might come out of a suggestion box, but it's a far cry from creating a culture that inspires and drives innovative thinking.

Innovation as a driver for the productivity outcome takes us back to the need for information flow up and down the organization. Information flow is the fuel of innovation and it's easy to illustrate why.

Schedule a meeting with three or four employees and inform them the topic to be discussed is a specific productivity issue that has been troubling the company. Prior to the meeting, give invited employees a one-page overview of the productivity issue with supporting data. On the day of the meeting, take 30 to 45 minutes to discuss the issue in detail and what the desired outcome could look like. Keep the meeting upbeat and targeted on the desired outcome. Give this micro-team 60 minutes of privacy to work on potential solutions and to be prepared to present their best idea. Trust me, you may be quite amazed at the results.

We regularly do this exercise in our business academy by dividing 30 or so participants into groups of five or six. We're consistently impressed with the innovativeness of the ideas generated, many of them stretching far outside the box. The compressed timeline gives the process a sense of urgency and focus on innovating one or two solutions that offer the most potential. Armed with the right information about a problem, a small team can innovate quickly. Getting concentrated team attention supported with the right information and data is a great way to switch on the innovative brain power in your company.

By the way, did you notice in the above exercise that I asked you to leave the team alone to work on the problem? Consider what would happen if you stayed in the room. You guessed it. You would most likely take over the meeting and stifle the innovative process before it begins. It would just be another meeting listening to the boss ramble about some problem.

The innovative culture in a no-compromise company is pervasive. Employees and teams work in an environment where ideas are encouraged, valued and given fair consideration. Productivity-enhancing innovation can be a simple change in the production process or service delivery or a better way to process an order. *It doesn't have to be a breakthrough idea... just a better way of doing the work of the company.*

What does innovation look like in your company? More importantly, how much of that innovation naturally occurs without your direct involvement? Ah, the no-compromise leader is emerging.

7. Systems

Sense of urgency says, "Let's get it done." Critical numbers are your performance targets. Information flow yields focus and understanding. Teamwork brings energy and vitality. Innovation unleashes creativity and efficiency. Systems hold it all together by bringing structure, discipline and predictability.

Systems give your business predictability. A system says, "Do this, and then that, and it will produce this outcome." That's about the simplest way to describe a system. *You design systems to produce predictable outcomes.* Got it? So, why are many essential processes in your business being executed every day without the structure of a clearly defined system? Don't like the way your company phone is being answered? What's your system for answering the phone? Don't like how long it takes to respond to a customer inquiry? What's your system for handling customer inquiries or problems? Consistently running out of inventory or raw materials? What's your system for managing and controlling inventory levels?

Another great way to describe a system (in a way that truly taps a nerve with leaders) is, "Systems set you free." No-compromise leadership is not about micro-managing people. In fact, leadership is not about managing people at all. It's about making sure you have the best systems in place to achieve the desired results and outcomes. I'll sum it up in two sentences. You lead people — you manage systems. If you don't like the results you're getting, change or tweak the system. *If you feel like you're constantly getting bogged down in the minutia of your business, the freedom you seek will only happen when systems are designed and put into play.*

The productivity business outcome is all about achieving efficiency and consistency in how work is done in your company. Systems can be simple or complex, depending the desired outcome. Systems eliminate the informality that comes with "invent as you go" or "show it to the next guy" approach. *Sooner or later, the failure to document the best system will create inefficiency and waste.*

Collectively, systems combine to create your operations or procedures manual. McDonald's ability to deliver consistency from store to store is grounded in its operations manual. Simply put, it's the "here's how a successful McDonald's works" bible. Managers lead people by working the systems. What does your operations manual look like?

Passivity versus proactivity; hands-off versus hands-on; unplanned versus planned. However you choose to look at it, the integrity of system design depends on whether you choose the former or the latter. When systems are self-created and loosely monitored, they are far less effective than when they are designed to achieve a specific and measurable end.

> You lead people — you manage systems. If you don't like the results you're getting, change or tweak the system.

An "invent as you go" system is akin to a "default" setting on a consumer electronic device. If you don't tell it what to do, it will simply do what it can, barring further input. Eventually the blinking lights will drive you crazy. To deprive your business of structure and discipline of systems is to invite inconsistency and all the costs and problems that accompany it. Inconsistency isn't always obvious or easy to spot. In fact, it is sometimes hidden quite well, until something "snaps." For example, client retention rates might fall below survival levels, but seasonal high traffic and a general feeling of "being busy" might mask the problem.

Other snaps are easy to see, often painfully so. These include client complaints, delayed delivery, incorrect orders and all those behaviors that drain time, money and resources. Some snaps can be gut-wrenching, such as the need to supplement what should be a self-sufficient, profitable business with borrowed or personal funds. These snaps can be brutal reality wake-up calls. Wake-up calls are generally the culmination of a series of low-key snaps. For example: Sales have been slacking off recently and you can't figure out why. The sales team seems to be doing its job, but something is clearly wrong. Actually, it began in the call center where turnover has been a growing problem. The manager of the department has been pushing hard for more phone sales to the point where staff are getting stressed and burnt out. They're trying hard to hit the numbers but the computer system is old, slow and doesn't provide sufficient customer data to personalize the sales call. Compounding the problem is the lack of a proven selling system that guides a call to a completed sale. *Systems produce outcomes. Pushing for results without a system is like heading to a new destination without a map.*

> **Neilism**
> Without systems, there is chaos, stress and waste.

Systems are safeguards. They greatly reduce the chances of things going awry, spinning out of control, or otherwise becoming more stressful than necessary. But a system's most significant contribution to a business is consistency and predictability. I'll end this with a Neilism: "Without systems, there is chaos, stress and waste."

8. Accountability

Of all the drivers in The BIG Eight, accountability is what defines you as a true no-compromise leader. "Being accountable" for all that occurs in your company, or your specific area, is a non-negotiable, no-compromise behavior. No blame, no excuses, no leadership blockages — just good old no-compromise accountability for getting it done and done right.

Accountability in the productivity business outcome has broad-reaching implications on two distinct levels.

1. Individual leadership accountability: This is all about you, the leader. *It centers on one key question; are you disciplined and tenacious enough to be accountable for your own productivity?* Sadly, too many leaders compromise when it comes to being accountable for their own productivity and get stuck in that "double standard" justification thinking that it's OK for them to compromise a little, but not anyone else. This thinking is dangerous in any leadership position because it communicates directly from you that compromise is acceptable within the company culture.

To be a no-compromise leader, you must be accountable for your own productivity. That sets the highest standards for your company's culture to emulate and broadcasts it loud and clear to everyone.

2. Overseeing accountability in others: You're driving on the highway and you catch a glimpse of the speed limit sign as it passes you in a blur. You're exceeding the speed limit — and you know it. Then you hear a siren, look in the rear-view mirror, see the flashing lights and feel your heart start doing that "I'm gonna get a speeding ticket" pounding in your chest. All the state trooper is doing is holding you accountable for your decision to exceed the speed limit. That's his job. (And he gets to wear a cool uniform, too.) Just as a state trooper must hold you accountable for your decisions and actions on the road, a no-compromise leader must unconditionally hold others accountable for their work and actions when compromise sets in.

For all the reasons already discussed in this book, accountability does not mean watching over the shoulders of employees or setting up camp in the security room to stare at TV monitors, hoping to catch a compromise in progress. It does mean practicing a higher level of leadership built around a clear understanding of the work that needs to be done and supporting that work with open and free-flowing information. Fairness and integrity must prevail, but accountability cannot be compromised.

Here is a quick hit list to connect accountability to the productivity business outcome:
  + As a leader, never compromise your own personal accountability.
  + Have systems in place to recognize and red-flag when productivity begins to slip.
  + Never ignore a problem, because it will only get worse.
  + Never hesitate to ask the status of a project or situation.

- Hold daily huddles or meetings focused on the productivity business outcome.
- Make sure everyone, I mean everyone, in the company understands and drives your critical numbers.
- Always ask if anyone is "stuck" and needs help with a project, issue or problem. It's so much easier to get things back on track today than discovering at deadline the project is in serious trouble.
- Whenever there is a lack of information flow coming from one area of the business, find out why. It's a sure sign of compromise and a brewing productivity issue.
- Address individual employee productivity problems quickly and thoroughly.
- Accountability takes on a life of its own, when the leader models no-compromise accountability.
- When repeated efforts fail to address an employee's productivity problems, it's time to give him a career opportunity elsewhere.
- Talk to customers directly to ask what it's like to do business with your company and what you can do to make the experience better.
- Remember, no-compromise leadership means, if has to get done — get it done.

A NO-COMPROMISE LESSON:
Are you clarifying your expectations?

You give your manager what you thought was a simple project. Three weeks later, she reports that it's done. Excited to check out the new system, you instantly see that procedures you had wanted are not only missing — but that no one was trained in the system. Your frustration meter goes critical.

The manager, who thought she did a great job, is devastated and feels she was set up to fail. Trust is compromised. Precious time and opportunities passed by your business yet again.

Such scenarios play out every day in the high-pressure — lead-on-the-fly — world of business. The good news is that the cure is simple and requires nothing more than the discipline to thoroughly clarify and communicate your expectations.

Here are some no-compromise strategies to ensure that expectations are clarified:

1. **Get the first 15% right:** The remaining 85% will fall into place. The first 15% represents vision, mission and objectives. It gives life, meaning and direction to a project. The "how" and "what" of the project live in the 85%.

2. **Paint a high-definition picture of your desired outcome:** Why does the company need this project? What should it look like? What are the pieces and how should it work? What results will you measure? Get it on paper.

3. **Communicate with clarity and intent:** Don't rush. Ask the recipient to describe the project back to you. Allow time for questions and be thorough in your response.

4. **Establish progress checkpoint dates and time:** Begin with shorter intervals to ensure the right start. Always ask, "Are you

continued...

stuck?" Better to know early when corrections are easier. Do not micro-manage. People learn by doing.

5. **Every project needs an "owner" and a deadline:** Creating a culture that consistently gets projects across the finish line will fail without project owners and deadlines.

6. **Celebrate your wins — learn from your mistakes:** Both go hand in hand.

CHAPTER  5   BUSINESS OUTCOME #2:
PROFITABILITY

*The profitability business outcome is all about
achieving predictable cash flow and bottom line
profitability — and doing so with the highest
level of no-compromise financial accountability
at all levels of the company.*

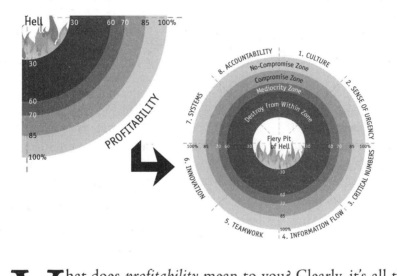

What does *profitability* mean to you? Clearly, it's all the money that can stay in the company coffers after all the bills are paid, but profitability is so much more. However, defining what profitability means to you is a significant question with consequences that tap the very essence of what business is all about. Think about what profitability means to the security your family and your employees' families. Think about opportunities that profitability creates for your company as it pertains to stability, growth and expansion. What about your customers, vendors, investors and stockholders — even your community? In just these few short sentences, it's clear how profitability touches everything in the most profound way. OK, now we're getting on the same page.

Interestingly, what many business leaders tend to overlook is best described in this Neilism: "Profitability is simply a way to keep score." You work hard to generate revenues and drop some cash on the bottom line. Your financial reports tell you how efficiently you're accomplishing this task. However, it's in the financial reporting process where compromise settles in.

Think about an entrepreneurial start-up business where it's essentially a mad dash to get past break-even and into the warm glow of financial daylight. The flaw in the thinking is that driving top-line revenue will somehow make everything else turn out just fine. Entrepreneurs are notorious for making that mad dash — and they're just as notorious for not understanding the financial mechanics of creating sustainable and predictable profitability. *They get so busy doing the work of the business that they never take time to understand how and why cash is flowing through the business.*

And it's not just entrepreneurs whose eyes roll back in their heads when handed a set of financial reports. There are multitudes of business leaders who are completely in the dark when it comes to reading and understanding what their own financial reports are telling them.

The flaw in the thinking is that driving top-line revenue will somehow make everything else turn out just fine.

Here is one statement I consistently hear that describes how profound this lack of financial connectedness really is, "We've got lots of money coming in and lots of money going out — and nothing left over." Asking just a few questions regarding their financial control systems instantly exposes how tenuous these situations are. No cash-flow plan. No regular financial reporting system. Even when a reporting process is in place, no formal system exists to use that data to make better financial decisions.

Heed these words: *Whenever a disconnect exists between leadership and the financial activity of the business, the business is flying financially blind.* When financially disconnected, the leader has little or no ability to control or influence profitability. By design, the business is setting itself up to stumble into one financial crisis after another. Profitability is one of The Four Business Outcomes. *As leader, you can neither avoid nor ignore profitability.*

It is impossible for me to know every reader's personal level of financial understanding. You might be a financial whiz kid who loves to build spreadsheets and dig deep to uncover the rich data found in your financials. But even financial whiz kids crash and burn in business, because they lack the essential no-compromise process of connecting the behavior of the business to its financial reality. Given this, even financial whiz kids are not excused from reading this chapter.

Neilism
Profitability is simply a way to keep score.

Likewise, you might be already squirming uncomfortably over this financial reality stuff and thinking about fast-forwarding to the next chapter to see if it's more palatable. *Don't you dare skip this chapter. If you're squirming, you need to take this chapter full strength.* Financial whiz kid or not, this chapter on profitability is essential to achieving balance across The Four Business Outcomes.

It's all about the financial literacy of your company

Did you notice that the headline above said, "… the *financial literacy* of your company?" There is a major flaw in the thinking of business leaders that financial literacy is something reserved for presidents, vice presidents, chief financial officers, accountants/bookkeepers and the various levels of management. That couldn't be further from the truth. Financial literacy is such an integral piece to achieving sustainable and predictable profitability that is must be embedded in the DNA of your company. That means that every employee possesses the ability to influence profitability in some manner. Therefore, they must be given the necessary financial literacy training to enable them to make the best decisions.

I'm not suggesting that you train sales staff, secretaries and maintenance staff how to read company financials. My point is that all employees have the ability, via their decisions and behavior, to influence profitability in a positive or negative way. Given this, leadership should be providing them with their own financial report (let's just call it a "scorecard") that they can read and understand so they can make the very best decisions. The higher up the leadership accountability ladder, the more detailed the financial reports. Remember, information flows from the top down and bottom up. As you'll see shortly, information flow is a profitability driver.

> **When a salesperson connects her decisions and behavior to what it costs to make a sale, more efficient processes emerge.**

What I'm describing here is the basis of *open-book management*. (Teach the rules of the business game, track progress with scoreboards, and incentivize achieving goals by giving everyone a stake in the outcome in the form of a bonus.) If all employees have the benefit of financial literacy training along with pertinent financial scoreboards and reports to show how their decisions and behavior effect profitability, you will unleash a previously untapped energy source in your own company. When a maintenance employee has the financial literacy knowledge and data to connect his behavior with profitability, more efficient ways of doing the work emerge. When a salesperson connects her decisions and behavior to what it costs to make a sale, more efficient processes emerge. In contrast, when employees operate in the financial dark, status quo is maintained and resistance to change remains part of the culture.

I wrote about open-book management in the Part I, especially how some leaders are reluctant to share their numbers as if it would break some sacred ancient trust. (Please forgive me, but too often I discover that these "I don't share numbers" leaders aren't looking at their own financials — or don't understand them at all.)

Whether you agree or not, financial literacy and the sharing of financial data so that everyone can influence the numbers is the no-compromise leader's most potent tool for driving profitability. It gets everyone focused on pushing the numbers in the right direction. It's also a proven approach to growing a fiscally responsible business. To learn more about financial literacy and open-book management, read *The Great Game of Business* by Jack Stack and *The Open-Book Experience* by John Case. There are some excellent workbooks available at www.greatgame.com, the official website for *The Great Game of Business*. I highly recommend their *Yo-Yo Company Workbook*. It delivers a fun way to teach business literacy to employees.

Now, let's begin applying The BIG Eight to the profitability business outcome. As we move through the remainder of this chapter, remember that profitability is an outcome driven by a no-compromise approach to fiscal responsibility. *Try as you might, driving top-line sales does not ensure that profits will occur when all the smoke clears.* No-compromise fiscal discipline is essential here, because an error in the financial business outcome can quickly send a company into a financial tailspin. Let's proceed.

1. No-compromise culture

I've worked with businesses that, by all outward appearances, were enjoying great success. They have a good brand identity, impressive customer list, a great looking facility, cool equipment (gotta have cool stuff) and all of the other trappings of an otherwise successful business. The owner drives a fine car and lives in an impressive house in just the right neighborhood. Yet, one look behind the curtain at their financial reality and you see that this company's success is more illusion than fact.

I've seen too many of these outwardly successful businesses that are starved for cash or on the brink of financial collapse. The most desperate are financially insolvent, meaning they don't have cash to meet payroll, pay the bills or the bank loan. Sadly, almost every one of these dire and stressful situations can be attributed to leadership's detachment from the financial reality of the business. A leader who is not fiscally responsible permits that thinking and behavior to infect and define the very culture of the company. That "just keep selling — we'll be OK" rationale is pure denial at its best. It's like announcing that the train won't crash while not knowing what track you're on, where it's going — or where it ends. A Neilism: "Only your financials tell you if the light at the end of the tunnel is daylight or an oncoming train."

In business, cash flow is king. Have you ever heard the expression *growing broke?* In order to comprehend how you can grow broke, think about all the cash you need to invest in payroll, equipment, inventory, accounts receivable, hiring, training staff, etc. In a start-up business, that cash will come from you, your lenders and suppliers that allow you a short period of time to pay them back (accounts payable). Sales are another source of cash and, of course, the most preferred source. But, depending on your business, a sale doesn't always mean you have the cash.

Neilism
Only your financials tell you if the light at the end of the tunnel is daylight or an oncoming train.

Many people get confused between a sale and the cash from that sale. If you sell on terms such as Net 30, a sale today means that you will not see the cash for 30 to 45 days or even longer. Why 45 days or more? Well, reality says that not everyone pays on time. All that time, you have this great sale but no cash, but you still have all of your bills to pay and other costs of doing business. Another example is winning that big contract. Problem is, you need to hire and train more staff and buy more equipment and materials to fulfill the contract — before you receive payment. *If you don't have a handle on cash flow, you can easily grow your company broke.*

I've seen the opposite occur in service and retail businesses that depend heavily on cash flow from gift card and gift certificate sales. On the surface, it looks like a windfall. Wow, you get the cash today in return for service or product redemption later.

Right? Wrong. Without being connected to the financial reality of the business and being fiscally responsible, that cash will flow through the business completely unchecked. Yes, it will help pay bills and buy stuff, but looming out there is the obligation to fulfill that gift card. When gift cards are redeemed, you will have to deal with payroll, product cost, inventory and other expenses attached to that sale that would normally occur if payment was received at time of delivery. If the cash wasn't managed and is all gone, you grew broke. With the dramatic increase in gift certificate and gift card sales, I've seen many businesses succumb to this "gift certificate dependency" affliction. They live for the next holiday season or Mother's Day, and if the gift card sales fall short, they're out of business. It's an ugly cycle — one that only a no-compromise leader can avoid.

When no-compromise leadership targets the profitability business outcome, it does so with a by-the-book discipline. That means that fiscal responsibility is practiced at every level of the business, from the leader and the leadership team to every salesperson, secretary, customer service representative, shop and maintenance worker. *Everyone pushes the numbers in the right direction.* This becomes a culture in which everyone is responsible — everyone is accountable. *Waste or cost without purpose is unacceptable.*

Just as you can see, feel and measure a business with a high-performance productivity culture, you can see, feel and measure a business with a high-fiscally responsible culture. It doesn't mean the company is "tight" and "penny-pinching;" it simply means that there are purpose and discipline with regard to how it deals with money, spending and cash-flow management.

Financial Compromises: It's important that I get the following on the table, too. By-the-book fiscal responsibility eliminates the following games that some entrepreneurs and leaders still play:

Paying wages "under the table." Giving unreported wages to employees or taking cash and not reporting it as taxable income is illegal. It's willful intent to defraud the government. *If you're playing this game, forget about becoming a no-compromise leader.* It compromises the ethics and values of your company. If you're paying wages under-the-table, stop. If you don't stop, close this book and give it away. It can't help you.

Paying personal bills or expenses through the company. This practice is no different than paying yourself unreported income. Personal and business expenses must never be mingled. It distorts your financial reports and flaws the data.

Never make personal credit card payments through the company's checking account. That is no different than running personal expenses through the company. If you have no choice but to use a personal credit card for business, submit an expense report and write a check to yourself and pay the credit bill through your personal checking account. Each item on that expense must then be allocated to the proper expense account.

I have to discuss this stuff because it's reality. It needs to be addressed. Compromise is compromise. Let's move on.

To get your no-compromise profitability culture going, think about the following:

+ Can you read and understand every line item on your financial reports? This includes your Balance Sheet, Income Statement, and Statement of Cash Flows. If not, what's your plan to learn how? This is non-negotiable.
+ How often should you receive complete financial reports? If it's not at least monthly (that's only 12 sets of financials a year) it is not often enough. Weekly is better. I'll explain why later.
+ How much time lapses from the end of the month until you receive your financial reports? If this exceeds two weeks, it's too long. Find out where the roadblock is and address it. If you have an in-house accounting department, there's no excuse not to have timely reports within days after the end of the month. Any good in-house accounting software and a competent book-keeper should be able to produce timely weekly financials. This is non-negotiable.
+ Do you have a cash-flow plan that guides your revenue targets and expense budgets? If not, why not? Financial reports tell you the score during and after the game ends. *Your cash-flow plan is your financial playbook.* Follow the plan, be fiscally responsible and your financial reports will show a healthier company. *You simply cannot grow a business without following a cash-flow plan.* The plan is a "best guess." The more you do it and work your plan, the better you predict the future. That is non-negotiable.
+ Do you have weekly cash-flow planning meetings? If not, why not? Having a cash-flow plan is pointless without comparing it

to actual revenues and expenses. Are you over or behind projections? Why? What do you need to do today or over the next week, month or quarter to get back on track? This is why I prefer weekly over monthly financials. I don't want to discover a problem at the end of the month that we could have fixed or avoided.

+ Who attends your weekly cash-flow planning meetings? (I hope you're still not stuck on the sharing numbers thing.) All leaders need to be present. In larger companies with many departments, separate cash-flow meetings focusing on numbers that are key to that area need to be held weekly.

+ Do employees know the score? If your response to, "Hey boss, how are we doing?" is something like, "Not good enough," the people responsible for doing the work have no idea what's going on. I'll address financial information flow in detail shortly.

+ Does your company require purchase orders to control spending?

+ Is your payroll percentage under control? What is the ideal target payroll percent for your company? What will it take to achieve and maintain that target?

+ Are your inventory levels under control? Money tied up in excess inventory is a cash drain. What's the plan to get it under control?

+ If you're a retail business, are you controlling inventory levels and turning your inventory as often as you need to? Slow inventory turns in retail kills cash flow.

+ As the leader of your company, department or division, are you setting the right example to create a fiscally responsible business culture. If not, why not?

There is no debating that the profitability business outcome begins with the right culture. Creating sustainable and predictable profitability begins with the right discipline and behavior at the leadership level. It cannot be faked or given lip service. The no-compromise leader lives it, inspires it and relentlessly builds a culture to support it.

2. Sense of urgency

Urgency is the energy that drives the profitability business outcome.
As I explained at the beginning of this chapter, I want to emphasize that
creating profit is not what business is all about. Profit is simply a measurement of business performance. It's the
reward for generating revenues, doing
the work well and staying within
budget. Job security, advancement,
better benefits, being able to invest
in the right research and development,
acquiring the best equipment, etc., are all part of profitability.
To achieve all of the amazing opportunities that profitability
can deliver, your company must maintain a no-compromise sense
of urgency. A Neilism: "Urgency is vital to achieving profitability."

Neilism
Urgency is vital to
achieving profitability.

When a business takes a lethargic and apathetic approach to profitability,
financial leaks begin occurring just about everywhere. When the leaks get out
of control, the business sinks. It's akin to letting go of the controls that allow
a leader to direct business activities toward its profitability goals. The cash-
flow plan is demoted to the "optional list," or it evolves into nothing more than
an annual planning ritual that is rarely looked at or put into play. Reviewing
financial reports or having cash-flow planning meetings rarely occur, if they
take place at all. Financial discipline and consistency are preached, but not
practiced. That's what happens when there is no sense of urgency.

Profitability will not take care of itself. Leaders must not only lead by
example (that means you don't ignore the budget and expect everyone else
to follow it), they must maintain a profitability sense of urgency at all levels
of the business. Doing so inspires a production worker to suggest a better
technique or adjustment in a process to improve quality and trim costs. It
causes retail staff to design a special promotion to move out that slow-moving
merchandise. It causes service providers to multi-task when there's downtime,
rather than hire more support staff. It causes sales representatives to make
that next sales call, or book that flight in advance to get the best fare.

Sense of urgency changes behavior patterns and does so quickly. It's like a steady drumbeat in the background that reminds all employees that their decisions and actions directly impact profitability. Sometimes the drum needs to beat a little louder, like during seasonal lulls, to uncover revenue opportunities and to conserve cash by controlling expenses. Likewise, the drumbeat should be faster to pick up the pace for things like new product launches, major expansion or to maximize a peak selling season. The no-compromise leader must maintain the right profitability drumbeat to match the needs of the business to the current opportunity or challenge.

Never use profitability as a "big stick." This will only create more animosity, stress and resistance for those on the receiving end. Profitability should be positioned as one of the key critical numbers to show how the business is performing so it can fund what the business needs and wants to do. (I'll get more into critical numbers next.) If you make it "all about the profit" and not what the profit can do to improve the quality of work and opportunity for employees, expect resistance rather than a dynamic sense of urgency.

So what does sense of urgency for the profitability business outcome look like? Here is a hit list to get your creative juices flowing:

+ If employees want better benefits, show them where and how they need to move the numbers in order to make the benefits happen. The no-compromise approach is to allow a team of employees to come up with the "how."
+ Make weekly financials the rule rather than monthly.
+ Look at and understand everything on your Balance Sheet, Income Statement and Statement of Cash Flows.
+ Live your cash-flow plan and budget. There's no sense creating a budget if the discipline to follow it isn't embedded into the company's thinking and behavior at the leadership level.
+ Have weekly cash-flow planning meetings with team leaders to review the numbers, pinpoint problems areas and rapidly adjust financial strategies when situations dictate.

+ Make each department responsible for its corresponding line item(s) on the financial statements. For example, make the office manager responsible for office supplies.
+ Create a company bonus plan based on profitability goals.

3. Critical numbers

It's easy to identify simple critical numbers for profitability, like gross revenues and net profit. And it's very likely that those numbers are the ones your business is currently focused on. But as you well know, growing a profitable business today means being able to expertly navigate through a seemingly endless minefield of obstacles, challenges and situations. Clearly, revenues and net profit are critical numbers to focus on, but the no-compromise leader must be savvy enough to identify and select the right critical numbers to drive — at the right time.

Contemplate for a moment the financial challenges faced by a seasonal business, perhaps a fine boutique hotel on Cape Cod, a ski resort in Aspen or the manufacturer of Christmas ornaments and decorations. These feast-or-famine businesses need to look beyond just revenue and net profit for their profitability-related critical numbers. Given that their window for generating revenue is so short, wouldn't it make sense for them to identify "cash reserves" on their Balance Sheet as a key critical number? Driving a cash reserve critical number sends a no-compromise message throughout the company to build cash reserves today in order to finance operations through the slow periods.

Consider a young business that has finally emerged from the tenuous start-up stage but is carrying a heavy debt and interest load. Reducing that debt would free up cash to finance its growth and expansion plans. Setting debt reduction as a critical number with a specific timeline is a wise no-compromise decision for this situation.

Here's the mother-of-all critical numbers. Nothing can drive a company into negative net profit faster than a payroll that's gotten out of hand. I see this all the time in many service and retail businesses that are traditionally commission driven. With a payroll that's a fixed percentage of service and retail sales, the ever-escalating increases in operating costs methodically squeeze the life out of profits until there's nothing left to squeeze. One very effective solution to get control over a runaway payroll is to eliminate commission and install an hourly/salary-plus-bonus pay program. (I'm referring to Strategies' Team-Based Pay program.) During these conversions, we make "service payroll" a critical number to drive until it reaches a manageable level. Payroll will remain a critical number until it is safely within the affordable target range.

Here's one last example you might find interesting. What would the profitability critical numbers be for a company that would like to position itself for sale? Let's just say the owner is looking to retire in five years. Clearly, the owner wants the financials to look impressive enough that they deliver a clear message that says, "You're going to pay a lot for my company." For this situation, a good critical number would be "Owner's Equity" on the Balance Sheet. Low debt load could be another. *I purposefully included this example to remind business owners that the time to start working on your exit strategy is the day you start or buy a business.* Entrepreneurs often wait too long before paying attention to "Owner's Equity" on the Balance Sheet, if they pay attention at all. And turning a negative owner's equity around can take a long time. Remember, your Balance Sheet shows the financial health of your business. If the business is sick and in pain, the Balance Sheet is going to show it — and that will have a direct and negative impact on the selling price of the business.

> **Nothing can drive a company into negative net profit faster than a payroll that's gotten out of hand.**

4. Information flow

It is within the information-flow process that profitability issues are either addressed or allowed to fester. If your business lacks an information-flow system to provide key profitability data to you, your leadership team and your employees, financial problems can, and often do, spin out of control. You cannot control the financial destiny of your business

Here are some examples of the most common critical numbers for the profitability business outcome:

- The tried and true — revenues and net profit
- Gross profit margin
- Service or production payroll
- Administrative and support payroll
- Cost of goods sold and/or cost of materials to do the work
- Cash and cash reserves
- Accounts receivable
- Reducing the average collection time on accounts receivable
- Accounts payable
- Short- and long-term debt
- Inventory on hand
- Inventory turnover
- Total general and administrative expense
- Owner's equity
- Percentage annual growth (in revenues and/or net profit)
- Travel and hotel expenses

when you, other leaders, your accounting department — or even your accountant's office — bottleneck profitability information flow. People all around your company are making decisions every day that will directly impact profitability. A well-conceived information-flow system will ensure that those individuals have the pertinent financial data to make the very best decisions. Imagine the positive impact on your bottom line if employees throughout your company connected their decisions to profitability.

Profitability is a fragile and precious business outcome that requires constant attention to detail and care. All it takes is one bad decision, one bad season or one expansion plan gone wrong, to wipe out not only profits, but your cash reserves, as well. Every day the business news has stories of weak profits, losses, layoffs and closings. Rest assured, a forensic analysis will reveal that compromise and lack of information flow played a role.

Here's a simple example of information-flow bottlenecking. Recently, the owner of a small business asked me to help identify her critical numbers. Staying profitable was a struggle, so much so, that her staff was picking up on her growing stress. As instructed, she sent me a cash-flow plan with an explanation that, although she was filling in her actual revenues, the expenses still showed projections. (I have a personal rule that I will not review incomplete financials. It's a waste of time and it involves me in someone else's compromise.) I could see from the revenue numbers that she was consistently falling short of her revenue goals. The problem was, she didn't have any actual expenses filled in for the first six months of the year.

> **Imagine the positive impact on your bottom line if employees throughout your company connected their decisions to profitability.**

When I asked when I could get a current, and complete, Balance Sheet and Income Statement, she said she's waiting for her bookkeeper to catch up. "Compromise — bottleneck."

When I finally got the reports about a week later, her financials really didn't look bleak at all. In fact, there was a six percent net profit. The Balance Sheet showed that cash was critically low. Some general and administrative expenses were red flagged, as well as cost of goods sold versus dollars tied up in inventory. When I asked how she connected spending to the budget, she explained, "My manager is really good at pinching pennies and does the ordering." "Interesting," I said. Then I asked two basic cut-to-the-chase questions, "Does your manager have a copy of the budget or any way of knowing how much of the monthly budget has already been spent? Do you meet weekly with your manager to review the cash-flow budget versus actual?" Like catching a kid who didn't do her homework, she painfully replied, "I don't give my manager any of that, and we never discuss or plan our spending." Geeezzz.

There are a couple of real lessons in this small business saga. First, the owner was getting emotionally stressed because cash was tight, not because the business was losing money. Second, her bookkeeper was bottlenecking the information flow process. Had she been providing accurate and timely financial reports, the owner might have been able to determine where the financial pain really was, worked on solutions and avoided unnecessary stress. Third, she disconnected with the numbers and allowed her manager to spend money without a plan and without essential financial data. This small business saga is played out on a grander scale in larger companies every day.

Open the floodgates of your information-flow systems. It's essential to protecting profitability. Scoreboards, daily huddles, weekly cash-flow planning meetings are all non-negotiable information-flow systems.

5. Teamwork

This one is easy and I'll say it in a Neilism: "Profitability is not a 'Lone Ranger' responsibility." Tiger Woods might be the highest-earning sports figure, but it still takes a team and teamwork to manage and grow his personal brand and assets. *Teamwork in business is all about profitability.*

I've been talking all along about sharing financial information, open-book management and focusing teams on driving your critical financial numbers. If you dream of the day when your employees will begin to think, act and make decisions like an owner, then it's time to give them the same information that owners have and use to grow the business. Treat them like owners. Give them the gift of financial literacy. If you think they won't get it or appreciate it, shame on you. That's compromise thinking that signals that it's time to get out of that box you're in.

Every Thursday is bookkeeping day at Strategies and the day we distribute a full set of financials to everyone. Balance sheet, income statement, year-to-date comparisons, statement of cash flows, accounts payable and accounts receivable. It is so cool to see everyone hovering around to get that first look to see what changed. Although there are only dozen of us, I'd rather have a dozen sets of eyes connected to a dozen brains looking for opportunities and financial leaks. Besides, those are their numbers. Good or bad, they made them happen. They have "ownership" in those numbers. When they're good, they celebrate. When they're not, they take it personally and work to figure out what happened and how to correct it. *That's teamwork in the profitability business outcome.*

Channeling and focusing the power of teamwork on profitability is the job of the no-compromise leader. Financial literacy, combined with the information, data and empowerment to put it to work, inspires a level of teamwork that most owners and leaders can only dream of. Otherwise, the burden of profitability will rest on the shoulders of the leader and the select few permitted to participate.

> **Neilism**
> Profitability is not a "Lone Ranger" responsibility.

6. Innovation

I'm always surprised at the responses I receive when I use innovation in discussions on profitability. It's like this whole profit thing is the exclusive domain of the numbers-crunching finance, accounting and bookkeeping departments. Well, it's not.

Innovation is the creative thinking that creates the "push" that drives numbers in the right direction. Innovation in the profitability business outcome is that great idea to spur sales in those slack periods. It's that innovative idea that pulls the company out of financial crisis without having to borrow money and go deeper into debt. It's using those innovative new systems and procedures your team creates to trim costs. It's the innovative partnership with a vendor or even a competitor that opens up new markets and growth opportunities. Innovation is definitely a factor in the profitability business outcome. *The no-compromise leader must inspire and create the opportunities for innovative thinking to flow freely throughout the company.*

One of the key drivers of profitability innovation is the need for urgency. As the cost of jet fuel skyrocketed, the major airlines saw their fuel costs nearly double in one year. Already in financial distress, the airlines scrambled for ways to offset fuel costs. They initiated fees for extra luggage, cut flights and retired as many of their fuel-guzzling jets as possible.

Only one airline will go relatively unscathed. Southwest Airlines might be one of the few U.S. carriers — if not the only one — to post a profit in 2008 while still offering bargain fares.

Southwest got innovative and locked in more than 70 percent of the fuel it expected to consume in 2008 at about $51 a barrel, far below the $126.62 a barrel at that time. With the huge cost advantage, Southwest hasn't had to hike air fares, or like other carriers, impose new fees and cut otherwise desirable routes.

Because of an innovative, calculated risk the airline took in 2007, essentially betting correctly that fuel prices would escalate, Southwest might be the only one left standing. Industry analysts expect most major carriers to post even greater losses with perhaps more joining those already in bankruptcy. Innovation in the profitability outcome paid off big for Southwest.

In 2001, Strategies' consulting business was growing faster than we could effectively handle. The pain of turning business away spurred our innovative thinking. We came up with a plan to create a new program that would train Certified Strategies Coaches (CSC). To offset the development costs and time to do the training, we made the program self-funding with a training fee. We promoted the CSC program to a select group of customers who were successfully using and living Strategies' programs and systems. Three years later, we graduated 22 CSCs. We now have coaches in key markets throughout the United States and Canada. The pain of turning business opportunities away created the urgency to get innovative. In the process, we created exciting, new earning opportunities for our best customers to partner in the work we do at Strategies.

7. Systems

Systems bring structure and discipline to the profitability business outcome. Accuracy and extreme attention to detail are nothing short of non-negotiable. As a consultant, I've seen more than my share of "garbage in — garbage out" accounting and financial reports. Blatant errors, improperly posted or categorized entries, expense line items that no one can explain and huge miscellaneous accounts are just a sampling of the financial nightmares that regularly occur when poorly designed systems exist. The end result is a collection of totally useless financial reports that cost you a bundle to produce. *You just can't make the best financial decisions with bad data.* Sloppy reports coming from the bookkeeping or finance office is a damn good signal that compromise exists at the leadership level. Otherwise, such nonsense would never be tolerated for even a nanosecond.

Profitability systems extend far beyond the accounting office. Wherever revenues are generated, financial systems must be in place to ensure proper reporting. And wherever money is spent and purchases made,

> **Sloppy reports coming from the bookkeeping or finance office is a damn good signal that compromise exists at the leadership level.**

financial systems must be in place. *Checks and balances. There is no other way to control and drive profitability.*

Remember, a system is a set of procedures that, when followed, produce a predictable and consistent outcome.

Here is a hit list of profitability processes that must be systemized:
- Proper categorizing of revenue streams.
- Invoice entry and generation (you just can't have errors on customer invoices).
- Accurate and timely posting of payables (improperly categorized expenses will make your profit and loss statements useless).
- Deadly accurate processing of payroll and payroll taxes.
- Purchase order system to control *everything* that gets purchased (if it's not in the budget, it doesn't get purchased.)
- System to run monthly, or even better, weekly financials — complete, accurate and on time.
- Distribution of weekly "Actual to Budget" comparison reports.
- Weekly accounts payable report (who do you owe money to?)
- Bill paying: What's the cycle? Who approves what gets paid?
- Weekly accounts receivable report (who owes you money).
- Quarterly review and update of your cash-flow plan and budget.

+ Competitive vendor cost analysis.
+ Debt management.
+ Inventory level management.
+ Creation of new project budgets.
+ Weekly cash-flow planning meetings (procedures needed to complete the meeting in 30 minutes).
+ Scoreboard updating (daily/weekly).
+ Financial performance data distribution to managers and staff.
+ Expense reports: Who's approving them? Are expenses verified and legitimate?
+ Office supplies: What's the budget, the system and who's accountable for it?

8. Accountability

What could be a more perfect topic for the profitability business outcome than accountability? *This is the end of the line for compromisers.* Go no farther. Only committed no-compromise leaders can pass this point.

Accountability in the profitability business outcome is extremely black and white. You make money or you lose money. You adhere to the budget or you violate it. You keep your financials accurate and current or you don't. You know your numbers or you don't. You make team bonus or you don't. *I'm confident my preceding rant has us on the same page.*

Imagine being one of the space shuttle astronauts thundering off the launch pad knowing that the individual in charge of your rocket fuel isn't paying attention to his systems monitor and controls. I put my money on you not having an overwhelming sense of confidence about being blasted into space. Considering the thousands of highly detailed systems required to prepare, launch and manage the mission, then bring the space shuttle back to earth safely, you begin to understand the importance of accountability at its highest no-compromise level.

The profitability business outcome is a perpetual measurement of your company's financial performance. Accountability at all levels of the company to adhere to its financial control systems is the determining factor

A Neil non-negotiable:

Depending on the size of your business, the following might come across as totally trivial. It's not. There are still multitudes of companies that still pay bills and write checks by hand. Today's excellent offering of accounting software makes handwritten checks something to see on display at the Smithsonian Institution next to Archie Bunker's favorite chair. Handwriting checks might have been fine for Fred Flintstone, but not for anyone doing business in today's automated world. (*QuickBooks Pro* by Intuit is the leading software for small business. I highly recommend it. www.intuit.com)

I'm making paying bills through your accounting software a non-negotiable. The speed and accuracy of computer checks allow you to produce accurate financial reports with the click of a mouse. Pay a bill by computer and the first thing it asks is, "Who are you paying?" Now you have vendor tracking. Next, it asks, "How much?" Now you have an expense amount. Then it asks, "What expense account should it be allocated to (e.g., rent, office supplies, cost of goods sold)." Insert your computer checks and hit "print." "Cash — Checking Account" on the Balance Sheet is reduced by the amount of the check and the expense is recorded on your Profit and Loss Statement. Out comes the check nicely addressed and ready for a double-window envelope.

I've been pounding away at running your financials weekly. The only way to do this is to totally and completely (that means 100%) automate all of your check writing and accounting procedures. No more handwritten checks or journals.

of your company's profitability performance. Accountability means "get it done, get it done on time and get it done right." It's honing your financial disciplines to a fine edge. Even if numbers are not your strength, you can develop and master the necessary skills to understand your financial reports and the systems required to keep them looking impressive. The reward is a sense of personal and company-wide pride.

> **The profitability business outcome is a perpetual measurement of your company's financial performance.**

Compromise is the curse of accountability. Unite no-compromise leadership with accountability and you will ensure balance in your profitability business outcome.

While writing this chapter, I received the following e-mail from a client. Her name is Mia Belliard, owner of Belliard's Salon and Spa in Cherry Hill, New Jersey. Mia's story eloquently captures the essence of this chapter on profitability.

I started the week with a leadership team meeting. I gave them each a copy of your Creating Urgency article that contained the Four Business Outcomes Wheel and had them review it for our meeting. We discussed why we missed goal and how we can get and stay focused. I had them each plot on the wheel where they thought we were in each of the Four Business Outcomes. The results were enlightening. We concluded that in July, we had too many people taking time off, as well as some unexpected hurdles. Then we discussed how to cut payroll when business is slow. It was amazing how the staff came up with deeper cost-cutting measures than I would have been comfortable bringing up. They truly do look at and understand the percentages on the scoreboards weekly. We all agreed that the energy started with us.

Two days later, we had a kick-butt staff meeting. This time, the entire team did the Four Business Outcomes Wheel exercise. I started by asking them to define The Four Business Outcomes. I'm happy to report that the entire staff knew them. I then drew a circle on the chalkboard and divided it into four parts and said, "Think of this as a wheel and each spoke represents one business of the business outcomes." We have a big dry-erase board that has our scoreboard numbers for the month. I asked them to look at the board for the month of July and tell me how we did in each area. We did the exercise as a group and they came out with the same results on the wheel as the leadership team.

Standing in front of the staff, I pretended to drive a car with the "off-balanced" wheel the team charted based on our monthly performance. Just as our business did last month, I started off fine, but veered off the road when I tried to pick up speed. The team understood that we must maintain balance in The Four Business Outcomes. I asked, "If we have all the ingredients for success — great staff, excellent skills, customer service — how can we be more profitable by creating balance in the Four Business Outcomes?" We went through each week and identified where the inconsistencies and problems were. That led to real solutions to create balance to not only drive a straight line — but to drive fast. Everyone was buzzing about the great opportunity we all created.

There was a time when I might have lacked confidence in myself. But given the no-compromise systems, the education we have, and the clear communication within the business, that is no longer the case. We have a great team that is dedicated to growth, profitability and excellence.

A NO-COMPROMISE LESSON:
The "gotta haves" of profitability

It's not luck or some cosmic force that allows a business to generate profits. You must focus on more than just top-line revenues. It takes making the best decisions about how to use the money you have. Here is a hit-list of essentials every no-compromise leader must follow:

- **Gotta have a cash-flow projection:** This is your financial game plan for required revenues and budgeted expenses.

- **Gotta live your plan:** If you don't connect your company's behavior to living and achieving your cash-flow projection, why did you waste the time creating it?

- **Gotta pay attention to all your financial reports:** The profit-and-loss statement tells you what came in, what went out and what was left. The balance sheet tells you if your business is healthy. The statement of cash flows tells you how cash is moving in and out of your business. Can't read these reports? Read the next "gotta."

- **Gotta understand your financials:** If you can add, subtract and divide, you can learn how to read financial reports. Stop making excuses. Make peace with your numbers.

- **Gotta be a financially literate company:** Want to see your revenues climb, expenses drop and profits soar? Teach financial literacy to your employees and open the books. Make them accountable for the line items they can control. Oh, and don't forget to give them a stake in the outcome with a bonus plan.

- **Gotta build cash reserves:** Investment counselors teach people how to save and invest. Shouldn't your company do the same?

- **Gotta manage debt:** It's hard to make money when the business is burdened with excessive debt. Debt creates financial drag. Cut up those credit cards.

- **Gotta enjoy the money:** You earned it.

CHAPTER 6

BUSINESS OUTCOME #3: STAFF RETENTION

The staff retention business outcome is all about creating a dynamic and empowering culture to attract and retain the best employees — and doing so with no-compromise leadership, open communication, integrity and respect.

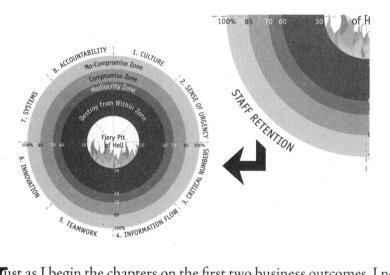

Just as I begin the chapters on the first two business outcomes, I need to ask a very simple question. What does *staff retention* mean to you? On the surface, it's your company's ability to get and keep employees. But as you move deeper into what staff retention really means, a more complex maze of human relationship dynamics begins to reveal itself. You quickly realize that there are forces at play, both internal and external, that influence the thinking, attitudes and job satisfaction levels of your employees regarding work and the company. How successfully you navigate your employees through all of these forces will ultimately define you as a no-compromise leader.

Winning in the game of business requires consistency in the execution of work. That ability to be consistent and predictable is what creates balance across The Four Business Outcomes. *Staff retention is the process of creating consistency in your workforce.* It allows your employees to bond as a team and to collectively build that exceptional high-performance momentum that only true teamwork can achieve. That momentum is so fragile that one player change or loss can derail it. That simple introduction of one new personality or attitude can shift the entire focus of the team from achieving goal to spewing toxic waste on one another. And it all happens in the blink of an eye. In football, a team has little chance of making the Super Bowl if the players keep changing. In business, if you want consistent and predictable outcomes in your business, you must retain staff. *You must keep your team as intact and in sync as possible.*

> **Neilism**
> Employees quit leaders, not companies.

We all know that employees come and go. Every business has employee turnover and attrition. However, getting stuck in the "employees just don't stay with companies very long anymore" thinking can lead business cultures down a dangerous path where employees are regarded more as commodities than the precious resources they are. Today's leaders should be fighting to change that thinking — not feed it.

The no-compromise leader cannot justify unacceptable employee turnover as a cost of doing business. That's the easy way — the compromise way. If an employee quits your company for any reason other than personal issues, relocation, health or for a career opportunity that doesn't exist in your company, your staff retention systems need work. There is no better way to drive this point home than this Neilism: "Employees quit leaders, not companies."

Employee turnover is a costly drain on your resources and cash flow. All that time and expense devoted to recruit, select, train and develop an employee into a productive contributor is lost when he or she walks out the door. Sure, you could have recruited and screened better, but consider this: What if you hired the perfect employee but something in the leadership process at your company turned him to the dark side and pushed him out the door? I totally support and encourage better employee screening, job profiling and job matching, and how these up-front hiring systems can improve employee retention. However, the fundamental question is what happens when that thoroughly screened and job-matched employee gets stuck working for a compromising leader in a contaminated culture? You guessed it, turnover. *Systems alone cannot overcome the turnover problems and related costs that compromising leaders create.*

It pains me to say that it's not uncommon to find myself coaching leaders who are their own worst staff retention problems. So much so, they appear to be blind to the problem or unwilling to see themselves as the root cause. I can only chuckle when I think about how many times managers have asked me, "Is there any way we can fire the boss?" Yes, it's disturbingly sad when the employees get it and their leader does not. In almost every case, these committed, "I believe in this company and its vision," managers leave out of utter frustration. *They are clearly the right hires that got stuck working for compromising leaders.*

> **What if you hired the perfect employee but something in the leadership process at your company turned them to the dark side and pushed them out the door?**

Every business has its own little society with its share of internal politics, disgruntled employees, and performance issues. It doesn't matter if your business has 10 or 10,000 employees, pulling them together into a cohesive, high-performance team is the true work of leadership. Do it with no-compromise leadership and you will attract and retain the best. Do it with compromise and you will get nothing more than a costly revolving door that employees pass through on their way to a better opportunity.

Staff turnover might naturally occur in business no matter what, but it still needs to be managed and controlled. Here are a few revealing signs that your staff retention efforts and systems need attention:

+ **Unacceptable behaviors, such as lateness, absenteeism, and poor attitude and productivity issues, have noticeably increased.** Abrupt and negative behavior changes are a sure sign that problems and frustrations exist and will likely further deteriorate. It's time for no-compromise leadership to open up the lines of communication to find out what's going on and what needs to be done to fix it. *Ignoring negative behavior shifts is a compromise.*

◆ **The work environment has been stressful lately and it's clear that managers and employees are far from content.** One or two employees quit or resign — then a few more follow. When clusters of employees begin leaving or walking out, it's a big red flag that demands immediate attention and open dialog with employees. *They need to vent and you and your leadership team members need to listen — really listen.* The right solution can always be found when you invest the time and reach out to understand what their "pain" is.

◆ **Employees are ratcheting up their complaints about the leadership approach of their department head or manager.** Performance reports also indicate that something isn't right. Interview some of the employees to gain their insights. Have that fierce conversation with that leader to discuss his or her challenges. Sometimes you can "save" a manager by helping him identify and address his leadership weaknesses — or by reassigning him to a role that's a better fit. Other times, you may need to let him go before problems get out of hand. One last thing, there are times when employees won't voice their concerns about a leader because the company is closed to such open dialog. Other times, there's fear of reprisal from that manager or the company for speaking up. It all leads to turnover and it's all driven by compromise.

Just like productivity and profitability, staff retention is a business outcome. It's the end result of all your systems, leadership and culture. Excellent staff retention is the hallmark of the no-compromise leader. All the time, effort and resources devoted to staff retention unite to drive performance and results in the other three business outcomes. Great staff retention drives productivity by minimizing disturbances in your workforce. That, in turn, drives profitability by improving output and efficiency while minimizing the costs associated with employee turnover. And when we get to the next chapter on the customer loyalty business outcome, you'll see how staff retention creates the foundation for delivering nothing short of world-class customer experiences.

Now it's time to apply The BIG Eight to the staff retention business outcome. As we move through them, remember that there is something special that exists in companies that attract and retain staff. It's not just one thing, system or approach, it's the company's ability to ignite and fuel the passion of its employees. It doesn't matter whether you make hamburgers at McDonald's or are a heart surgeon who save lives, there must be passion — not only for the work, but also for that greater vision and mission of the company. If you work at Starbucks, making that special custom-crafted cup of coffee or latté is your personal contribution to making someone's day. And if you do it well enough — if you understand the process well enough — you could become a manager or even own your coffee shop one day. If the

> If the vision and work of your business cannot ignite some level of passion in your workforce, you will have turnover.

vision and work of your business cannot ignite some level of passion in your workforce, you will have turnover. *Staff retention is all about finding and keeping the passion.*

1. No-compromise culture

The staff retention business outcome requires that I seriously ratchet up the intensity of my discussion for creating a no-compromise culture. In the 38 years I have worked in, owned, consulted, instructed, studied and wrote about business success, it is each and every company's unique culture that defines its success.

It's the culture that makes companies work — that allows world-class performance to take place. *It is your business culture that attracts and retains staff.* It's your culture — your company's collective behavior patterns — that lifts and draws your company toward its vision. And when compromise begins to spread, it's your contaminated culture that drags your company down, makes it inefficient and causes staff to lose faith.

If turnover is an issue in your company — your culture is contaminated. And if you're the leader, you allowed it to happen. *You compromised.* By contaminated, I'm referring to the negative behaviors that so easily, quietly and methodically infect a company's culture. It's all that drama and drag that interfere with productivity and forward momentum. It's when the self-proclaimed backroom managers spew their toxic waste on everyone they come in contact with. Simply put, a contaminated culture is one that lost its focus, sense of purpose, passion for the work and determination to grow due to compromise at the leadership level. Just like every garden has weeds that are determined to spread, every business has contaminating behavior looking for opportunities to spread. *The no-compromise leader is ever-vigilant to catch it and pluck it before it spreads.* To do so, leaders must be engaged and present.

> Simply put, a contaminated culture is one that lost its focus, sense of purpose, passion for the work and determination to grow due to compromise at the leadership level.

Five years ago, a hard-working couple purchased a busy service business. They were working in the business and when the owner informed them he wanted to sell, they jumped at the chance. They took a loan on all the equity in their home and borrowed from friends and relatives. Still, they were coming up short to close the deal. Anxious to sell, the owner agreed to hold a note on the balance but insisted on a three-year payout at a high interest rate. The couple's entrepreneurial seizure to purchase the business had them oblivious to the consequences of what they were getting into. Neither had hands-on experience in business ownership, leadership or financial management. Needless to say, these spirited entrepreneurs were overburdened with debt. Even though the business was generating $2.5 million, they quickly found themselves in a perpetual cash-flow crisis.

The stress of their financial woes became so severe, staff began questioning what was wrong. "Everything is fine," was always the message, but employees read the situation differently. Even though progress was being made in restructuring the debt and installing much-needed financial control systems, contamination set in. A few key service providers quit, but before doing so, spewed their toxic waste on other employees. Before quitting, they methodically collected customer contact lists and records of clients they were servicing.

The over-stressed entrepreneurs caught wind of the impending exodus from a client. However, weeks passed before they addressed the "rumor" with the technicians. They didn't want to believe that their once fellow teammates would leave and go work for a competitor. They were stuck in a full-blown leadership blockage. Well, it was true and the technicians not only quit, they had the time to collect all they needed to take clients with them. Oh, they had time to do one more thing. They influenced and incited enough of the remaining technicians that, of the 30 technicians employed, over half quit within a matter of weeks. Just 12 months after the acquisition, they filed for Chapter 11 bankruptcy protection.

Put on your no-compromise leadership hat. What could our young entrepreneurs have done to avoid the mass exodus of experienced technicians, not to mention the loss (theft) of proprietary company data? Consider the following strategies that could have prevented the internal collapse of the business.

Chaos yields to vision: Nothing is as stressful as worrying how you're going to make payroll or pay the bank loan. But allowing that stress to become apparent to staff and giving them nothing but an "everything is fine" smoke screen only accelerates contamination. Open but measured communication about the issues the business was facing, along with specific projects and goals to engage staff, could have channeled team energy in the right direction. Instead, the rumor mill and toxic waste spewers were allowed spin up the discontent.

Confront reality: Our entrepreneurs waited too long to get a handle on their debt load. They never paid attention to their financials. They didn't have the foggiest idea how to get control over their cash flow. Moreover, they not only resisted asking for help, but refused help that was being offered. They simply waited until the pain became so excruciating, they had to seek help. Had they addressed their financial woes early, it's likely they could have managed their debt load and even put money on the bottom line. *No* *business can work itself out of a financial crisis if it focuses only on sales and avoids controlling cash flow.*

Fierce conversations: When the entrepreneurs learned that two key employees were planning to leave, a meeting should have been scheduled — not to confront, but to discuss and resolve issues. Even if the situation was beyond resolution, all parties would have been able to discuss an ethical and organized departure.

Neilism
Change allows cultures
to adapt, grow
and strengthen.

Embrace change, don't fear it: The culture of the business was weak and contaminated when the business was acquired. Any business acquisition is the opportune time for implementing necessary change. Employees are expecting it.

Our entrepreneurs didn't want to rock the boat. Unfortunately, it was already rocking and taking on water. No-compromise leadership dictates that when change is needed, change happens. A Neilism: "Change allows cultures to adapt, grow and strengthen."

Always recruit: Recruitment efforts in a contaminated culture are difficult at best. New hires are quickly exposed to the contamination and their fate is often uncertain. If the company is actively and aggressively working at implementing positive change in the culture, new hires can be that breath of fresh air that's needed to accelerate cultural change.

I'm happy to report that our young entrepreneurs embraced no-compromise leadership and turned their company around. They restructured their debt, got a handle on their financials and cash flow and created a "let's grow this company together" culture. The contamination dissipated and the culture shifted in the right direction — the entire team felt it. What they felt was the shift that occurs when lift replaces drag in the culture.

It all began with our young entrepreneurs' decision to go no compromise. Yes, it was a slow and painful transition that required them to confront their weaknesses and change their thinking and behaviors. The shift to no compromise was so profound, one of them wrote me the following, "It's amazing how the business is a reflection of how we are feeling,

thinking and behaving. That's why business is not work or play, it's life."
No-compromise leadership had them out of Chapter 11 in less than a year.

Culture is everything when it comes to staff retention. A no-compromise culture is damn near super glue for retaining staff. It's also powerful at weeding out those who just don't fit. No compromise keeps your business culture as close to pure and pristine as possible. It keeps leaders actively engaged with the business and its employees.

True, I used an example of an ailing business to drive home the power of no compromise, because every business has contamination festering in its culture. Every business has issues that distract leaders from the most important work of leadership — protecting its culture and its people. *You can hire the best recruiters and do the best screening and job matching, but your ability to create a no-compromise culture is the ultimate factor to attracting and retaining the best staff.*

2. Sense of urgency

Perhaps you're wondering what "sense of urgency" has to do with the staff retention business outcome.

> **Neilism**
> If you lead a thirsty horse to water and it refuses to drink, get another horse. You don't have time to waste."

The answer is simple, everything. Like me, I'm sure you've worked for, done business with or visited companies that are just lethargic and slow moving. Service is slow. Response is slow. Decisions are slow. Delivery is slow. Leaders are slow. *Everything is slow.*

Lethargic businesses drive me nuts. They're totally frustrating to do business with. It's even worse to have to coach them. For me, it's just painful because any forward progress requires energy and comes from a sense of urgency. Urgency fuels change and drives growth. Urgency makes a company dynamic. Urgency "lifts" a company to the next level.

I haven't done a Neilism in a while, so here's a good one for sense of urgency: "If you lead a thirsty horse to water and it refuses to drink, get another horse. You don't have time to waste." OK, it sounds cruel and you feel bad for the horse. But how many times do you play out this scenario in your own business? You see that your business is stuck, you see the solution, but only stare at it and do nothing. Do you think this mode of behavior impacts your company's ability to recruit and retain staff? You bet it does.

The no-compromise leader creates a dynamic, all-inclusive work environment. These dynamic companies are always on a mission, chasing a goal and moving toward its vision. They're just exciting companies to work for. They're never boring. They're never lethargic or slow. There is always something new and opportunities abound. Employees are involved and engaged in the work of moving the company forward. Job satisfaction is high because the sense of urgency drives individual, team and company achievements. When job satisfaction rates are high, so is staff retention. *For employees, leaving means giving up too much.*

The no-compromise company is like a magnet for recruiting the best players. At Strategies, we are always receiving inquiries from individuals who know about the work we do, or attend our seminars, asking how they can become involved or what opportunities we have available. When qualified individuals come to us seeking career opportunities, it reinforces that we're doing our job right.

Urgency begins at the hiring process. Does your hiring and orientation procedure begin the process of instilling a sense of urgency in your employees? Think about FedEx and the role sense of urgency plays for its culture. Remember the opening scene from the movie *Cast Away?* Tom Hanks is teaching the Moscow FedEx office about the urgency of time. With passion, he says, *"Tick tock, tick tock, tick tock. Time rules over us without mercy. It's like a fire; it can either destroy us or keep us warm. That's why every FedEx office has a clock — because we live or die by the clock. We never turn our back on it or allow the sin of losing track of time."*

Time is the ultimate urgency generator. At FedEx, the pride of beating the clock is nurtured and shared throughout the company. How often and in how many places is your company losing track of time? More importantly, are you hiring employees that are compatible with your company's sense of urgency? If an employee prefers a nice relaxed pace, he won't survive in a company culture that is fueled by sense of urgency.

Here are some do-it-now strategies to connect sense of urgency to the staff retention business outcome:

- **"Empower to the people."** The no-compromise leader sets the vision, objectives and timelines for the company — then empowers employees to get the job done. Employee involvement and ownership in the design of how work gets done directly influences staff retention. For example, if the mission is to cut delivery time without compromising quality, empower those that do the work to design the solution. Given the right data and accountabilities, employees will work harder and faster to successfully complete their mission.

- **Design games and mini-games to keep the action exciting and staff actively engaged.** Tie games to prizes or bonus payouts when goals are met. Create a game design task force in each department to keep games fresh and new. Assign game leaders and scorekeepers. Never underestimate the energy from games.

- **I said it before — teach financial literacy to your staff.** Teach them how a business makes money. Give them costs to manage that are directly related to their work. Want them to think, act and make decisions like a business owner? Teach them how to use the financial data and tools business owners use.

- **Take time to be your company's best cheerleader.** Get out of your office or away from the work to cheer your employees on to victory. Get your hands dirty. Show that you care about more than just numbers — show that you care about your people.

3. Critical numbers

Clearly the most important critical number for staff retention is your employee turnover rate. However, for some companies and situations, it's not always the easiest number to nail down. If you're a small business with just a few employees, it's possible to go for a year or more without losing staff. That zero annual turnover rate is pretty impressive until a few employees jump ship and drive that number to 20 or 30 percent. Large or small, turnover is a disruptive and costly occurrence.

Here's another example: If you start the year with 100 employees and end the year with 100, and 84 of those employees were the same ones you started the year with, then your turnover rate is 16 percent. Now, let's make this interesting by throwing some reality into the equation. Let's say that one of the 16 new hires was fired and was replaced three times. The employee quit in January, the replacement quit in April, and another person was hired who lasted only until November. Then you might want to count every time an employee left the company and another one was hired, in this example your turnover would be 18 percent.

Estimates of the total cost of losing a single position to turnover range from 30 percent of the yearly salary of the position for hourly employees to 150 percent...

Estimates of the total cost of losing a single position to turnover range from 30 percent of the yearly salary of the position for hourly employees (Cornell University) to 150 percent, as estimated by the Saratoga Institute, and independently by Hewitt Associates. Even a conservative estimate, that the loss of one person is equal to his or her annual salary, clearly illustrates the negative financial impact of employee turnover. For example, for a company with 500 employees at an average salary of $40,000 and a turnover rate of 10 percent, the cost of that turnover equals $2 million. A reduction in turnover of two percent would result in an immediate savings of $40,000.

Here is a hit list of strategies to address and reduce the cost of employee turnover:

- **Hire right by matching employee profiles to the requirements of the job.** Willow Creek Consulting, www.willowcc.com, specializes in employee profiles and job matching. Potential or existing employees take an online test and the results are matched to a job pattern you define for the job. The job match report gives the best indication if there's a fit. From sales clerk to CEO, getting the right individual in the right job is the very first step to reducing turnover.

- **Refine your orientation process.** Ensure that new employees get all the information they need to understand the vision and objectives of the company and their jobs. Too often, new employees are thrown to the wolves, expected to perform and quit out of frustration.

- **Once and for all, dismantle and tear down the command and control military-style of management.** You'll never get employees to think and make decisions like an owner until you do. Empowerment is just a buzzword until you not only allow it to happen, but encourage and drive the process. "Dictator" is certainly not the definition of the no-compromise leader.

- **Never keep your employees in the dark.** I'll address this in detail when I discuss information flow.

- **Never allow the business to become lethargic and slow.** Keep the energy alive. Cheer-lead every day if that's what it takes. Play games. Always have a goal. Create short-term wins to feed and inspire enthusiasm.

- **Keep the passion alive in your company.** Keep your vision fresh. This alone does wonders to build employee pride and loyalty in the company they work for.

4. Information flow

From 1981 until 1985, I was editor-in-chief for a small Connecticut-based business publication. I was initially hired to build the company's seminar business but quickly found myself at the typewriter writing articles — yes, I said "typewriter." Actually, I brought in my own electric typewriter, because that big non-electric Underwood they gave me was a tank. By tank, I mean that even Arnold Schwarzenegger couldn't punch those keys for more than 10 minutes straight. *Lesson: Don't expect quality work and high productivity if you don't provide the best tools and equipment for your staff to do their work.* And the owner/publisher wouldn't even pay for the special ribbon cartridges my typewriter used. *I loved the work — but I was not a happy camper.*

We were all concerned for our jobs. Because there was no information flow, that's all we had to focus on.

About five months after I arrived at the publication, I noticed that the owner was having unusually long and almost daily closed-door meetings in his office. This was clearly a contrast from what I observed in my first few months. Then I began to notice projects getting placed on hold. Being a small office with about a dozen staff, sightings of the owner were becoming less frequent. He would simply hunker down in his office. He even resorted to entering and exiting the building through the sliding doors in his office. *The non-verbal messages were disconcerting.*

Not being one to hold back when I have concerns, I frequently asked if everything was OK. Each inquiry got me the same, "Uh, sure, everything's fine," response. *There was never direct eye contact.*

Clearly something was going on and I didn't have a very good feeling about it. I had just moved my wife and son from Southern California 3,000 miles to Connecticut. The last thing I wanted to hear was that the company was in trouble. The other employees were just as anxious. Needless to say, productivity ground to a halt and staff stress levels were high. We were all concerned for our jobs. Because there was no information flow, that's all we had to focus on.

Finally, after weeks of speculation about what was really going on in those closed-door meetings, the owner announced that he was selling the company to Prentice Hall, a major publishing company. Now, the owner of the company was always "all about the money." Sadly, he often regarded employees more like commodities to be leveraged — not loyal teammates who shared his vision of growing a great business publication and education company. *Being a key employee, I was deeply troubled, not to be privy to the fact the company was being sold.* We were finally informed that all employees were going to receive employment contracts, so our jobs were assured. Had this been shared, it would have defused the stress and anxiety that permeated the company for months. *More importantly, we all could have shared in the excitement of the greater opportunity Prentice Hall's recourses could bring.*

As it happened, the sale fell through. And because many important projects and mailings were put on hold for the pending sale, the company found itself in a serious cash crisis. An interesting shift occurred. The owner brought us all into the loop and we got creative. Within months, the team brought the company back into the black. Sadly, it didn't take long before the owner was back in his office holding closed-door meetings and most certainly conniving his next big scheme.

That was a trend that went on for the next four years. Closed doors, secret meetings and lawyers' letters always piled high on our leader's desk. We never really knew how the company was doing. *Nothing was ever shared.* At one company meeting, the owner announced that he was giving me stock in the company. That was cool — and unexpected. Then a year passed. Whenever I would ask about the stock, he would laugh it off and say, "It's coming — keep checking your mailbox."

I loved my job and the work I was doing, but I was working too hard for a leader I didn't trust. Ethically, and for the security of my family, I resigned at the end of my fifth year. *I quit the owner — not the company.*

> I loved my job and the work I was doing, but I was working too hard for a leader I didn't trust.

Here is a hit list of information-flow strategies you can put to work in your company:

- **Share critical numbers, such as units made or shipped, customers serviced, sales goals, profit goals and more.** This keeps employees tightly connected to the numbers that are vital to company growth. By design, the sharing of critical numbers creates an inclusive business culture and sense of "ownership" in the operation and growth of the business.

- **Every employee wants and needs to know how he or she is doing.** Leaders and managers must do regularly scheduled one-on-one performance evaluations. They must be open and honest without candy coating or holding back. That's compromise.

- **Make a weekly "Presidential Address" to your company.** Take 10 minutes to give a status report on your critical numbers, new opportunities, challenges and to celebrate a win, such as a new client acquisition, a department that hit goal or a new cost-cutting measure that worked.

- **Use company newsletters to keep everyone informed.** Make them look great. These days, you could even consider a weekly e-mail update to everyone in the company.

- **Take a hard look at your new-employee orientation programs.** Are they up to the task? Are they up-to-date? Poor information flow at the orientation and training stage is asking for turnover problems.

- **Use scoreboards.** Keep them up-to-date. Scoreboards might not seem like a retention tool, but rest assured, they are. Anything that keeps employees involved in the business game keeps them involved in the business. Remember, scoreboards and huddles go together. A quick Neilism: "A scoreboard without a huddle might as well be invisible."

- **Empower your employees to make decisions.** Create special task forces or teams to spearhead new projects or to solve problems. To do so, they need information. An inclusive company retains staff.

Information flow is a powerful retention tool. It builds trust. It communicates the respect a company has in its employees and that everyone has a stake in its health and success.

In September 2000, a major publisher approached me expressing an interest in acquiring Strategies. Remembering not only how I felt about not being privy to acquisition discussions, but how it created false assumptions and stress through the company, I purposefully kept my entire team informed every step of the way. At the very first meeting, I introduced them to the president of the company and had key staff sit in on most of the meetings. *Not once was a conversation held behind closed doors.* Yes, there were questions about "what will happen," but the process never created anxiety or stress. I never sold, but the experience taught me a lot about acquisitions. Above all, I was proud of my team and how open the process was handled at Strategies. Our no-compromise culture held true, as did productivity throughout the three months of acquisition talks.

> **Neilism**
> A scoreboard without a huddle might as well be invisible.

I hope my story drives the point home of just how vital information flow is to the trust, integrity and culture maintenance of a company. Most of all, I hope it locks in how the information-flow driver works to drive the staff retention business outcome.

5. Teamwork

Everyone wants to be part of something — to belong. Team momentum and excitement are infectious. Teamwork pulls people together in the most positive and inspiring way. When the team spirit is strong enough, even those self-proclaimed diehard loners will find themselves subtly seeking a way to align with the team. Call it teamwork, camaraderie, or your family at work, the effect teamwork has on staff retention is the magic that every company can and must strive to achieve.

Throughout my working years, I've been part of three teams that stand out. With two of those teams, I was an employee. We were truly tight as co-workers and relentlessly focused on goals and vision. Both companies had inspiring leaders who kept us on task and totally accountable for our actions and results. We were proud and WOW, were we ever productive. In both cases, when our teams' fearless leaders moved on, the team energy and focus left with them. For me personally, I yearned for the involvement, camaraderie and growth I experience on those teams. So much so, that without the team connectedness, I found myself looking for other opportunities — even if that meant looking beyond the company I was working for at the time. In both instances, my searching led me to start my own companies.

For the no-compromise leader, the team and the company must endure above all else.

Clearly teams will go through up-and-down cycles as people come and go and as the business environment changes and evolves. But the no-compromise leader does the best job of maintaining high-performance teams. For them, the lows are not so low. They inspire teamwork. They attract and nurture the right players. *For the no-compromise leader, the team and the company must endure above all else.*

The third and very best team I have ever been on is my team at Strategies. Some of us have been together for over 13 years. Since founding Strategies in 1993, we've only lost eight employees, six who moved on — two more by invitation. Not bad for 15 years. Every change was good for the team and the company. Every addition added energy to the team. It all comes back to creating a culture and level of personal involvement that make people want to stay. They stay because they're part of a special team that can't be found elsewhere.

How good is my team? They gave me the time I needed to write this book. They essentially ran the company and made big decisions. That's how we designed it. That's what we were working to achieve, because once the book is published, I'll be on the lecture circuit — out there promoting and bringing business to Strategies. That's going to be a big part of my job over the next few years. *That's what I've been working for.*

Here's a hit list of teamwork strategies you can use to drive the staff retention business outcome. Some were discussed previously, so this will be down and dirty:

- **Keep operational tasks off your plate.** Delegate and empower those tasks to individuals and teams.
- **Set up task teams.** These teams work on special projects, problem solving and system development.
- **Do daily huddles and mini rallies.** Teamwork should be fun, exciting and inspiring.
- **Create orientation teams.** Indoctrinating new employees into your no-compromise culture is key and teams hasten the process.
- **Set up games to create friendly competition between teams.** Don't forget to include some cool prizes for the winning team. Games keep employees engaged, and engaged employees are easier to retain. Games bring life, energy and opportunity to slack periods or during seasonal trends.
- **Take a day or so to play on a team.** Nothing like having their fearless leaders get down and dirty with the troops.
- **Create a mentor program.** Mentors are key for employees moving into new positions within the company, or to help employees with specific challenges to overcome them. Set strict qualifications to be on your mentor's team. Make it a privilege and position of respect. This is a powerful approach to not only improving staff performance, but to retain your most-gifted and productive employees as well.

6. Innovation

When Jack Stack implemented open-book management at Springfield Remanufacturing Corp. (now SRC Holdings Corp.) in the early 1980s to save it from closing, he did more than start The Great Game of Business. Through open-book management, scoreboarding, driving critical numbers and giving SRC employees a stake in the outcome, he discovered a way to tap into the entrepreneurial spirit of his employees that traditional management structures typically squelch. By 2008, Stack's innovative approach took SRC from a dying company and grew it into 44 companies doing over $450 million in revenues. Stock value has risen from 10¢ per share in 1983 to $134 in 2005.

I interviewed Jack Stack in late 2004. We talked about how open-book management and playing The Great Game of Business created an ownership culture that provided opportunities and security for SRC employees. Stack's tone went super serious. I could feel the passion in his voice as he spoke about what SRC had done for its employees. *"SRC has 840 shareholders at present. We face that liability to make the right investments to make sure the liquidity is there so we can cash them out when they're ready. In 1987 a decision was made to start other companies to build liquidity. We invested in a bank, bought properties, started a venture capital company and other companies. All these startups turned into great new ventures and became part of the SRC family. Then, interestingly, no one wanted to sell off any of these companies. So, we found other ways to build liquidity. Today, we earn a 19 percent return annually from our venture companies. More importantly, these companies provide a great quality of life for our employees and the community as well."*

Stack got innovative to keep the bank from foreclosing on SRC. In the process, his open-book approach to business, teaching employees financial literacy and creating an ownership culture became a powerful staff-retention tool. It's no wonder why such notable companies, like Harley-Davidson, Southwest Airlines and Roadway Express, all came to The Great Game of Business to learn and build an open-book management culture. *These companies came to play "the great game of business" at the highest level. To do so requires no-compromise leadership.*

How a company does business is only one aspect of how innovation drives the staff retention business outcome. Innovation in a company's products and service is just as vital, because it fuels forward momentum and growth. Innovation is a natural motivator that inspires employees and keeps a company and its culture fresh and vibrant. Employees engage and feel a sense of shared company pride.

Here is a tough story that shows how the failure to stay innovative can devastate a once-great company. In early 2005, I was in Rochester, New York, to do a no-compromise leadership seminar. Rochester is the corporate home of Eastman Kodak, the famed camera and film manufacturer. During the seminar, conversation turned to the depressed local economy spurred on by mounting losses and layoffs at Kodak. The company announced in 2004 that it would cut 15,000 jobs. In July 2005, Kodak announced an additional 10,000 layoffs. Kodak posted losses of $142 million in the first quarter of 2005 preceded by a $59 million loss in the fourth quarter of 2004.

Digital cameras have experienced one of the fastest growth rates of any new technology. As rapidly as consumers embraced digital photography, demand for traditional cameras and film, where Kodak was the major domestic supplier, tanked. Kodak took another lethal broadside from the rapid shift away from film when demand for photo processing and paper also plunged. Like other companies that jumped on the digital bandwagon, Kodak enjoyed brisk growth of its digital products. However, the company failed to innovate fast enough to make up for the rapidly shrinking film-based photography business in which the company had always been perceived as an invincible market leader.

Leadership was clearly asleep at the wheel at Kodak when the shift to digital cameras was taking place. They failed to innovate as fast or faster than the marketplace and their competition. It cost the company not only hundreds of millions of dollars and tens of thousands of jobs, it cast a dark cloud on its ability to attract and retain the best innovative talent it desperately needs to recover — if it can recover as a market leader at all.

7. Systems

I'm still amazed at how many companies fail to adhere to the most basic system of doing consistent employee reviews. Studies consistently reinforce that performance and job satisfaction are directly related to employees knowing and understanding how leadership views their overall performance. *Failure to communicate and give detailed feedback on a scheduled basis is about the easiest way to show an employee that the company just doesn't care.*

Here's a very appropriate and thought-provoking Neilism for systems and staff retention: "Do you do quarterly employee reviews at least once

Here's a hit list of thoughts on innovation to drive the staff retention business outcome:

- Don't assume that you know and understand what your employees value most about your company. Learn what and why they stay. Make sure every leader and manager is privy to this information.

- Benefits are great retention tools, but only if those benefits are meaningful to employees. Survey your employees to find out what benefits they value most and what benefits they desire most.

- Is it time to re-engineer how your company works with respect to layers of leadership, jobs and job titles?

- Who are the emerging leaders in your company? What programs or training do you have in place to prepare them for leadership?

- Are you tapping into the innovative thinking of employees for new and better products and services?

- Are you tapping into the innovative thinking of employees for better ways to run the company?

- Are you creating an ownership culture that engages employees?

- How do you communicate career and growth opportunities to employees? Do they really understand what those opportunities are? How can you improve the delivery of this vital information?

a year?" I get audience chuckles every time I use this line and I can always tell by the seat squirming and facial expressions that I touched a leadership accountability nerve. If you or any leader in your company is so busy that there just isn't time to do periodic scheduled employee reviews — then you shouldn't have employees. It's that simple and 100 percent non-negotiable. *No compromise.*

> **Neilism**
> Do you do quarterly employee reviews at least once a year?

No-compromise companies with high staff retention have systems in place to ensure high levels of employee satisfaction. *The most powerful systems that directly impact staff retention target six key areas:*

1. Communication
2. Information flow
3. Job performance
4. Training and development
5. Career growth paths (including compensation)
6. Hiring and job matching

8. Accountability

As always, accountability is what distinguishes the no-compromise leader from all others. When it comes to a company's most precious resource, its people, accountability demands nothing less than center stage. However, leaders can easily fall short in the disciplines of staff retention by losing that key connection of accountability that drives two critical support legs.

> **If you or any leader in your company is so busy that there just isn't time to do periodic scheduled employee reviews — then you shouldn't have employees.**

First, the no-compromise leader, no matter where he or she is in the company structure, is accountable to the productivity, efficiency and security of its employees. *Staff retention is an outcome.* Accountability to the company's systems,

Systems bring consistency and discipline to the staff retention business outcome in the following areas:

- Recruiting and hiring systems to attract and screen the best candidates;
- Communicate clear and specific job expectations;
- Match the right employee with the right job through profiling and job matching;
- Formal, scheduled periodic performance evaluations;
- On-going performance feedback systems to communicate on what's going great and what needs improvement;
- Training and development systems to expand and refine skill sets;
- Grooming and preparation for leadership advancement at all levels in the company;
- Meaningful and flexible benefit plans;
- Flexible work schedules;
- Systems to feed the research and development of new products and services;
- Bonus systems to inspire performance and give employees a stake in the outcome;
- Systems to engage employees in supporting an ownership culture, such as open-book management;
- Financial literacy training and getting employees engaged in the operational and cost management process of driving profitability;
- Scoreboard and huddle systems to ensure consistency in communicating progress toward goal;
- Reward and recognition systems to identify, celebrate and share outstanding individual and team performance and contribution.

sales, profitability, procedures, communication vehicles — anything and everything that impacts staff retention — is non-negotiable to the no-compromise leader. Remember Kodak's fall from grace as the market leader in photography and film? Kodak's leaders let their guard down. They didn't read and respond to the obvious signs that photography was shifting at high speed to digital. They compromised the integrity of the company and the security of all its employees.

> **It's hypocritical to complain about staff retention problems when compromise at the leadership level is the root cause.**

Let's take this one step further. Consider a leader who doesn't pay attention to numbers or budgets. What happens to staff retention when the leader can't afford to give raises or bonuses that employees worked hard for and met the requirements to receive? What happens to staff retention when the company gets stuck in a perpetual cash-flow crisis, because its leaders can't live the very budget they created and approved? The answers are obvious. The no-compromise leader must be accountable to his or her employees to run an efficient, productive and enduring company. It's hypocritical to complain about staff retention problems when compromise at the leadership level is the root cause.

The second accountability support leg is open and honest communication, growth paths and information flow for each and every employee. Poorly defined job expectations, absence of or inconsistent performance reviews and inadequate training or tools to do the work are all open invitations for employee frustration and turnover.

Two years after graduating college, my son, Eric, took a position as the Northeast regional sales manager for a manufacturing company of professional salon products. His first task was to attend a sales meeting in Florida. After the meeting concluded, he called me to express concern that his orientation to the company was not going well. Essentially, Eric had no idea what was going on or what he was supposed to be doing. Although the meeting did discuss sales and sales strategies, he received no specific training in the product nor was he given any insight or history on the distributors he would be servicing. There was no product knowledge

— not even product samples for him to try. To top things off, he didn't have order forms or any training on how to place an order. He basically returned from the meeting with a $1 million sales quota, a laptop and a company car. Eric, who is a natural achiever and prides himself on delivering nothing but his best, was freaking out.

During that conversation, he delivered a fierce no-compromise assault on how the company set him up to fail.

Eric placed a call to one of the more experienced salesman he met at the meeting to ask a question that epitomized how poorly prepared he was to achieve his sales quota. He asked, "Can you tell me what your typical day and week look like?" When his fellow salesman said, "Why do you ask?" Eric responded, "I don't have a clue what I'm supposed to be doing in this job." I really felt for Eric and how totally frustrated he was and how he was grasping for any help he could get. This calls for Neilism: "No-compromise leadership is not, 'If I think it, they'll do it.' You've got to prepare them and clarify expectations."

After about two weeks, Eric had enough. He called the vice president of sales to advise her that he was resigning. Now, you need to know that my son is a chip off the old block. During that conversation, he delivered a fierce no-compromise assault on how the company set him up to fail. Trust me, that vice president needed a stiff drink and some band-aids after that phone call. She accepted full responsibility and agreed to give Eric the training and support he needed if he would agree to stay. Eric did hang in there for nine more months until he couldn't take it anymore and resigned.

Within one year after Eric resigned, each and every one of the sales people he worked with left the company. Compromise at the leadership level fueled the company's staff retention problem. First, the company failed to be accountable to the business and how it did business. Second, it failed to be accountable to its employee by providing proper training, support and open communication. This scenario is played out every day at businesses large and small.

A month or so later, Eric walked into my office, sat down and slid a piece of paper across my desk. I picked it up, turned it over and saw a rather serious salary figure. He came to talk about coming back to work at Strategies. (I was hoping he would.) I slid the paper back and asked, "What will the company receive in return for this salary?" We both smiled and talked about what his job and responsibilities would be. He became Strategies' vice president. That was thirteen years ago. Today, he runs the marketing and internal operations of the corporate office. Will he take over the company some day? I tried to make him president once and he gave it back. We'll see.

Here is a hit list of do-it-now strategies that you can use to address accountability in the staff retention business outcome:

+ **All employees want to know where they stand at work.** Do frank and open performance reviews at least quarterly. Never let behavior or performance issues go unaddressed.

+ **Your company has systems, procedures and rules.** Follow these just as you expect every employee to follow them. Leaders must be accountable first and lead by example.

> **Neilism**
> No-compromise leadership is not, "If I think it, they'll do it." You've got to prepare them and clarify expectations.

+ **Employees cannot be held accountable for abstract and poorly designed tasks, projects and duties.** Remember the story about my Eric. He was accountable for producing $1 million in sales but was never given the training, tools or support to do his job. A Neilism: "Poorly designed work will always be poorly executed."

+ **Being accountable to your business is the real work of leadership.** Be aware of what's going on in your company and the marketplace. Stay connected, involved and ever vigilant in driving The Four Business Outcomes. You can't build a secure and enduring company for you and your employees if you don't.

+ **Accountability is a discipline.** Adhere to deadlines and schedules. Never promise anything you cannot deliver. Once compromised, employee trust in leadership is difficult to regain.

+ **Along with accountability comes consequence.** *Accept it.* If you fail to be accountable, take responsibility for the outcome. If an employee fails to be accountable, you must adhere to your set policies — no matter how painful. A consulting client discovered that his manager was stealing from the company. Against the very policies he established, and the recommendations of his leadership team, the president of the company refused to terminate the manager. In effect, it sent a message throughout the company that, "You can steal and nothing will happen." A side note: The failure to check references would have revealed that the manager in question had a history of stealing.

Neilism
Poorly designed work will always be poorly executed.

+ **Create a steering committee for the purpose of monitoring and refining staff retention in the company.** The committee should consist of representatives from all levels of the company. The task of this committee is to analyze not only why employees leave, but to further develop all of the wonderful things the company does to retain staff. Recruitment and employee development strategies must also be addressed.

+ **Accountability demands free-flowing information and data on company, department, team and individual performance.** You simply cannot hold employees accountable for performance and outcomes without a system for providing information and data. *If you want accountability, they need to understand the game and what the score is.*

+ **You cannot hold others accountable if you refuse to let go of the controls.** Empowerment and accountability are inseparable.

A NO-COMPROMISE LESSON:
Tuff Stuff: Leave nothing unsaid

You're getting ready to do a performance evaluation with a key employee. There have been behavior and performance issues that have surfaced a while back that you had hoped were temporary and would just fade away. But, as they often do, the issues continued and now they are beginning to impact other members of your team. You know this employee is highly sensitive to constructive feedback and the process often produces all kinds of drama, emotions and funk. Because of this, getting into the tough stuff with this employee always produces a knot in your stomach.

So, the evaluation begins. You navigate through the process until you reach that point where all that remains to be said is the tough stuff. You feel like you've cornered a wild beast and you're just trying to find the best moment and angle to capture it without getting mauled. And then it happens — you ask the employee if she has any questions and you end the evaluation. You hesitated. You left essential things unsaid. You wimped out. You compromised.

This scenario gets played out in business every day. You see behavior and performance issues and for some reason, you fail to engage. Interestingly, it only occurs with certain individuals when your pre-conceived mental picture of the process and the immediate fallout cranks up your anxiety levels high enough to hit the compromise button. To make matters worse, you beat yourself up for missing the opportunity to address a growing problem that will only continue to escalate.

Here are some red-hot strategies to ensure that you leave nothing unsaid:

- **Just get it over with:** When it comes to confronting reality and dealing with the tough stuff, if you hesitate, you lose. That's it.

continued...

Address it and move on. Lingering issues do more damage to the performance of the business. More importantly, allowing issues to linger means you're allowing contamination to infect your culture.

- **Focus on the desired outcome:** It's easy to get stuck in the emotions and stress of addressing highly sensitive and seemingly explosive issues. When emotions surface, help yourself and the employee by focusing attention on the desired outcome. Doing so gives purpose to the process — that addressing the tough stuff today you're both creating a better tomorrow.

- **How bad did it get before you engaged?** Here's the real kicker. If you've observed and even acknowledged that a behavior and performance problem exists and did nothing, you compromised your leadership role. Had you engaged when the problem surfaced, the probability of it going critical is greatly minimized.

- **What's the worse that could happen?** OK, the employee might get so upset that he or she quits. Is that a bad thing? Typically when behaviors and performance head south, the ripple effect can degrade performance and create distractions throughout a department or even the entire company. If your respectful efforts to help an employee grow and prosper are met with a resignation, consider it a favor. Accept the resignation, open the windows and allow the fresh air in.

One of the most challenging aspects of being a no-compromise leader is the ability to engage in open and constructive dialog with employees on behavior and performance issues — and to do so when the issues surface. Hesitate today and you'll just have a bigger problem tomorrow.

CHAPTER 7

BUSINESS OUTCOME #4:
CUSTOMER LOYALTY

The customer loyalty business outcome is all about delivering extraordinary service, quality and value to achieve maximum client retention — and doing so with a no-compromise passion to be nothing less than world class.

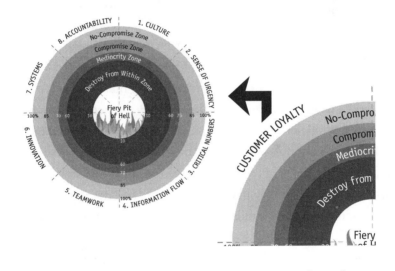

W hat does *customer loyalty* mean to you? If you focus on just this one business outcome called customer loyalty, what would the results look like in your business? If there were one key ratio to measure customer loyalty in your business, what would it be? Prepare to completely immerse yourself in this topic, because the implications to your company are profound. At the core of every business entity resides a fundamental customer loyalty component. It doesn't matter whether you're a service business, manufacturer, distributor — or even a government agency — you have customers to satisfy. And here's the catch: You can merely "satisfy" or you can take the no-compromise approach and create fiercely loyal customers beyond your wildest expectations. For the no-compromise leader, to just satisfy just isn't good enough.

Let's kick this chapter off with a Neilism: "Why strive for mediocrity when no compromise can make you world-class?" Striving for mediocrity is easy. Though few business leaders would confess that's what they're doing, their customer retention rates and slow growth prove otherwise. Frankly, any business can be designed to be world class. By "designed," I'm referring to the systems that drive the highest level of customer loyalty. A coffee shop, printing company, accountant's office or global manufacturing company can deliver world-class service if it designs systems worthy of the task. And what's wrong with the corner coffee shop being world class? Why can't it deliver consistent and memorable service to its customers to keep them coming back? *The only thing standing in the way is leadership's decision to either compromise or to install a no-compromise culture.*

Neilism
Why strive for mediocrity when no compromise can make you world-class?

Of The Four Business Outcomes, customer loyalty is the undisputed ultimate driver. So much so that if you compromise customer loyalty in any way whatsoever, there will be an immediate and degrading ripple effect in the productivity, profitability and staff retention business outcomes. Marginal customer service and experiences contribute little to generate the lift needed to grow a business. Quantum leap growth is totally out of the question. *Given that, when it comes to customer loyalty, "no compromise" must be your company's ultimate battle cry.*

My parents owned a dry cleaning business where, as a teenager, I worked afternoons and weekends. Reflecting back, I have to say that my parents tried their best to deliver a world-class dry cleaning experience. My father was the resident comedian and was always ready to give customers his latest joke or funny story. My mom packaged each garment with extreme care. There wasn't a garment that would leave their store if it didn't look spectacular and when possible, better than new. The customers just loved the care and attention both they and their clothing received. Their reward was a loyal clientele which helped to fetch a good price when they sold the business to retire.

The relentless customer service that I learned from my parents has served me well throughout my career. To me, it never mattered if I was working as editor of a magazine, owner of a printing company, CEO of Strategies, a trainer, consultant or public speaker — I was in the service business of identifying and satisfying needs. Customer loyalty has always been the true measure of my success. *Without customer loyalty and retention, I have nothing, my company has nothing — your company has nothing.*

Some argue that today's high-speed economy and virtual web-based companies have diminished the value of customer loyalty and that loyalty is not what it used to be. That's outright nonsense and a total compromise to everything that business stands for. It doesn't

> **It doesn't matter what industry you're in, it's customer loyalty that's driving the true growth leaders.**

matter what industry you're in, it's customer loyalty that's driving the true growth leaders.

Think about the value of one retained customer that might spend an average of $75 per purchase. If that one customer buys six times a year from you, she will spend a total of $450 a year. If the average lifespan of a customer at your company is five years, this one client is worth $2,250. If you retain 2,000 of these customers, it's worth $900,000 a year in predictable sales. If you retain 5,000, it's worth $2.25 million in predictable annual sales. Increase that average purchase to $750, six times a year with 5,000 retained customers and you'll get $22.5 million a year in sales.

Do the math for your company using your own average sale, annual purchases and number of retained customers to see what your potential is. Before you get permanent dollar signs in your eyes, remember, all business growth hinges on customer loyalty — and your ability to convert first-time buyers to retained customers. I'll get more into this shortly when I discuss critical numbers for customer loyalty.

At the heart of the customer loyalty business outcome is the acquisition and retention of customers. If your company's performance is marginal, sputtering, or lacking a pulse, it's likely that you have customer retention problems that must be addressed.

Why did I focus on customer retention first rather than acquisition? Simple. If you're having trouble retaining customers, the difficulty factor of acquiring new customers increases dramatically. Simply put, would you rather have 60 or 70 percent or more of your first-time customers saying wonderful things about doing business with you — or a mere 20 percent? That 80 percent that your company failed to "wow" is out there in the marketplace working against you. *Simply put, your company is its own worst enemy.*

Let's start applying The BIG Eight to the customer loyalty business outcome and no-compromise leadership:

1. Culture

When it comes to customer loyalty, no other single factor plays a greater role in your business than your culture. *It's your culture that every customer comes in contact with.* It's your culture that allows positive and memorable experiences about doing business with you to occur. It's your culture that inspires your employees to go that extra mile to ensure complete satisfaction. Call it "wow" or "exceeding expectations." If your culture is contaminated with toxic behavior and compromise, any pursuit of "excellence" or "world class" is nothing more than wishful thinking propped up by buzzwords, hype and a reality disconnect.

OK, I just need to rant on one thing before going forward. What's your company's USP? You know, your "unique selling proposition." No doubt you'll come back with USPs, like your product, service, location, selection or convenience. However, not once have I heard a business leader say, "It's our culture." You may have the best product or service offering out there, but if doing business with your company is anything less than world class, each and every one of your customers is fair game to the predatory attacks of your competition. It is not my intent to knock or degrade the importance of having a unique selling proposition. You certainly better have one if you intend to compete in today's fierce and unforgiving econ-

No-compromise culture in action...

As my cab pulled up to the Toronto Four Seasons Hotel, as if on cue, a bellman opened the cab door with a warm and friendly greeting. Collecting my bags, he escorted me to the front desk. As he turned to walk away, I reached for my wallet to give him a tip. He smiled and said, "That won't be necessary, Mr. Ducoff. Please let me know if there is anything else I can do to make your stay at the Four Seasons a pleasurable one." This was pleasantly unexpected, not because I saved a couple of dollars on the tip, but because the bellman knew my name. How he knew it doesn't matter, addressing me by name certainly does. This simple act communicated volumes about the culture of this hotel and its no-compromise commitment to world-class service.

While checking in at the front desk, the courteous representative informed me that an important letter was waiting for me with details for the seminar I was delivering the next day. When she handed me my voucher and room key, something really cool took place. The young lady said, "Please wait one moment while I retrieve your letter. I'll bring it around to you." As promised, she came to my side of the check-in desk, smiled and handed me my letter. She then escorted me to the elevators. She reached in to push the "up" button while informing me that the seminar hosts were on the 14th floor and awaiting my arrival for dinner. As the elevator doors began to close, she reached in to shake my hand, wished me a pleasant stay and a successful seminar. She returned to her station at the desk.

I've been traveling most of my working life. This is the first time a front desk representative at a major hotel came to my side of the counter to deliver an envelope and push the "up" button for me. What I was experiencing was the no-compromise culture of the Toronto Four Seasons Hotel. The remainder of my stay was a thoroughly enjoyable "meet and exceed my expectations" experience.

omy. But first and foremost, you must create a "no-compromise world-class customer loyalty — or we die" culture. This culture must be capable of not only supporting your USP, but be capable of lifting it as high as it can go for all to see. A Neilism: "Customer loyalty begins and ends with your culture."

There's something inherently special about doing business with a company that has a no-compromise customer loyalty culture. Response is faster. Needs are identified and addressed faster. Problems are resolved easier and faster. Phone experiences are a joy. Even when scripted, there's something personable and engaging. There's a willingness to please. If there is a date for delivery, a return phone call or a problem resolution, that date commitment is going to happen as promised. It's like every commitment, large or small, is a contract to be filled on time, on budget — as promised. *Yes, systems create consistency, but it's your company culture that brings your systems to life.*

Neilism
Customer loyalty begins and ends with your culture.

A number of years ago, Strategies hired a marketing firm to help us refine and communicate our message to the business-to-business marketplace. One of their "let's figure out what Strategies is really all about" exercises was to survey our customers at one of our seminars. This particular seminar had about 130 participants, of which 40 percent were repeat Strategies' customers. They explained their mission to the audience, distributed questionnaires and did lots of one-on-one interviews.

A few weeks later, the marketing people returned with their findings. I must say, we were all excited to hear their findings and recommendations. We gathered in the conference room where we were handed a very official looking bound report containing, as they explained, raw unedited feedback from our customers. As I began to read page after page of our customers' comments, I truly began to glow. *This report was a bullet-by-bullet testimonial that captured the true essence of Strategies, our secret sauce — our mojo.*

The general theme of the comments read like this, "The Strategies team was always there for us. From early morning into the late evening, the Strategies team was available to help and answer questions. The Strategies' course workbook is so full of valuable information and guidance, it will be an invaluable tool to help implement new systems when I get back to my business." And my personal favorite, "Neil was always present and available for questions and private consultations."

By the time we finished reading the comments in the report, we were all feeling pretty good about who we are, what we do and our company culture. Then came the initial recommendations from the marketing experts. First, they said, "Your trainers are too accessible to your customers — especially Neil." They emphatically recommended that none of us enter the conference or classroom until it's time for us to present. They looked directly at me and said, "This especially applies to you, Neil." These marketing experts were telling us that immediately following a presentation, we should leave the area and return to our hotel rooms, of course taking time to sign books and shake hands. Once again, they said this policy most specifically applied to me. Then they held up our course workbook and proclaimed that we're giving too much information away — that the workbook needs to be edited down by at least 50 percent.

They wanted to turn us into something that we are not, something that is contrary to everything our culture stands for.

While listening to their recommendations, I looked around to see the expressions on my team's faces. I saw the same look of utter disbelief I was feeling. I then broke into the marketing presentation and said, *"You totally missed the key messages that our customers were communicating to you about who we are as a company — about our culture. We are there for our customers and always will be. We won't hide in our hotel rooms to create what we believe is a phony and egotistical image. If necessary, we will stay all day and try to answer every question. We will give them the most complete and information-rich course workbooks possible. This meeting is over."* And with that, so was the contract with the marketing firm.

This marketing firm wanted to turn us into something we were not, something contrary to everything our culture stands for. Most importantly, they wanted to change the very culture that our customers identified as what makes Strategies special. It was my responsibility to protect our culture. To this day, I know I made the right decision.

Bring no-compromise leadership, thinking and behavior to your culture and you will see your customer loyalty business outcome soar. That means achieving the highest first-time customer retention rates. That means larger and more frequent purchases per year. That means more positive reviews and referrals. All this adds up to a quantum leap in growth for your no-compromise, world-class, company.

Here's a hit list of do-it-now strategies to create the right culture for your customer loyalty business outcome:

+ **Show them what it looks like.** You can talk customer loyalty all you want, but until you show your employees what it should look and feel like in your company, nothing is going to change. Everyone in your company needs to see it, feel it and understand why and what needs to change. Shift into a serious behavior training mode. Show how it's done, then observe and coach until the execution of the process meets your no-compromise standards.

+ **Take a small team of employees on a field trip.** Visit a company that has the type of customer loyalty culture you would like to have in your company. Be sure to build in a debriefing and strategy meeting when you return to implement what the team experienced and learned.

+ **Customer focus groups.** Formally tapping customer insights can help to quickly identify where your company needs to improve. Be sure to hire a professional with the experience to moderate a focus group. Video tape the sessions to be edited down into a video presentation you can use throughout the company.

+ **If you're a business-to-business company, send teams to your customers' companies to see what it's like to do business with you.** This is a sobering way to get employees to see and feel the problems customers have buying products and services from you.

+ **Hire a "secret shopper" firm.** This works for any business as a means to evaluate and provide feedback on their service experiences. (Employees should not be made aware of the secret shopper evaluation or when it will occur.) Be sure to plan the presentation of the findings for maximum impact. I've seen too many companies invest the time and resources in secret shopper evaluations and blow it with a poorly planned presentation. The worst I've seen is a company that simply distributed the reports without explanation, emphasis or delivery of the strategies to resolve and correct customer loyalty issues. This is about your customers and your company's future. *Make it a big deal.* Get the message out that customer loyalty is going "no compromise."

> **Rekindle the passion for service excellence throughout your organization.**

+ **Get back in the trenches with your staff.** This means it's time for you and your leadership team to be present and engaged with your staff and your customers. Rekindle the passion for service excellence throughout your organization.
+ **Identify your customer loyalty champions.** Have them lead or participate in mentoring new employees, as well as existing employees, who need to refine their behavior and customer loyalty performance.
+ **"Good for the customer" story time.** Build in a quick "It was good for the customer" story into your daily huddles to showcase one employee's customer loyalty efforts. Over time, you will assemble a powerful collection of real life examples that will help indoctrinate new staff quickly and ensure the continued integrity of your no-compromise customer loyalty culture.

2. Sense of urgency

Sense of urgency takes on new meaning and purpose when discussing the customer loyalty business outcome. Think about the times you walked into a business and waited for someone to notice and take care of you. OK, now think about the times you waited while watching employees talk to one another as if they're totally oblivious to your presence. How about those times you sat in a restaurant watching other tables that were seated after you being served and you can't even find someone to get you a cocktail? What about that sales or customer service representative who said he would call you back in an hour and that call never happened? These are all symptoms of a breakdown in sense of urgency.

A Neilism: "Urgency and customer loyalty are inseparable." *If your business fails to deliver on a customer expectation, it will show in your retention rates.* It's that black and white. Nothing infuriates me more than shoddy or substandard service. If a business fails to deliver on a promise, I consider it a breach of contract. Likewise, I relish great service and the efforts any business makes to exceed the ordinary and deliver the extraordinary. It's always a reflection of the culture and systems of the business. Here's an interesting question to ponder. Think about those times when you experienced a true, no-compromise, high sense of urgency service from a company. Were you experiencing the culture and systems of the business, or the service and work ethic of an individual who functions with a sense of urgency? *An employee who embraces no-compromise customer loyalty behavior might hide a company's warts once or twice, but eventually the company's true culture, thinking and behavior will be exposed for customers to see.*

Neilism
Urgency and customer loyalty are inseparable.

Here's a hit list of do-it-now strategies to create a sense of urgency to drive the customer service business outcome in your business:

+ **Videotape staff servicing customers.** Watching their own behavior, posture, body language, attire and the visual responses from customers can be a real wake-up call. It's so important to find ways to communicate the need to change in compelling ways that employees can truly feel and internalize.

+ **Videotape or take staff on a tour of your own facility.** Have them take notes of everything they see and observe that would either support or detract from customer loyalty. Time for a Neilism: "Why is it that only leaders can see dirt that seems

Create your company's own "Non-Negotiable Customer loyalty Standards." Here's one we did for Strategies:

1. **Return all calls within 24 hours.** If you can't, ask a team member to contact the customer with a date and time you will be able to return the call.

2. **Return all e-mails within 24 hours.** If you can't, ask a team member to call or e-mail the customer with a date and time you will respond to the e-mail.

3. **Change voicemail when not in office or in Training Center.** State when you will return calls. Offer the customer options for assistance in other Strategies' departments.

4. **Check voicemail at least once a day.** This is crucial while on the road or in our Business Academy. You must be accessible.

5. **Complete all coaching session reports by next business day.** Coaching session progress reports must be entered into the system within 24 hours.

6. **Complete expense reports the next business day.** This is crucial after an on-site session or business trip that requires expenses be charged to clients. Receipts must be attached.

7. **Meet all deadlines.** Projects, articles, reports, lesson plans, etc.

8. **If you hear a phone ringing, answer it.** It's a customer trying to reach us. Letting a call go into voicemail that we could have answered is a compromise.

9. **Always deliver on what you promise...** when you promised it.

10. **Manage customer expectations.** Be clear on what you are promising to customers and what they will receive.

11. **Always go above and beyond.** Strategies must be the shining example of the no-compromise company.

12. **Have Fun.** Support and praise each other, appreciate all we do, find ways to make our jobs easier — and make money.

invisible to employees?" Be sure to have a debriefing and strategy meeting afterward to create a decisive plan of action to improve customer loyalty.

+ **You're putting on a Broadway show:** Every successful Broadway play demands that every actor know his or her lines and be in the right position on cue. There is a sense of urgency to relentlessly rehearse until everyone gets it right and every scene is executed flawlessly — not just on opening night, but to do it consistently every night. How many of your employees know their lines and cues? How many employees can execute those lines and cues flawlessly every day?

Neilism

Why is it that only leaders can see dirt that seems invisible to employees?

+ **If you have a call center or telephone sales office,** install call sequencing monitors so employees can see how many customers are on hold, for how long and how many calls were lost. Mount the monitors so all employees can see them. Nothing creates urgency more than seeing the action live. I'll get to the accountability aspects in a bit.

+ **Huddles and sense of urgency issues.** Make sense of urgency issues and strategies part of your daily huddles. Keep them short and focused. The intent is to keep the drumbeat set on urgent. These daily reminders will ultimately shape your customer loyalty culture.

+ **Leadership cheerleading.** The no-compromise leader never hesitates to use the tried and true method of cheerleading employees with the "let's pick up the pace — we've got customers to satisfy." When direct instruction or "wake-up calls" are needed, don't hesitate. I'm not suggesting that you turn into a Marine drill sergeant, it simply never hurts to apply a little leadership nudge, or more, when necessary.

3. Critical numbers

As with all the business outcomes, customer loyalty has its own critical numbers. Too often, leaders tend to get stuck in tunnel vision by monitoring sales, units sold or shipped, cost of goods sold and net profit. What is easy to overlook is that these critical numbers related to other business outcomes — not specifically and uniquely to the customer loyalty. The no-compromise leader's primary responsibility is to drive and maintain balance across ALL four business outcomes to create consistency and predictability. This cannot occur without monitoring customer loyalty behavior and performance via its own set of critical numbers.

The critical numbers for customer loyalty will certainly vary depending on the nature of your business. For example, if you're a seasonal or resort business, your critical number will have to be adjusted to reflect seasonal fluctuations. Customer loyalty terminology might also be specific for your business or industry. For example, in subscription- or membership-based businesses, like magazines, newsletters, fitness centers and associations, first-time customer retention (first renewal) is often referred to as the "conversion rate." From the second renewal forward, it's called

> **There's no positive retention data to track if there isn't a second purchase.**

"renewal rate." The intent is to focus attention on the all-important second purchase renewal. *There's no positive retention data to track if there isn't a second purchase.*

Let's look at some of the key critical numbers you can use to monitor your company's customer loyalty performance:

First-time customer retention rate: This is the ratio of how many first-time customers return for a second purchase or visit. I suggest that you monitor specific time frames, such as how many first-visit customers in the month of January made another purchase or visit within 60 or 90 days. It will throw your ratios off if you do not allow sufficient time for the customer to return. The return cycle should be based on the purchase patterns of your customers. If the purchase pattern is six times a year, the

Is your software giving you the correct data?

The accurate and timely tracking of critical numbers and customer retention will require computer software. Most business software applications collect the necessary data, but don't always generate the specific retention reports needed to monitor your customer loyalty performance. If you're not sure that your software can generate the necessary data and reports, or if you are questioning the validity of the data, talk to your software provider.

I've seen enough cases of inaccurate data and mislabeled reports that it's prudent to make a call to your software provider to ask what data they use and how they make their calculations.

Here's a quick example of a faulty reporting that was driving a consulting client crazy. The software report for how many first-time customers in one month returned for a second visit was showing dismal retention ratios. So much so, if those ratios were true, my client would have been out of business. I called their provider and learned that the formula was flawed. It actually calculated how many first-time customers in month X returned for second visit in month X. The customer visit cycle was 60 to 90 days. The formula never allowed enough time for customers to return. Always verify how your software calculates retention.

Here's another programming error I discovered while working with a large salon and day spa. This particular client was touting that his company's first-time client retention rate was 95 percent. With 450 new clients a month, how does he accommodate them all as they keep returning? It was simply an awesome ratio that didn't make sense. I called the developer and found the problem. The software recorded the "appointment" as first visit and the actual "first visit" as the second visit. Still with me? Simply put, 95 percent of first-time clients who booked appointments showed. Interesting, but not the right data.

60- or 90-day return cycle should work fine. (The more time you allow for customers to return, the higher your retention ratios. However, they do tend to level off quickly once you hit your natural return cycle.) I suggest you stick to same return cycles to ensure you are always communicating consistent retention rates to staff.

The ability of your business to convert a first-time customer to repeat customer is truly the defining and tell-all ratio for driving the customer loyalty business outcome. If you're only tracking retention after multiple visits or purchases, or simply track-ing the current number and percent of repeat sales, you are not getting a true read on your company's abil-ity to convert first-time clients to retained clients.

> **Neilism**
> If a first-time customer doesn't return for at least a second purchase, there's nothing left to track.

A Neilism: "If a first-time customer doesn't return for at least a second purchase, there's nothing left to track." All of the customer relationship building is either positively established or damaged during the first buying experi-ence with your business. Another Neilism: "First-time retention is your company's customer loyalty score." Simply put, you cannot call your busi-ness world class if 60, 70 or 80 percent of your first-time customers never buy again.

The last key factor about your first-time customer retention rate is that the higher you drive it — the better your business gets at satisfy-ing all customers. It's like your "no-compromise loyalty" or "total quality" performance score. Why? Because all of the positive behavior and systems that caused first-visit retention to improve have an immediate and positive impact on all other aspects of customer relationship building.

Existing customer retention: This is the ratio of how many customers with two or more visits or purchases returned to your business. Again, I suggest you target existing customer visits/purchases for month X and how many returned within 60 or 90 days (or your customers' natural purchase cycle). This is an interesting ratio because it can also give you an indication of what your customer attrition rate is. For example, if 500 exist-ing customers made purchases from you in January, how many returned in 60 or 90 days? If 350 returned, your existing retention rate is 70 percent. This also says that 30 percent of January's customers have not returned or made another purchase since. In most cases, if your attrition rate is

Neilism
First-time retention is your company's customer loyalty score.

30 percent, you have warning lights flashing and need to be on a quest to find out why. *Your business cannot grow if 30 percent of its customer base is defecting to the competition.*

Annual purchases: It makes sense to include annual customer purchases, because it does reflect on the buying and customer service experience, as well as the quality of your relationship. It's also an interesting indicator of the level, content and quality of your company's contact with customers. For example, annual sales with a customer could be down because your company is having insufficient contact or simply passively waiting for cus-tomers to make another purchase. Remain passive long enough and you'll see your aggressive and hungry competitors snapping them up.

Referrals: When I find a company I enjoy doing business with, I tell everyone. I'm the best walking-talking referral system for Rabbit Hill Inn, Apple, great business books — you name it. If I'm happy, I tell everyone. On the flip side, if I'm unhappy with a buying experience, I'm just as vocal, if not more so. When I get to innovation, I'll give you some ideas for building referrals.

4. Information flow

One of the issues of delivering consistently high levels of customer loyalty and retention is the seemingly subjective nature of exactly what customer loyalty is and looks like. Simply put, what one customer regards as qual-ity service may be completely different to another. *In business, that same subjectivity exists with employees.* Given this, the task of the no-compromise leader is to define, communicate and train employees to deliver customer loyalty — as the company envisions it. Without this absolute level of clarity, individual interpretations will lead to compromise and inconsistency.

One of the most powerful tools in the no-compromise leader's toolbox is the ability to adjust the content, quantity, frequency and intensity of information flow throughout the company. When used effectively, information flow can quickly elevate the sense of urgency throughout your business. For example, during peak periods when customer loyalty systems are being put to the test, information flow can help keep your staff motivated and focused.

Information flow systems are vital to keep your critical numbers for customer loyalty in front of employees. It doesn't make sense complaining about low customer retention rates if employees can't see and monitor the same numbers that are frustrating you.

I've done countless staff meetings where, for the first time, I introduced the company's first-time customer retention rates. I like to project their numbers up on a big screen and watch their looks of utter disbelief. "No way we're losing that many first-time clients," is what I always hear from staff. Then I hit them with one of my favorite Neilisms: "We're hanging a banner that says, 'We piss off 68 percent of our first-time customers. Enter at your own risk.'" I always get a painful chuckle, but the message gets through loud and clear.

> Without this absolute level of clarity, individual interpretations will lead to compromise and inconsistency.

Information flow rules when it comes to driving customer loyalty and retention. Here is a hit list of do-it-now strategies you can use:

+ **Post and discuss your first-time customer retention rates monthly.** There must be a scheduled debriefing session to relate the importance of the score, what went right and what needs to improve. Keep it short. *Under any circumstances, do not post numbers without a debriefing session with staff.* If posting isn't possible, put out a monthly one-page "how do our customers rate us" report. My issue with distributing reports without group discussion is how quickly vital monthly reports become invisible.

+ **Track the first-time and existing customer retention rates for individual sales or service employees who work directly with specific customers.** When customers have most of their contact with your company through their sales representative or service provider, retention accountability carries more weight on these front line individuals. *Tracking individual retention rates quickly reveals who your best performers are and which employees need additional training.* Individual retention reports help identify if an employee is a "black hole," which means you put customers in her care and never see them again. The no-compromise leader must weed out "black holes."

Neilism
We're hanging a banner that says, "We piss off 68% of our first-time customers. Enter at your own risk."

+ **Daily huddles must include a "hot list" of current customer-loyalty issues.** It's best they know that they will be short-handed today or that you're expecting a large order or shipment. You can even give your team a heads-up that a prospective or special customer is visiting your facility and will be taking a tour.

+ **Business is all about relationship building.** Nothing is more frustrating to a customer than building a relationship with an employee only to have the individual leave — especially when that employee knew her preferences and systems. For the customer, it's like starting a new relationship with your company all over again. *During such transitions, customers are fair game to your competitors — or even that dearly departed employee who now works for your biggest competitor.*

> Individual retention reports help identify if an employee is a "black hole," which means you put customers in their care and never see them again.

+ **Create one knowledge vault.** Whenever unique customer data resides solely with an employee, the customer/company relationship is quite tenuous and vulnerable. In such cases, the customer's relationship and trust are primarily with the employee — not to company. All employees who have one-on-one contact with customers must be able to access customer data that contains personal preferences, procedures, key contacts — even the president's wife's birthday. Nothing builds customer relationships faster than when the company and its employees "know" the customer. *Your company must have a system to collect and share customer data.* I'll discuss this more when I get to the systems driver for customer loyalty.

+ **Information flow is critical when a customer's job, service or order must be completed on time.** Employees responsible for the work must be totally aware of the status of the work and time remaining for deadline. Information flow is essential to synchronize workflow, especially in those "this must get done" situations.

> **Nothing builds customer relationships faster than when the company and its employees "know" the customer.**

+ **Celebrate your customer loyalty victories.** Big or small, a victory is a win for the company and the customer. It can be a pizza lunch with balloons or have the local high school marching band parade through your plant. *The point is to send a message throughout your company that world-class customer experiences are taking place all the time.* This is the type of information flow that builds and sustains a world-class customer loyalty culture.

+ **Use company and individual retention rate reports in all performance reviews.** Every employee wants income growth and advancement. The no-compromise leader must connect that desire to customer loyalty and retention.

5. Teamwork

Nothing adds greater lift to the customer loyalty business outcome than teamwork. When it works, teamwork is a beautiful orchestration of shared responsibility and accountability to do whatever it takes to satisfy the customer. Everything runs more smoothly when teams are in sync. Customers are serviced faster, orders are filled faster and shipments go out on schedule. Inventory ordering is done with that extra care to ensure that the products or materials are in stock when needed — no customer likes to hear about delays due to back orders. Maintenance keeps everything running smoothly to avoid breakdowns that can cause production delays. Your sales staff knows that the team back at the company will process and fill orders on time. From manufacturing plants, restaurants and spas, to retail stores, building contractors and hospitals, *customer loyalty truly is all about teamwork.*

Consider Dell Computers. You can go online and build a computer system to specifically suit your needs. Or, if you're not sure, you can call Dell and speak to an "all-about-the-customer" representative who will ask you some questions and help you design just the right system. Once that order is placed, it takes perfectly coordinated teamwork to pick the right parts out of inventory and get them to the designated assembly team. Within a matter of days, your custom-configured computer system is delivered to your door. Dell's approach to mass customization is truly world class and represents teamwork and customer loyalty at its best. That's what elevated Dell to the top slot as the world's largest computer maker.

Just like in sports, teamwork takes discipline and practice. You cannot mandate teamwork.

Amazon.com is another interesting study in teamwork. I'm continually in awe of how this completely virtual company can offer a zillion products for sale and get them to me the next day if that's what I desire. Teamwork makes it happen. Yes, technology and some very elaborate and finely tuned systems all play a key role, but it's still teamwork that gets those orders correct and out on time. That's what makes me a regular Amazon.com customer.

The no-compromise leader, whether in the president's office or on the plant floor, takes special care to monitor, inspire, coach and lead employees to do whatever it takes to drive customer loyalty — and to do it as a team. More importantly, the no-compromise leader knows all too well that anytime an employee or team loses the vital connection between their work and customer loyalty, there will be a measurable drop in customer retention.

Here's a hit list of do-it-now strategies you can use to drive teamwork and the customer loyalty business outcome:

- **Put the time, effort and training into developing highly functional and empowered teams.** Just like in sports, teamwork takes discipline and practice. You cannot mandate teamwork. It takes leadership, systems, discipline and focus on a goal.
- **Connect your customer loyalty dots.** To achieve coordinated teamwork throughout your company, all the players and all the teams must see and understand how all the pieces, procedures, standards and systems work together to deliver customer loyalty. *If you're not pleased with your customer loyalty ratings, you haven't connected the dots.*
- **Teams must be ego-free.** I can't write about teamwork without tackling a common teamwork buster. Keep egos grounded and in check. If you have a sales team or service providers, then you understand the drag big egos can create. It's sad when "superstars" think the world revolves around them — that the company can't survive without their royal presence. Such behavior is simply disrespectful to everyone in the company who works hard to fill those orders or support the service provider so the customer is satisfied.
- **Teamwork and games go hand in hand.** Create some healthy competition or games between teams that focus on customer loyalty with a focus on first-time retention, on-time delivery, customer problem resolution, increasing buying frequency, etc.

+ **Mix it up to share knowledge.** Implement cross-functional team development by rotating employees to other teams for a few days or a week. Nothing creates an appreciation for the ripple effect one team's performance, or lack of, can create for other teams throughout the company.
+ **Empower customer loyalty decisions to be made within the teams.** Set the guidelines and cut the apron strings. The job of the no-compromise leader is to lead, not bog things down by holding on to decisions that teams are capable of making.
+ **Keep celebrating customer loyalty wins.** Allow your teams to experience the sweet smell of success.

6. Innovation

Here are three quick stories about some simple, yet innovative, strategies for customer loyalty.

The first time my wife and I stayed at Rabbit Hill Inn in Lower Waterford, Vermont (*yes, I'm "referring" to them again*), they asked if there were any allergies or special needs they should be aware of to make our visit just right. I advised them that Joanne has an allergy to corn products. For the remainder of that visit, they made sure that Joanne wasn't offered or served anything containing corn. We enjoyed that first visit to Rabbit Hill Inn so much, we decided to return a few months later to wrap up our vacation tour of Maine, New Hampshire and Vermont. We arrived just in time for their delightful afternoon tea and pastries. As I headed straight for the delectable pastries, Leslie, the innkeeper, asked Joanne to wait a moment. A minute later, Leslie emerged from the kitchen and said, "These are for you." She handed Joanne a plate of pastries that the pastry chef made special for her without corn. That evening in the dining room, Joanne was handed a menu that had "Especially Prepared for Joanne" printed across the top and listed her selection of corn-free dishes. (My menu didn't even have "Occupant" on it. *Sorry, just seeking attention.*)

> It's sad when "superstars" think the world revolves around them — that the company can't survive without their royal presence.

A few years ago, we decided to spend the Thanksgiving holiday at Rabbit Hill Inn. While having breakfast Thanksgiving morning, Leslie approached our table with a concerned look. She said, "The chef woke this morning in a fright. He realized that turkeys are usually corn fed. He called the farmer immediately to confirm if the turkey we bought was, in fact, corn fed. It was." Leslie asked Joanne if she can eat turkey that was corn fed. Joanne said it wasn't a problem. That brought an immediate sigh of relief and smile to Leslie's face. We all got a good chuckle out of the turkey incident — but greatly appreciated the chef's concern. A Neilism: "A no-compromise culture naturally and routinely creates memorable customer experiences."

> **Neilism**
> A no-compromise culture naturally and routinely creates memorable customer experiences.

This attention to detail always makes Joanne feel safe and cared for while at Rabbit Hill Inn. This is world-class, no-compromise thinking and behavior nestled away in Vermont's Northwest Kingdom. These are just some of the many reasons we go to Rabbit Hill Inn several times a year and refer it to friends and customers all the time.

Strategies held a special gathering for our team of Certified Strategies Coaches at the Fairmont Chateau Lake Louise in the majestic Canadian Rockies of Alberta, Canada. The service was extraordinary, as it should be at a five-star Fairmont property, but two simple, yet innovative, touches stood out. The first occurred as I was checking in. Apparently, when I gave my name at the front desk, a message was sent to the catering manager who handled our function arrangements in the most enjoyable and accommodating way possible. Just before I was handed my room key, the catering manager approached, welcomed me by name and introduced herself. Before leaving, she handed me a special Fairmont lapel pin with instructions to wear it throughout our stay. That little pin identified me as "the decision maker," as well as the guy paying the bill. Needless to say, for the next four days I was treated like royalty.

The second innovation occurred at the end of our first day of meetings. We had a formal dinner in a private dining room overlooking Lake Louise.

(If you have never been to Lake Louise, it is simply the most amazing sight to behold. Definitely put it on your list of places to visit.) At each place setting was a small, tassel-bound menu. On that menu was the Strategies logo. The Chateau Lake Louise catering manager had gone to our website and downloaded our logo to customize the menu. That menu became a nice memento that everyone took as a reminder of a wonderful evening the Strategies team had at Chateau Lake Louise.

My wife fell in love with a bright red Chrysler Crossfire that was sitting in front of the dealership we pass on the way home. Well, that little Crossfire eventually ended up in our garage. About two weeks later, a big box arrived at our home. In that box was a special and complete set of Crossfire luggage, complete with the Chrysler hood ornament and embossed Crossfire logo. The roller suitcase had design elements from the hood of the Crossfire. Even the wheels were mini black and chrome replicas of

That little pin identified me as "the decision maker" as well as the guy paying the bill. Needless to say, for the next four days I was treated like royalty.

the Crossfire's wheels. There was also a nice, personalized note from Chrysler. *What an innovative surprise this was.* Needless to say, Joanne takes that luggage on all our trips and when asked about them, she tells the story. *Great luggage. Great customer loyalty strategy. Great customer relationship builder.*

Here is a hit list of do-it-now strategies to drive innovation and the customer loyalty business outcome:

+ **If you ship products to customers, try putting some candy, like a Tootsie Roll Pop, in the box.** Whoever unpacks that box will find it a friendly touch. It may also get inventory staff to get to opening and unpacking those boxes faster.
+ **Put a team together to come up with new ways to make orders and packaging special.** I must say that every new Apple computer I ever bought had a lot of creativity put into the packaging. So much so, unpacking a new computer or product from Apple is all part of the experience. Remember that "Think Different" motto Apple used years ago? *They live it every day.*

- **If you have a service business, what can you do to make each visit extra special?** I once worked with a salon that put heat lamps in the towel bins at their shampoo stations. Clients loved the feel of that warm towel after a relaxing shampoo.

- **What are you doing to officially welcome new customers to your business?** Consider creating a "users guide" to fully inform first-time customers about how you do business and who to contact for questions or service. How about a personalized letter from the president of the company thanking them for their business? Every time I purchase a custom suit from The Tom James Company, I get a personal letter from the president. *They have 225,000 customers, so don't say it can't be done.*

- **What are you doing to show appreciation to loyal customers?** Personal "thank you for your business" notes really stand out in these days of e-mail and instant messaging. How about honoring a selection of your best customers at your annual company meeting or holiday season party?

- **Show your civic-mindedness and sponsor a local or national charity event.** If you're raising funds for a worthy cause, get your customers to participate with you. It's a great way to partner with customers and do something good for others in the process.

- **Use technology to its fullest.** Use e-mail or voice messaging to let existing customers take advantage of special buying incentives before the general public. This is also a great way to move extra inventory or sell open time in your service business. Offer the incentives to your existing customers first.

- **Create a special "Customers Only" section on your website.** Make it a user name and password-protected section that contains information, discussion boards, product manuals and special incentives. Receiving special access lets customers know their business and loyalty are appreciated.

7. Systems

A quick Neilism: "Systems set leaders free." If you want consistency in cus-tomer service, satisfaction and retention, you must use systems. A football coach has his playbook — a collection of systems designed to produce specific results. *What does your company's playbook look like?*

Customers are on the receiving end of your systems. If those systems are designed well and your team follows those systems with discipline and resolve, you have the best chance of achieving consistent and predict-able results. If you're lacking systems, or they're poorly designed and not adhered to, your customers are on the receiving end of compromise. Your company phone won't be answered correctly. Customers will be on hold too long. Problems will take longer to resolve. *Retention will suffer.*

Simple or complex, customer loyalty systems just make work move more smoothly. I stopped at a diner for breakfast with a client. It was one of those popular and very busy local spots with lots of character. The waitress would come by and pour some decaf for my client and some high-test for me. She had a lot of tables to handle and I began to wonder how she could remember who had decaf or regular. I decided to ask. "It's simple," she said, "the decaf cups have two red rings around the top and the cups for regular have one black ring." Duh. What a simple and efficient system.

> **Neilism**
> Systems set leaders free.

Here is a hit list of do-it-now strategies you can use to implement systems to drive the customer loyalty business outcome:
+ **Go critical.** Begin identifying the critical areas in your business that have the greatest impact, positive and negative, on customer loyalty. Prioritize this list and assign teams to design, test and implement the new systems.
+ **Set time standards for all points of contact with custom-ers, including** answering calls within three rings, greeting and

acknowledging customers with 30 seconds, never leaving a customer on hold for more than two minutes, etc.

+ **Connect the dots.** Tie your critical number for customer loyalty, specifically your first-time retention rate, as one of the qualifiers for a bonus payout. This sends a clear message to employees that if the company can't maintain satisfactory retention rates, it can't afford to pay bonus. We have a customer who bases 50 percent of the bonus payout on his company's ability to maintain a first-time retention rate of 50 percent or better. He's been working this for over a year and his first-time retention has never dropped below 54 percent.

> **If you're lacking systems, or they're poorly designed and not adhered to, your customers are on the receiving end of compromise.**

+ **Collect key data.** Are you collecting data on customer preferences, order history, birth date, what their favorite sport is or any other data that can help your company personalize and customize each customer's buying experience? What are your systems for collecting this data and getting it into a central database for sales and customer service representatives to access?

+ **Dealing with customer problems.** What's your system to ensure that problems, even the smallest concerns, are documented and reported so follow-up actions can be initiated? What's the paper or document trail? Who follows up with the customer? When?

+ **Identifying and filling customer needs.** Is there a system for your sales or customer service staff to follow to design the best solutions? The last thing you want in your business is an order taker. Taking an order is ordinary. *Customizing an order to truly satisfy a customer's needs is extraordinary.*

8. Accountability

Here it is, short and sweet: Everyone is accountable for customer loyalty. Everyone. No-compromise.

Yes, customer loyalty begins with leadership and that's where the problem can begin. Leaders are notorious for going on those infamous rampages when a major customer quits the company or when customer retention rates go critical. The no-compromise question that must be asked in such cases is, "Where is the accountability and how far down in the company does that accountability go?" Playing the blame game is a compromise and totally unacceptable.

The no-compromise leader places accountability for customer loyalty in the hands of every company employee. It cannot be any other way. For this level of accountability to exist, employees need to understand just how accountable they are. What I'm talking about here is a business culture at its highest level, a no-compromise business culture. At this level, employees feel the pain of a lost customer. They feel the pain when a customer has a problem that could have been avoided. This is what an "ownership culture" functions like. It's when employees are accountable to the numbers of the business, and most importantly, to the critical numbers that drive customer loyalty.

I'll give you a simple example that I'm proud to share. At Strategies, everyone knows that our payroll target range is 30 percent. They know that our incremental bonus plan has two activation criteria. First, sales must be 20 percent or more ahead of last year. Second, we must be on track for our target net profit goal. In 12 years, no one has ever asked me for a raise. If we're within our financial revenue and profit targets, and payroll is within budget, raises will be given. To accomplish that, we must tenaciously work our customer loyalty systems and critical numbers. If we lose a good customer or if our coaching client retention slips, believe me, everyone feels the pain. Everyone at Strategies is accountable. They know it, I know it, and our customers know it. No compromise.

Here is a hit list of do-it-now strategies you can use to drive accountability and the customer loyalty business outcome:

- **No entitlements.** Once again, tie raises, bonus payouts and employee incentives to your customer loyalty critical numbers.
- **Define what they're accountable for doing.** If you don't have one already, create an ongoing training and coaching program that specifically targets every employee's accountability to customer loyalty.
- **Ensure that your information flow systems are working.** You cannot hold anyone accountable if they don't have access to what's going on. Leadership cannot compromise or ignore its accountability to maintain fast and furious information flow.
- **If you're the leader, admit when you failed to be accountable.** The no-compromise leader always take the high — and the right — road. You'll only gain respect for doing so.
- **Never hesitate to engage issues.** You must address behavior or performance that impacts customer loyalty.
- **Know when it's time to give someone a "career opportunity."** Never hesitate to terminate an employee who, after coaching and corrective measures, continues to compromise customer loyalty. *Failure to act sends all the wrong messages to the rest of the staff.*
- **Make time.** You and your leadership team must schedule time to talk to your customers about the service and quality they receive from your company. Too many leaders just don't do this and lose touch with what their clients are really thinking. Jet Blues' CEO and founder, David Neeleman, takes a no-compromise accountability approach to assessing his airline's customer loyalty level. Neeleman can be found regularly servicing and talking to customers on board flights. That's right, the CEO of the company makes it a point to work the beverage cart on flights to talk to customers. He simply asks, "How is Jet Blue doing and what can we do better?" That's powerful stuff. And when he addresses

issues with his leadership team, he's talking based on his personal interaction with customers.

+ **Monitoring quality.** Establish a customer quality assurance team to monitor customer loyalty and to provide monthly feedback for the entire company.

+ **You put all that effort into creating systems.** What are you doing to hold staff accountable for following those systems? Where are the challenges? What are the fixes? How long will it take? What needs to change? Do you need to change?

+ **Never hesitate to replace or reassign a member of your leadership team.** In most cases, you'll be saving that leader by reassigning him to a different position. Termination is always an option if no other position exists. If the leader is in over his head, reassigning or terminating, although tough, is actually helping the individual in the long run.

+ **The no-compromise leader must exemplify accountability to customer loyalty.** *Anything less is compromise.*

A NO-COMPROMISE LESSON:
Are you keeping your promise to the customer?

These days, terms like "brand promise," "exceeding customer expectations" and "the customer is always right" are so overused that their message is barely audible above the daily activities and routines at your business. Of course, you and the rest of your team know how essential it is to deliver amazing customer experiences all day, every day. In fact, strategically placed at the core of your business thinking, there is a promise you've made to your customer. That promise is something special and unique that only your business can deliver. That promise says your business is committed to delivering extreme value with extraordinary consistency. It doesn't really matter what your price point is or what segment of the market you cater to, it just matters that you deliver on your promise to be your best.

The question I pose to you is simple: Is your business keeping its promise to your customers? It's a "yes" or "no" answer. An answer like, "Most of the time," is unacceptable because it compromises your promise. Actually, the reality at your business might be that some people believe in and deliver on the promise, while the rest of your team delivers something less. That's breaking your promise. That's compromise.

Here are three red-hot strategies to keep your promise to the customer:

1. **You need to commit first:** If your business compromised its promise, as the leader, you watched it happen. It will take a major initiative and a lot of pushing to get your entire team back up to speed. You must be resolute.

2. **Define your promise:** Create a two- or three-person team charged with the responsibility to define every aspect of your promise

continued...

What does it look like, feel like and sound like from a customer perspective?

3. **Skill certify EVERYONE:** Build skill certification training modules that address phone skills, greetings, consultations, client interaction, service closing procedures, client assistance procedures, problem procedures, ending-the-visit procedures, you name it — train and skill certify everyone on how to be world class.

4. **Across the board accountability:** This is where no-compromise leadership needs to engage and stay engaged. It's a 100% commitment to keep the promise or it's compromise.

All too often, customers are at the receiving end of a company's indifference and apathy. And sadly, too many customers have gotten accustomed to inconsistent service and the breaching of a company's promise to deliver amazing experiences. The winners invest the time and energy to master the disciplines of customer service and respect. By doing so, the no-compromise winners stand out like shining stars in a sea compromising mediocrity. **Can you deliver on your promise?**

PART III

Putting No-Compromise Leadership to Work in Your Company

PART III
Introduction

A t this point in the book, it would be easy to say, "OK, I've got this no-compromise leadership thing down. I'm ready to go." From one perspective, it's easy to believe you're ready. In Part I, I delivered a compelling argument on the cost of compromise. Then I gave you the 10 non-negotiable requirements to be a no-compromise leader. We journeyed into the thinking of the no-compromise leader and how the transition can only take place when your shields are down and open to new thinking. I took you through the 10 "install requirements" that integrate a no-compromise leadership operating system into your personal leadership thinking and behavior. In Part II, I took you through The Four Business Outcomes and strategies for using The BIG Eight Drivers to create consistency, predictability and quantum-leap growth.

So, that's it. You have the tools and you think you're ready. Go right ahead. Take one more sip of my no-compromise Kool-Aid and charge decisively into your company and flip that no-compromise leadership switch. Oh, this is going to be fun to watch, as your employees gaze upon you like some alien from another planet. Go ahead, throw out your first

> **Go ahead, throw out your first "this is non-negotiable" and watch it get shot down like a clay pigeon at a skeet shoot.**

"This is non-negotiable" and watch it get shot down like a clay pigeon at a skeet shoot. *Yup, I want a ringside seat to watch that show.*

If you believe you can skip Part III and charge head first into no-compromise leadership, you're still compromising. You know enough to be dangerous — you're not ready. More importantly, your staff isn't prepared to accept, let alone embrace, no-compromise leadership. *There's simply much more to learn.*

In Part III, I'll take you through the steps necessary to put no-compromise leadership to work in your company. As I stated from the beginning, you just can't flip a switch and instantly transform into a no-compromise leader. You just can't flip a switch and expect your company's culture, behavior and thinking to go no compromise. If it was that easy, I would have written a short article on the subject instead of an entire book.

> **Having just completed your own personal transformation into a no-compromise leader, the most crucial and daunting task now stands before you.**

The culture shift to no compromise

Having just completed your own personal transformation into a no-compromise leader, the most crucial and daunting task now stands before you. *You must successfully lead your entire company through the culture shift to transform into a true no-compromise company.* That means converting the ever-present change resisters into avid supporters of the new no-compromise culture. This is where the character, tenacity and courage of your leadership skills will undeniably be put to the test.

I don't want your no-compromise culture shift initiative to turn into a clay pigeon. *Yes, you are going to encounter resistance.* You might discover members of your leadership team and trusted employees clinging to old, compromising thinking and behaviors that were once acceptable — even practiced — by you. What will you do if their resistance persists? Will you make the tough no-compromise decisions? How long will you wait? If you are committed to becoming a no-compromise leader, you must work through that resistance. I'll give you strategies to make it work.

In Chapter 8, I'll provide you with an 18-month sequence for leading a culture shift to no compromise, complete with timelines, must-dos and what you should see as you and your company move through each stage. This is where the complexities of a full-blown culture shift to no compromise become vividly apparent. By the end of Part III, you'll understand why no-compromise leadership is in no way a passing fad. It's an approach to leadership that requires a life-long commitment to personal development and adhering to the highest leadership standards.

Let's get to work.

CHAPTER 8

LEADING THE CULTURE SHIFT TO NO COMPROMISE

Changing your own behavior is difficult enough. Changing and shifting the culture of an entire company is the ultimate right of passage for a true no-compromise leader.

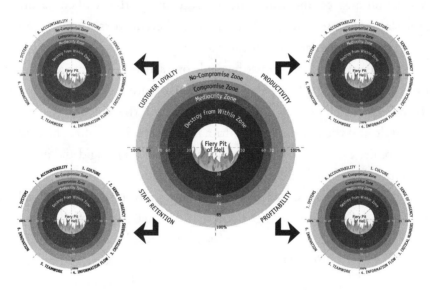

F
rom a business culture viewpoint, no-compromise leadership is about ensuring the integrity of your company's values, performance and financial wellbeing. It is about creating a culture that defines and shapes the collective thinking of the business to drive The Four Business Outcomes. No compromise is about creating a high-performance business culture that gets things done through its ability to be consistent and systems driven. A no-compromise culture is dynamic, inspiring and it attracts and retains the best employees like a super magnet. It's a fast-track culture that just doesn't get distracted, tripped up or even derailed by the inevitable obstacles and road hazards that always seem to litter the road to success.

Now that you're on your way to becoming a no-compromise leader, the next phase of your transition is leading the shift to a no-compromise business culture. Think of it as deputizing every one of your employees as a *duly-authorized, no-compromise leader*. That is a truly worthy voyage — but you must be prepared to lead your company *all the way through* the culture shift that must take place. Failure to complete a culture shift

> **Failure to complete a culture shift will set off a cascading avalanche of compromise that will contaminate every facet of your company.**

will set off a cascading avalanche of compromise that will contaminate every facet of your company. Make no mistake, culture shifts are about as dicey a challenge as any leader can take on.

A Neilism: "No compromise has only one setting — whatever it takes." However, charging off into a no-compromise culture shift can really rock the boat when employees don't fully understand the concept, the leadership style and the culture it will ultimately create. Rapid-fire shifts to no compromise can easily broadcast that you're installing a rigid and inflexible structure that is void of emotion and compassion.

It's so easy for employees to interpret no compromise as, "So, if I'm late, I'm fired," or, "If we miss our goal, there will be hell to pay." *This is not what "no compromise" is all about.* It's about

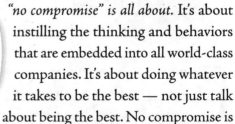

Neilism
No compromise has only one setting — whatever it takes.

instilling the thinking and behaviors that are embedded into all world-class companies. It's about doing whatever it takes to be the best — not just talk about being the best. No compromise is the collective thinking and behavior that creates dynamic lift. It's positive. It attracts and gains momentum. It breaks through obstacles. Compromise is pure drag.

Heed this warning: Attempting to flip your leadership switch to a hard line and dictatorial style will likely backfire on you. Doing so will send all the wrong messages by defining no compromise as something negative, overbearing and arrogant. This is especially so in companies that are functioning in the mediocrity, destroy from within or fiery pit of hell zones on The Four Business Outcomes and The BIG Eight Driver wheels. *The more a company falls below the no-compromise zone, the more challenging the culture shift.*

The BIG shift

All culture shifts, positive or negative, are successfully led or derailed by the leader of the company. If the leader is hesitant, indecisive or reluctant to lead, the business culture will remain status quo — or plunge farther into the fiery pit of hell. This also applies to leaders who are more talk than action or have a dismal track record with accountability.

A Neilism: "Culture shifts are fueled by deeds — not words and grand visions." This entire book is about leadership and execution — about getting things done and done right. It's time to put aside those leadership blockages, procrastination, fears and self doubts. Such behaviors will slow, prevent or even kill a culture shift to no compromise. *Remember, anyone can initiate a culture shift, but only a no-compromise leader can see it through to completion.*

> **Neilism**
> Culture shifts are fueled by deeds — not words and grand visions.

If this book has inspired you to look at yourself, your company and what can be achieved through no-compromise leadership, you know that the culture shift begins and ends with you. You must be prepared to see the transition through. Sure, there will setbacks and times when you may question your abilities, decisions or effectiveness as a leader. Throughout the culture shift to no compromise, your true character as a leader will be revealed. In every way imaginable, it will test how you handle tough decisions, resistance to change — and your resolve to stay the course.

Creating balance across The Four Business Outcomes demands the presence of a no-compromise business culture. As a no-compromise leader, the task of creating this culture rests squarely on your shoulders. In no way am I attempting to make this task appear more daunting than it is, nor is it prudent for me to oversimplify the challenges of leading a company through a culture shift. Just be prepared for the hard work ahead of you. I'd rather have you prepared to bust through any and all obstacles than be stopped by them.

I've witnessed more attempted culture shifts during which the leader charges off in a new direction only to discover that his culture is still locked on the old heading. That occurs when employees lack the clarity on why the company changed course. There was no detailed mission plan or map to follow. There was no information flow to share progress or challenges. In such cases, it doesn't take long for the change initiative and culture shift to sputter and fizzle out. *Yes, culture shifts can collapse in an instant.*

Warning: If you equate shifting a business culture to a speedboat making a 360-degree, full-throttle turn — you just compromised.

It is vital that you understand the complexities of the task ahead. Rest assured, a culture shift will occur in your company. It will require tremendous energy and relentless focus from you and your leadership team, most being expended in the early implementation stages. It's the equivalent of turning a massive aircraft carrier around. All of the forward momentum of the ship must be shifted in a new direction...and maintained until it aligns on the new course heading. More importantly, that wide turn and new heading must be free of any navigational hazards. Yes, in business you must be prepared for the unexpected, but plotting the best course that is free of hazards certainly improves the odds of achieving your goals.

WARNING: If you equate shifting a business culture to a speedboat making a 360-degree, full-throttle turn — you just compromised. Culture shifts take time — significantly more time than you might realize.

Good or bad, fast or slow, your company is currently on a specific course heading. Like the captain of that aircraft carrier, you are responsible for keeping your company on the right course. More importantly, you are responsible for the culture that shapes the collective behavior and thinking of your employees. If that course heading needs to change, you need to communicate that change to all employees — and do so with absolute clarity. If that new no-compromise course takes your company into uncharted waters, you need to communicate the why, where, how and when of this change. You must ensure that your team's focus is at high alert, your systems are ready to engage and the necessary resources are at hand. *Everyone must be in perfect sync on where you are going to take the company. Absolutely everyone. No compromise.*

What's the GAP?

There is a difficulty factor to navigating your business through a culture shift. To understand your difficulty factor, you must assess how wide the gap is between your current business culture and the no-compromise culture you want to install. Be absolutely clear on how wide that gap is before launching the transition to a no-compromise culture. If you underestimate the gap, you might find your newly launched culture shift colliding head on into deeply embedded behaviors — behaviors that are highly resistant to even the smallest change initiative. Likewise, if your business has a history of quickly adapting to change, this may indicate a smoother transition. *The larger the gap, the more energy and focus your culture shift will require.*

Change efforts and culture shifts succeed or fail for many reasons. Clearly, leadership's approach to the process is largely the deciding factor.

> **If you underestimate the gap, you may find your newly launched culture shift colliding head on into deeply embedded behaviors...**

However, if your company has a track record of failed change efforts, this is an indication that compromise exists in both its leadership and culture. *The size of the change effort doesn't matter.* In fact, if small and seemingly basic change efforts routinely failed in the past, it's a sure bet that a major culture shift could quickly go down in flames. If this describes your company, expect intense pressure for the no-compromise leader in you to emerge.

The best indicator of how wide the culture gap is to examine how balanced your company is across The Four Business Outcomes. Go back to The Four Business Outcomes wheel at the beginning of Part II. How did you rate your company's performance in each of The Four Business Outcomes? How out of balance was your wheel? The more out of balance, the more inconsistent and compromising your company and its culture is. A Neilism: "Compromise ensures consistently inconsistent business outcomes." The degree of imbalance in The Four Business Outcomes wheel is a solid indicator of the gap between your current reality and achieving a no-compromise culture. I say this because balance in The Four Business Outcomes and your business culture are intrinsically inseparable. *Compromise and contamination in your culture will create imbalance in The Four Business Outcomes and vice versa.*

Neilism
Compromise ensures consistently inconsistent business outcomes.

The Four Business Outcomes wheel, and corresponding BIG Eight Driver wheel for each outcome, provide a visual mechanism for you to pinpoint where to focus your culture shift efforts. For example, if the profitability business outcome is in the "destroy from within zone," the BIG Eight Driver wheel might identify compromise in the sense of urgency, accountability and information flow drivers. The BIG Eight Driver wheel for profitability guides you to work on these drivers first to infuse fiscal responsibility into your culture. Accountability to the numbers must flow from leadership to every single employee of the company. Budgets must be created and meticulously adhered to. Financial reporting must be timely and accurate. Financial decisions must be carefully weighed to determine *value* versus *impact* on the financial integrity of the company. Information flow systems must be in place to track your financial critical numbers. *Use the wheels. No compromise.*

As you isolate what must be done in each of The Four Business Outcomes, the true depth of navigating a culture shift can appear daunting. Imagine how those NASA engineers and astronauts felt when President Kennedy made his memorable address before Congress in 1961. Kennedy proclaimed a national goal of landing a man on the moon and bringing him safely back to earth before the end of the decade. The technology gap in 1961 was essentially as big as the quarter-million mile gap between the earth and the moon. Methodically, the gap was closed until, on July 20, 1969, Neil Armstrong put the first human footprint on the surface of the

Lee Iacocca and the Chrysler turnaround

Lee Iacocca's famous turnaround of Chrysler is a true no-compromise leadership story. When Iacocca arrived at Chrysler in late 1978, it didn't take him long to figure out that Chrysler was in a crisis state. Chrysler was drowning in red ink. There was a leadership gap and no vision, purpose or urgency. Teamwork was nonexistent. Operating units functioned as if they were working in a vacuum. Iacocca had to make some drastic decisions. He was forced to fire many of the executives. He tried to set up a partnership between Chrysler and Volkswagen, but when they realized the extent of Chrysler's massive debt, the deal fell through. Iacocca had no choice but to make the unprecedented move to ask Congress to grant federal guarantees for all of Chrysler's loans.

With the company's loans backed by the federal government, he bargained with the union for cuts in salary and benefits. Iacocca even reduced his salary to $1.00 per year to show how everyone at Chrysler must be willing to sacrifice for the automaker to survive. Because he was able to understand and relate to workers, as well as executives, he rallied them together to save the company. By 1983, Iacocca's no-compromise leadership had Chrysler back on its feet. On July 13, 1983, Chrysler paid back all its government-backed loans. In true Lee Iacocca style, he made the following short public statement, "We at Chrysler borrow money the old-fashioned way. We pay it back." No compromise exemplified Iacocca's management style at Chrysler. He created balance across The Four Business Outcomes and successfully led Chrysler through a massive culture shift.

moon. No-compromise leadership created a no-compromise culture at NASA. *No-compromise leadership fulfilled President Kennedy's vision creating a sense of national pride in the process.*

Once you define the gap, the next step is to design and build the bridge to cross it. Just remember, it took years for the gap to evolve. It's going to take time to build a no-compromise culture that is capable of closing it. *Let's begin the process.*

Creating your transition team

No-compromise leadership is not about you becoming the Lone Ranger or some super-fearless leader. Installing a no-compromise culture will require the creation of a special transition team to participate in fulfilling the requirements of The BIG Eight. (Notice I used the word "participate." No-compromise leadership is about inclusion and empowering your employees. It's not about the leader making all the decisions and keeping a grip on the controls.) The BIG Eight are the building blocks to creating a no-compromise company and culture. The culture shift to no compromise cannot and will not occur if any of the The BIG Eight are compromised.

The culture shift to no compromise cannot and will not occur if any of the The BIG Eight are compromised.

Your transition team will consist of key leaders and managers. However, the team must also include employees in key areas throughout the company. Those employees might have special skills or unique knowledge about the company, its systems and customers. More importantly, employees throughout the company might view those team members not only as mentors, but an integral part of the information flow system to ensure that their voices, concerns, ideas and solutions are heard.

Bringing together this transition team is key to a successful culture shift. Inclusion in crafting the details and requirements of The BIG Eight instills a sense of ownership in becoming a no-compromise company. More importantly, this team has a *multiplying effect* in each member's area of influence to maintain urgency, information flow, teamwork — and accountability.

This team should be powerful enough and large enough to drive and guide change throughout the company. They will need to create and maintain the sense of urgency not only to change, but to keep the process going. Think of it this way. In order to install all aspects of a no-compromise culture in a company with 250 employees, what creates the highest probability for success — a transition team of five or 50? If you picked five, those poor souls will quickly find themselves head-butting change resisters as well as the embedded behaviors of the old culture. The change effort will die as quickly as it began. *Pitting one change agent against 50 is pure short-sighted compromise.*

The ideal culture-shift ratio is one transition team member to five employees. To shift the behaviors of 250 employees, a team of 50 can generate the momentum needed to influence and inspire change in more areas of the company — and do so simultaneously.

The ideal culture-shift ratio is one transition team member to five employees.

Keep in mind that you don't need to start the planning phase with a large transition team. Additional managers and employees can be added to the transition team as you near the launch. You can even create sub or department teams. *The point is, you need sufficient team energy to complete a successful culture shift to no compromise.*

Mapping your culture-shift course

The initial communication to employees on where the company is going, why you chose such a new path and detailing how it's going to get there, is the critical first step. *Maintaining absolute clarity is non-negotiable.* This requires a comprehensive strategy to map out what exactly needs to take place and in what sequence. *Focus your culture shift on driving The Four Business Outcomes and you will find absolute clarity.*

Let's go back to The BIG Eight I used for each of The Four Business Outcomes. The BIG Eight encompass the must-dos for creating your culture shift map. Think about The BIG Eight in terms of presenting change to your employees. Here is what they look like in relation to beginning your shift to a no-compromise business culture:

Four Business Outcomes refresher

Your vision of shifting to a no-compromise culture must be linked to The Four Business Outcomes.

Productivity: The productivity business outcome is all about doing the work of the business — and executing that work in the most efficient and timely manner possible to the highest no-compromise standards. Productivity is the <u>output</u> of a business.

Profitability: The profitability business outcome is all about achieving predictable cash flow and bottom-line profitability — and doing so with the highest level of no-compromise financial accountability at all levels of the company. Profitability is the <u>fuel</u> of a business.

Staff retention: The staff retention business outcome is all about creating a dynamic and empowering culture to attract and retain the best employees — and doing so with no-compromise leadership, open communication, integrity, and respect. Staff retention is the <u>heart</u> of a business.

Customer loyalty: The customer loyalty business outcome is all about delivering extraordinary service, quality and value to achieve maximum client retention — and doing so with a no-compromise passion to be nothing less than world class. Customer loyalty is the <u>strength</u> of a business.

1. No-compromise culture

Defining the culture you will need to support no compromise in each of The Four Business Outcomes gives you the detail needed to paint a high-definition picture of what the company will look and feel like. For example, predictable and controlled growth, expansion, dramatically improved career and income opportunities, better equipment, better benefits, etc. You must communicate not only the "why" that's driving the no-compromise change initiative, but the "how" that is built into The BIG Eight Drivers. No compromise.

Culture shift points to consider:

Even when change is needed and expected, it's natural for employees to fear and resist it. This is especially so when installing no compromise in a business that has a history of compromising behavior and performance. Your task in initiating a no-compromise culture shift is to deliver a compelling and sustainable message to employees on why the company is changing and how this change is a win for all.

> **Neilism**
> Leading a culture shift to no compromise is more of a long-distance marathon than a 50-yard dash.

+ Can you describe in detail what the new culture will look and feel like? What exactly is going to change? What's inspiring about it?
+ What will employees find challenging during the culture shift?
+ How long will the culture shift take?
+ How will the shift to no compromise benefit employees? What growth opportunities will it provide? When will they see some of those opportunities?
+ How will no compromise impact individual employees? What will they see and feel that's different in their daily work? What makes this culture better for them?

A Neilism: "Leading a culture shift to no compromise is more of a long-distance marathon than a 50-yard dash."

2. Sense of urgency

Launching a culture shift to no compromise without creating a sustainable high sense of urgency is a setup for failure. Urgency provides the initial burst of energy that launches a change initiative in the right direction. Once a culture shift is underway, a sense of urgency maintains and builds momentum to keep the shift going. *Urgency pushes and prods the culture shift* *process along.* And when your culture shift encounters those inevitable speed bumps and hurdles, sense of urgency provides the horsepower to get over them. The no-compromise leader's role during a culture shift is to create and maintain urgency throughout the company. No compromise.

Culture shift points to consider:

President Kennedy set a goal to put a man on the moon and beat the Russians in the process. Iacocca saved Chrysler from going under and taking tens of thousands of jobs along with it. What creates a sense of urgency is different for every business and situation. Consider where your company is positioned in relation to The Four Business Outcomes. Can you identify which of The Four Business Outcomes requires immediate sense of urgency? If so, what are the most urgent "gotta get done" issues that you can rally your team around? Here are some quick examples:

> The no-compromise leader's role during a culture shift is to create and maintain urgency throughout the company.

- **For productivity,** it could be the urgency to sell time, units produced, orders shipped or resource utilization.
- **For profitability,** it could be urgency to reduce costs by streamlining processes or to improve cash flow by reducing accounts receivables.
- **For staff retention,** it could be creating project teams to engage employees in discovering and implementing growth solutions.
- **For customer loyalty,** it could be creating that "wow" factor that drives up customer retention rates by reengineering the customer's buying experience via faster response time, rapid problem solving, or one-to-one consultative relationship building.

Sense of urgency is like a starting gun for a marathon or countdown clock to a space launch. It's the catalyst that starts and maintains forward momentum. *How will you communicate the sense of urgency to get your company out of the starting gate?* It could be the introduction and launch of a major growth initiative or expansion plan that creates new opportunities for everyone in the company. Perhaps knocking your top competitor out of the number one market leader slot is an inspiring challenge. What about the reward for employees in the form of better benefits or team bonus opportunities? If your company is in pain, the urgency to implement a cure is one of the best ways to rally your troops. An urgent Neilism: "There's nothing like a good case of business pain to ignite urgency around a long-overdue culture shift."

> **Neilism**
> There's nothing like a good case of business pain to ignite urgency around a long-overdue culture shift

It's one thing to initiate a sense of urgency, but maintaining that sense of urgency will challenge all leaders. Some leaders are great at getting out of the starting gate, but their culture shifts run out of gas halfway around the track. Don't forget no-compromise tenet number nine: **Resolute:** *Be tenacious and courageous.* Leadership tenacity to stay the course — to stay true to your no-compromise mandate — is what gives the perpetual push to maintaining sense of urgency.

3. Critical numbers

A culture shift to no compromise must be guided and measured by the critical numbers you define for each of The Four Business Outcomes. Critical numbers are targets that you, your employees and your company fight and strive for. They provide the measurements to indicate and illustrate progress and to identify where more focus and effort must be applied. Without defining the critical numbers for each business outcome, your culture shift can wander aimlessly off course. An inspiring vision is great at launch time but its energy fizzles out quickly without critical numbers to guide it. A critical

> **Without defining the critical numbers for each business outcome, your culture shift can wander aimlessly off course.**

Neilism: "Critical numbers eliminate the abstract interpretation of what work needs to be done." More importantly, they keep the culture shift on course and, when consistently monitored, they sound an alarm when things go off course or move too slowly. The only way to measure the progress of your culture is to see your critical numbers moving in the right direction. No compromise.

Culture shift points to consider:

To get your culture shift going, limit the critical numbers you want to drive to two or three. *These two or three critical numbers, when moved in the right direction, should be the most significant indicators that your culture is changing.* For example, if the three numbers are revenue growth, net profit and first-time customer retention rate, positive change in all three numbers communicates progress and a win throughout the company or department. The objective here is to initiate a culture shift and track its progress. Overloading staff with too many critical numbers will do more harm than good. *Find those initial wins and build from there.*

Neilism
Critical numbers eliminate the abstract interpretation of what work needs to be done.

Invest the time and resources to educate all employees on what your key critical numbers mean, why they were selected, and how you will measure progress. The shift to a no-compromise culture is your opportunity to fully engage everyone in building the company. This is the time to educate and coach your employees.

4. Information flow

Information flow in a company must be fast, furious and relentless. It must flow to everyone at every level. Remember, I'm not talking about distributing an internal bulletin or meeting once a month, I'm talking about daily updates on scoreboards, status, progress, wins, challenges and team success stories. *Don't expect to complete a major culture shift by making a grand presentation at a general meeting and following it up with a few memos.* Think of a war room at the Pentagon with its constant inflow and outflow of real-time data. Want to win a war? Then your information and intelligence — your information-flow system — must be up to the task.

It's no different in business. *If you stifle information flow, you can kiss your culture shift good-bye.* No compromise.

Culture shift points to consider:

Information flow connects your employees to your critical numbers and the overall goals of the company. Too often, information flow is under utilized or overlooked when, in reality, it is the key driver to achieving a successful and lasting culture shift. What does your information-flow system look like now? Where is it lacking and what needs immediate fixing?

> **Think of a war room at the Pentagon with its constant inflow and outflow of real-time data.**

Remember, you're taking your company on an exciting voyage and everyone on board needs key information on progress, resources available and consumed, and what is and isn't working. Chances are, there might be holes in your information-flow system. Find them and fix them.

A simple information-flow acid test

Take a walk around your company and randomly ask employees if they can tell you what a company goal is for the current month and what the progress is to reach that goal? Chances are, you'll see just how inadequate your information-flow systems are.

One of our best consulting clients did just that to test his systems and was shocked. When he asked some employees in the breakroom what some of the numbers on the scoreboard meant, they didn't know. This is a business that has been doing daily huddles and scoreboards for years. It was a wake-up call that their information-flow systems needed beefing up.

Information flow brings understanding and clarity. It eliminates the "but I thought…" or "I didn't know…" excuses that occur when a company engages in a major change initiative. *Scoreboards are a must.* You must be able to answer these key scoreboard implementation questions:

+ Who will design them?
+ Who will update them daily?
+ Where will you strategically place them so all employees can watch the action and keep score?
+ When, where and what time will team huddles take place?
+ What's the hit list of key information that will be communicated at huddles?
+ What are the non-negotiable rules for huddle attendance?

Take the information flow process seriously. No compromise.

5. Teamwork

A business culture is the collective behavior of its employees. Given that, teamwork is the essence of a business culture. In culture shift, teamwork is a natural catalyst that gives momentum by pulling staff together in the pursuit of company goals. Rally your teams. Empower your teams. Lead your teams. The more disciplined and focused your teams are on driving your critical numbers, the higher and tighter the level of teamwork. The higher and tighter your level of teamwork, the more resistant your culture is to contamination from change resisters. Intentional or not, change resisters are intent on derailing your culture shift. Teamwork shapes and strengthens your culture. No compromise.

> **The higher and tighter your level of teamwork — the more resistant your culture is to contamination from change resisters.**

Culture shift points to consider:

I wrote earlier about the necessity of creating a transition team to lead the culture shift to no compromise. Consider each member of this team as an essential change agent empowered to coach and inspire the change process to the farthest reaches of the company. These change agents should be readily identified and their roles clarified to all employees. They should also be charged with recruiting so-called "change deputies" to accelerate the process. This *multiplying effect* is powerful and essential to creating the higher level of teamwork a no-compromise culture shift requires. It's also an efficient way to break through the natural resistance that accompanies any degree of culture shift.

Teamwork is all-inclusive. It's a decree that sounds like, *"Everyone is getting on the bus. No one will be left behind."* By design, culture shifts rock the boat and some employees will fall off or get left behind. This is unacceptable for the no-compromise leader. True, if an employee fails to make the grade, it might be best to part ways. However, is that employee's failure due in part to leadership's failure to train, mentor and coach? If so, you might be losing a valuable employee resource who's worth saving. A Neilism: "Compassion is the heart of no-compromise leadership." It's so easy for leaders to forget this basic leadership principle when engrossed in a major culture shift.

> **Neilism**
> Compassion is the heart of no-compromise leadership.

The key ingredient to teamwork's secret sauce is "empowerment." Empowering teams is the opposite of the traditional top-down, dictatorial management hierarchy that stifles creative thinking at a dynamic level. Teamwork is about collective growth and achievement. As you begin your no-compromise culture shift, look to empower your teams with clearly defined decision-making authority. Start with the basics and give them more control as their skills and confidence develop. If you don't empower your teams, you will be de-powering them — and nothing will change.

> **If you don't empower your teams, you will be de-powering them — and nothing will change.**

Teams need goals. Teams flourish through healthy competition with other teams. *Teams need to celebrate.* And teams need that regular dose of reality to get them back in the game. *The no-compromise leader succeeds based on how well he or she inspires and empowers teamwork.*

6. Innovation

Let's be honest, you're not going to capture and ignite the passion of your employees by announcing a grand plan to maintain status quo. "Hey, let's shoot for more of the same," is not the battle cry that inspires a major culture shift. A Neilism: "A culture shift is a voyage to a place of greater opportunity." This is the time for innovative thinking. Get your shields down (your personal resistance to change) and get innovative. Here's the guiding rule of change: *No one person, group or system can be excluded. Be prepared to go all the way or don't change at all.* Innovate new ideas, systems, leadership structures, products, services, job content and roles. *If you want to achieve quantum leaps in business growth, everything is on the table and subject to innovation.* No compromise.

Neilism

A culture shift is a voyage to a place of greater opportunity.

Culture shift points to consider:

Culture shifts are doomed when leaders cling to the past and refuse to lower their shields and allow new thinking and behavior into their companies. The whole purpose of no-compromise leadership is to create a dynamic, world-class company by driving The Four Business Outcomes. *It's impossible to bridge the gap between where you are now and becoming world-class without embracing innovative thinking.* As if by design, your culture shift to no compromise will allow innovative thinking to flow throughout your company. Innovation will only flourish in a culture that nurtures, encourages and celebrates it. *So, put those shields down and enjoy the ride.*

Create four special projects teams; one for each business outcome.

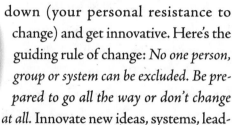

Charge each team with the mission of innovating new ideas, systems, procedures, products, services, etc. Give the teams crazy names like the Jedi Knights, System Geeks or how about your very own NCL Team (No-Compromise Leadership Team). Set the guidelines and let their innovative thinking fly. Have each team hone their ideas down to one or two potential winners. Once they identify their top one or two ideas, have the teams expand the details and develop an implementation plan to be presented to the entire leadership team for consideration. Just to spice it up, have a special prize for the team that presents the most innovative idea and plan.

Time to dust off that old suggestion box so all employees can play the innovation game. And what makes better sense than to have those who do the work — who really know and understand the work — to innovate better, faster, cheaper ways of creating and delivering your service or product?

Employees are highly capable of innovating breakthrough ideas — if you give them the opportunity and freedom to do so. In his book *Success Principles*, Jack Canfield said this

> **"I'll give you 80 percent of my 100 percent — you can have the remaining 20 percent if you allow me to use it."**

from an employee perspective, "I'll give you 80 percent of my 100 percent — you can have the remaining 20 percent if you allow me to use it." Are your employees giving you 100 percent of their 100 percent? If not, compromise exists in your culture. Again, consider a reward or bonus payout for the best new idea or cost-cutting system. The innovative ideas are there. *Create a culture and a system to let them out.*

7. Systems

Culture shifts fizzle without structure and explicit road maps to guide and illuminate the way. A culture shift to no compromise cannot survive without systems. I'm not talking about a few systems here, I'm talking about a company-wide initiative to create, redesign and/or bulletproof all the systems that drive The Four Business Outcomes. Just get comfortable with the reality that many of your systems will need to be upgraded or replaced entirely with innovative systems that are up to the task of creating no-compromise results. *The goal of no-compromise leadership is to instill consistency and predictability.* Gotta have systems. There's no other way. No compromise.

Culture shift points to consider:

A no-compromise business culture is a systems-driven culture. That being said, how many of the essential daily activities in your company occur without a system to efficiently guide them? Systems development is a great place to focus the innovative energies of your special projects teams. Start with basic systems in key result areas like customer service, production, financial controls and, most importantly, on your information-flow systems so they function at high speed throughout the company.

Implement systems at a pace that your current culture can handle. Mastering new systems takes time, repetition and a high accountability factor before they're locked in. Incremental progress builds confidence and momentum in a culture shift. Overload your team with too many new systems to master and you'll be doing more to elevate frustration levels. You'll de-motivate your team rather than lead and inspire a culture shift. *Know what your current culture can handle and gradually increase the pace of systems implementation as the culture shift gains momentum.*

8. Accountability

Of all The BIG Eight, accountability is the definitive make-or-break factor to complete the shift to a no-compromise culture. Accountability to yourself, your vision, your team, your systems, your ethics, your integrity, your communication and your ability to be consistent is going to be put to the test. Once launched, the success of your voyage to no compromise rests squarely on you being the accountability driver. You set the accountability standard of behavior in your company. The curse of the accountability driver is your own procrastination and leadership blockages that you alone allow into your leadership behavior. *If it needs to be done, get it done. No hesitation and absolutely no procrastination.*

> The curse of the accountability driver is your own procrastination and leadership blockages that you alone allow into your leadership behavior.

Yes, compromise will inevitably creep in, but the no-compromise leader must address compromise quickly and decisively. No compromise.

Culture shift points to consider:

A Neilism: "Accountability is the backbone of no-compromise leadership." The strength of that backbone and the weight it can bear will be the defining factor, not only of your transition to a no-compromise leader, but your ability to lead your company through the culture shift to no compromise. Culture shifts die when leaders compromise the accountability driver. All you need to do is drop one ball and your employees will see and hear it. You can acknowledge it — even take responsibility for dropping that one ball — and your employees may let it slide. *Drop two balls and it's over. Excuses don't drive culture shifts.*

> **Drop two balls and it's over. Excuses don't drive culture shifts.**

As the no-compromise leader, every aspect of your behavior is under the microscope. Given this, you are accountable to higher standards of behavior and performance. At no other time in business is leading by example so critical than during a culture shift. *Rest assured, your personal accountability is going to be put to the test.*

The game is now in play.

The culture shift to no compromise is underway. It's your ultimate responsibility to hold your leadership team and employees accountable for execution and driving The Four Business Outcomes. *You must be present and engaged. You must be a visible leader.* If that means spending time working alongside employees…do it. If that means video or print updates from you…do it. The more visible your commitment to seeing the culture shift through, the more energy, lift and life you give to those you lead.

> **Neilism**
> Accountability is the backbone of no-compromise leadership.

The accountability driver will demand that you make even the toughest decisions. If a member of your leadership team drops that second ball, what are you prepared to do? Will corrective and decisive measures be taken? If balls continue to drop, are you prepared to fire one of your leaders? Remember what I said about your behavior being under the microscope as well. If you fail to take decisive action, including termination if that's what's called for, everyone will know it. A Neilism you can trust: "Once compromised, the high trust that accountability builds is difficult to regain."

Neilism
Once compromised, the high trust that accountability builds is difficult to regain.

Your resolve to be accountable and lead by example must cascade through all levels of leadership in your company. Your leaders must follow your lead and hold their teams accountable. Team members must "feel" and respond to the urgency to be accountable for their own performance. *No-compromise leadership is where it begins.*

A no-compromise culture emerges when accountability becomes embedded in every fiber of a company's behavior. It's when empowerment and accountability merge into an unstoppable and dynamic force. Empowerment in action is the Holy Grail in business. It is the genetic fingerprint of the no-compromise business culture. It signals when the culture shift is complete… for now. (Rest assured, the process will begin again. Change is relentless.)

A no-compromise culture emerges when accountability becomes a embedded in every fiber of a company's behavior.

The BIG Eight provide the framework for creating a thorough culture shift map. Use it as a checklist to ensure that your plan has the absolute clarity to not only kick off your culture shift, but to see it through to completion.

❧

Thoughts on culture shift timelines…

Now that you're all fired up and ready to go, I need to offer some words of caution. This is clearly a pivotal juncture for you as the leader of your company. *You are about to initiate a culture shift that will test the limits of your leadership abilities.* Changing your own behavior is difficult enough, but changing the behavior of an entire company is what earns you the coveted right to refer to yourself as a no-compromise leader. So, let's be sure that your culture shift timelines are realistic.

FACT: Culture shifts take time — a lot of time. The amount of time your culture shift will take is based on on three factors:

1. **You:** Your ability to relentlessly communicate, stay focused and stay the course.

2. **The size and complexity of your company:** This includes layers of management, departments, divisions and the geographical nature of your company, such as multiple locations or multinational operations.

3. **The current state of your company and its culture:** Specifically, the more out of balance your business is with respect to The Four Business Outcomes, the more energy and time it will take to move it through a culture shift to no compromise.

CAUTION: I've seen companies make wonderful culture-shift strides in a matter of months. However, too many leaders misinterpret these rapid and positive "strides" as being farther along in the culture shift than they actually are. Such misinterpretations can cause you to ease up on the urgency factor far too soon, causing the culture shift to stall. Once stalled, it's extremely difficult to get a culture shift moving again. *It's simply human nature for old, comfortable behaviors to snap back in a heartbeat when discipline and focus are compromised.*

The best leadership mindset for a culture-shift timeline is six to 24 months. That allows sufficient time for new behaviors to become embedded in your culture. For any leader to think he or she can complete a culture shift in less than six months is simply short-sighted. It's difficult enough to change your own behavior in six months, let alone the behavior of an entire company. *It doesn't matter if you have five or 500 employees, the no-compromise approach is to think beyond the "quick fix" and settle in to drive consistent change over the long term.*

> Once stalled, it's extremely difficult to get a culture shift moving again.

I'm sure some readers will feel their entrepreneurial "get it done" nature balking at the prospects of a culture shift taking up to, or beyond, 24 months to complete. Allow me to interject some clarity here. No-compromise leadership is not a license to jump into the leadership driver's seat and slam the accelerator to the floor. *You can't lead a company through a culture shift with employees hanging on for dear life.* A culture shift begins with a mission and a sense of urgency fueled by no-compromise leadership. It gains momentum and lift like a jetliner gaining altitude. *Maintaining your culture shift's speed, lift and altitude is the duty of the no-compromise leader.*

A complete culture shift can take years until all remnants of the old culture and the behaviors that defined it are purged. And just when you think you've got it right, relentless pressure for your company to adapt and stay ahead of the competition can signal that it's time for the culture to shift once again. *The message here is that no business culture is immune to change, upgrading — or a complete overhaul.*

And just to ensure you're really grounded, I might as well tell you that many culture shifts never succeed. They crumble under the weight of compromise radiating from leadership. It's simply impossible for any change initiative, especially one as all-consuming as a culture shift to no compromise, to achieve the lift necessary to gain altitude in the presence of compromise. *Compromise is pure drag.*

> A complete culture shift can take years until all remnants of the old culture and the behaviors that defined it are purged.

The culture shift to no compromise begins and ends with you. A no-compromise business culture will remain a pipe dream if you do not rise above the fray and become a no-compromise leader yourself.

This can be one of the inspiring and fulfilling transformations you can make as a leader. It will create opportunities for growth throughout your company. And when balance is achieved across The Four Business Outcomes, you and every employee who worked to achieve that balance will see and experience the rewards of no compromise.

What a culture shift to no compromise looks like...

The charts on the following pages illustrate the timelines, must do's and outcomes of a culture shift to no compromise over a span of 18-months. As you read through the charts, keep in mind that the charts are for demonstration purposes only. Based on your current reality, the timeline for your culture shift might be quite different.

As you study the charts, focus special attention on the flow as the timelines methodically progress. You'll clearly see your role as a no-compromise leader intensify and why being tenacious and courageous is non-negotiable. One constant is the incessant need for communication and information flow. *What you won't find in the timeline is room for compromise in the form of procrastination or leadership blockages.*

Timeline	No-Compromise Must-Dos	What You Should See
Before the Launch: Plan until there is absolute clarity on where you are going to take the company. This is the time to confront the good, the bad and the ugly of your current reality.	Get your leadership and change team into the game. You can't do a culture shift alone. The more disciples you have to spread the vision of the new, no-compromise culture, the better. You'll need "believers" to win over the fence-sitters and change resisters. Begin ratcheting up the sense of urgency for change. Determine where the company stands on The Four Business Outcomes wheel. Which zone is your company in? How out of balance is your wheel? Define the critical numbers for each of The Four Business Outcomes.	Buy-in throughout your leadership and change team. Leadership and change team members should exude a passionate resolve regarding the shift to a no-compromise business culture. A heightened sense of urgency and excitement to begin the culture shift. Culture shift champions on your team should begin to emerge.
The First 30 Days **The Kickoff:** It's all about communication and getting company-wide buy-in to your vision and plan for a no-compromise business culture.	Make the kickoff a powerful and meaningful event. Communicate with passion the need for change, new vision and no-compromise culture. Introduce The Four Business Outcomes wheel. Introduce the critical numbers that will drive each of The Four Business Outcomes. Kick your communication and information flow systems into high gear. Use all communication tools: meetings, one-on-ones, e-mail, video, webinars, on-site visits, posters, banners, inserts in paychecks, etc. Relentlessly communicate the vision and details of the change effort with extreme clarity. Open dialog is key. Watch for pockets of resistance or "fear of change." Coach and counsel quickly.	Buy-in and growing support should become evident throughout all levels of leadership and all employees. Employee champions for no compromise should emerge. If you do not see a heightened sense of urgency, you and your leadership team are not leading and driving change. Engage. Get out there and lead your team. No compromise. Employees should be asking questions about the change and culture shift. Questions mean employees are listening and thinking. Relentless communication is non-negotiable. If you think you're comminicating enough, you're not. Double your communication efforts.

Timeline	No-Compromise Must-Dos	What You Should See
1 – 3 Months: Change becomes the new reality. Letting go of the old behaviors and culture can lead to discouragement. No-compromise leadership must focus on communication and information flow to build momentum for the culture shift.	Use the strategies in Part II to fuel the sense of urgency in all four business outcomes. The BIG Eight Drivers must be embedded as non-negotiables throughout the company. Begin rolling out your newly designed systems. Begin teaching The Four Business Outcomes at all levels of the company. Begin daily huddles and scoreboards to drive critical numbers. Look for and celebrate the right no-compromise behaviors. Celebrate every win. A "win" shows progress and success — and eventually leaves the change resisters without an audience.	A sense of urgency should begin to translate into early measurable improvements in your critical numbers in each of The Four Business Outcomes. Team performance should be shifting to a more efficient and consistent level. New systems should be in the early stages of development and implementation. Employees should experience and celebrate some wins. A win, no matter how small, is a win worth celebrating. Execution and accountability should reveal positive and measurable improvement.
3 – 6 Months: **This is where most culture shifts can crash and burn.** Complacency will set in at the first sign of compromise and spread like wildfire. No-compromise leadership must tenaciously lead the company through this crucial development period.	No-compromise leadership consistency is critical. You must hold yourself and leadership team accountable. Accountability creates consistency — and trust. Keep fueling your communication and information-flow systems. Any slowdown or interruption can signal an end to the culture shift and change initiative. You and your leadership team must be present and engaged. Evaluate what's been working and what needs fine-tuning or a completely new system or approach. CHANGE RESISTERS: Get them into the game or get them out. Allowing toxic waste spewers to remain in the company is a compromise.	Your no-compromise culture should be taking hold. You should be able to see it, feel it and measure it. If not, find the compromise. It's there and it might be coming from you. (I never said it would be easy.) Performance across The Four Business Outcomes should be improving, as The BIG Eight Drivers move into the no-compromise zone. Morale and focus on company growth should begin to turn in a positive direction. Employees and teams should be getting more comfortable and engaged in the no-compromise business culture.

Timeline	No-Compromise Must-Dos	What You Should See
6 – 12 Months: It's all about getting the new culture to stick. Continued refinement, execution and driving The Four Business Outcomes is the focus of no-compromise leader.	Work on consistency and accountability. You guessed it, keep your communication and information-flow systems persistent and consistent. Continue to develop new systems and refine those that are not yet delivering consistent results. Continue to celebrate the wins and spotlight great examples of no-compromise leadership and behavior. Nothing drives a culture shift faster than positive recognition, celebrating wins and real examples of what success looks like. Re-evaluate your critical numbers based on progress to date. Don't hesitate to set goals to make your team stretch. Just be sure goals are attainable.	Continued signs that your no-compromise culture is taking hold. If not, (you guessed it) you compromised. Leadership team members, department leaders and employees in general should be settling into higher levels of no-compromise behavior and performance. There should be measurable progress in creating balance in The Four Business Outcomes. Even if it's minor progress, the fact that progress is being made is what you're looking for. Specifically look for progress in the productivity, profitability and customer loyalty business outcomes. (I left out staff retention because your culture shift might prompt some necessary turnover.)
12 – 18 Months: Consistency, focus, urgency and no-compromise behavior. It's all about creating lift and eliminating drag.	Continue refining, reinforcing and fueling the company's sense of urgency. Be vigilant of your personal behavior and accountability. The no-compromise leader sets the trust, integrity and accountability bar for the entire company. Keep your communication and information-flow systems persistent and consistent. Continue systems refinement. Empower your emerging no-compromise leaders. Let go of the reins. Trust your systems and new culture. Begin focusing on developing and building your bench of no-compromise leaders.	This is a critical transition period. Your no-compromise culture should be vividly apparent throughout your company. As leader, you should find your role and focus shifting to longer-range growth plans and projects. You now have the culture and leadership infrastructure to allow you to chart your company's future. Creating balance across The Four Business Outcomes should become easier to control and more predictable. More no-compromise leaders should emerge. This is critical to ensure seamless leadership succession at all levels of the company.

A NO-COMPROMISE LESSON:
The time has come to shake things up

The body language of the employees I was about to address oozed negativity and resistance. You could cut the tension in the meeting room with a knife. As the business owner prepared to introduce me, my mind was in rapid creativity mode, crafting my opening for this launch of a major change initiative that included a new compensation system.

It was showtime. "Good morning," I began. "As your consultant, I examined every conceivable aspect of your company, and I'm happy to announce that absolutely nothing needs to change."

As I stood silently, allowing my words to sink in, almost in unison the employees responded with, "You've got to be kidding. Everything here needs to change!" With the ice broken and everyone in agreement that significant changes were needed, I was able to proceed.

There are two lessons to learn from this story. First, the owner waited too long to implement the tough changes the business truly needed. This "fear of change" caused a deterioration in the business culture that trashed morale and productivity. Second, employees are more ready and open for change than most leaders think. It doesn't mean that all change will be welcomed with open arms. It means that, in general, employees know when change needs to happen.

I love change and the sense of urgency it ignites in a company. Change not only stirs the pot, it often gets people focused on a specific project, behavior, objective or goal. When necessary, change can snap a business out of its complacent stupor.

The question is: What do you need to change in your company? I'm not talking about little tweaks, I'm talking about that vision-driven, courageous, fearless, heart-pounding kind of change that transforms a company and offers unlimited possibilities.

I'll bet you already know the answer. So what's standing in your way?

continued...

Let's get the fear-of-change thing out of the way. Get over it! Leading a company is not about you — it's about ensuring the health, profitability and growth of the company. You are responsible and accountable to do what needs to be done. When you allow your fears and leadership blockages to get in the way, you are compromising the company, its employees, suppliers, investors and customers. It's the leader's job to make tough decisions (even if they're unpopular) if those decisions are right for the company as a whole. Get over it, or get out of the way.

It's easy to get caught up in the daily mayhem of business and not be aware that your vision is getting stale. Companies with strong, inspiring and vibrant visions have a distinct bounce in their step. It's as if the entire company is focused on and moving toward one laser dot on the horizon.

If your vision has become rusty, it's time to get out the polish and work on it until it shines brightly enough to guide everyone in the company. Shake things up. Get your company moving until its heart is pumping at an invigorating rate.

At different points, change is the perfect prescription for every business. Change is simply part of the evolutionary process of creating an enduring company.

Change is a process of identifying obstacles and opportunities on multiple levels, which impact the behaviors and culture of a business. Change can be described on a scale that ranges from critically urgent (survival change) all the way to steady, incremental growth change. No matter where your company is on the scale, change is a non-negotiable part of business. Failure to change is an invitation to failure itself.

- **Put everything on the table.** Too many leaders fall into the trap of keeping individuals, groups, systems or elements of the business off limits to change. Be prepared to go all the way, or don't change at all. Anything less is a compromise of the change process.

- **Stay true to your values.** Don't allow the need for results to compromise your values; those values must guide all change initiatives.
- **Go deep.** If you're going to begin a change initiative, don't dance around the issues. Go deep enough to create positive change where it counts — in your business culture.
- **Think big, think long-term.** There are times and conditions which call for big-thinking change that will prepare your company for the future. Evaluating what needs to change means out-of-the-box thinking.
- **Change takes collaboration.** You can't change a business all by yourself. The energy of change comes from collaborative innovation and the recruitment of change-friendly disciples.
- **Change takes time.** Most change initiatives fail because of unrealistic expectations and timelines. Basic system changes can take up to 18 months to stick. Major culture shifts can take years. Be tenacious and courageous.
- **Re-think strategic planning.** Based on your growth rate, today's strategic plan can quickly become obsolete. Do strategic planning as often as necessary (quarterly, if that's what it takes), to keep on top of change, and to stay realistic with your goals.

CHAPTER 9

JUMP STARTING NO-COMPROMISE LEADERSHIP

The "doing" of no-compromise leadership is all about consistency and execution. This chapter delivers 12 practical lessons to ensure that your no-compromise culture endures.

I just took you through the culture shift to no compromise. If anything, I hope the scope and complexity of shifting your culture to no compromise has you both enlightened, excited and even a bit cautious. Perhaps you're asking questions like, "What does the work of no-compromise leadership look like on a daily basis or in certain situations?" To help jump start your transition to no-compromise leadership, I prepared 12 lessons. Each lesson targets either a specific situation or a leadership discipline. Collectively, the intention of these lessons is to get you into the thinking behind no-compromise leadership and how to apply it.

Lesson 1: Trust

How is trust impacting your business? The simple answer is massively more than you realize. Trust, or the lack thereof, is deeply embedded into every relationship with an individual or group. So much so, that Steven M.R. Covey's book, *The Speed of Trust*, not only became a bestseller, but an insightful workshop, as well.

If there is any point that Covey drives home, it's how our individual behaviors can so easily compromise and degrade trust in business and our personal lives. For example, something as basic as not clarifying expectations when communicating projects or tasks to others can propel trust into a downward spiral. The same holds true for not delivering or doing what you said you would do, talking straight even if it's the tough stuff, breaking commitments, not listening and not being first to extend trust. Those are just some of the 13 behaviors Covey identifies as trust builders or detractors.

When Lorinda Warner, a Certified Strategies Coach and owner of Lorinda's in Mill Creek, Washington, invited me to a two-day Speed of Trust course she was presenting to her staff, I eagerly accepted. Immersing myself in the trust behaviors for two days was a profound experience, not just for me, but for all of Lorinda's staff and other invited guests. The process challenges you in each of Covey's 13 trust behaviors by allowing participants to express trust issues that have been lurking below the surface, sabotaging productivity and feeding those ever-present hidden agendas.

We asked and responded to the toughest of questions safely and openly.

When the class ended, Lorinda asked me what I would like to do. I said, "I would like you and me to sit in private and go through all 13 behaviors one by one to assure that we have total mutual trust." It's not that we had any known trust issues, but with Lorinda promoted to heading up Strategies education, this was a unique opportunity to ensure clarity and trust. For over five hours, Lorinda and I "talked straight" to one another and left nothing — absolutely nothing — unsaid. We asked and responded to the toughest of questions safely and openly. Tough questions that often exist, yet are rarely asked. Simply put, it was a profound experience for us both, as we agreed complete trust was achieved.

Imagine a scale of one to 100 with 100 being complete trust. Now consider each of your employees and, one by one, rate your overall level of complete trust in them. Now imagine the potential speed your business can achieve if everyone on your team lived The Speed of Trust. No more drama, hidden agendas, failed commitments or poorly defined expectations. Imagine how dynamic your culture can be — no-compromise all the way.

Lesson 2: Success — How badly do you want it?

Success is something deeply personal. It's that aching in your gut to achieve something so special that you're willing to dedicate every fiber of your being to attain it. In many ways, success is about achieving your full potential — that special point in your life journey where you can finally say, "I've made it." However, the one undeniable fact about success is that success comes from hard work. A Neilism: "Success is not a gift that can be bestowed upon you. It must be earned."

I was 12 years old when my parents decided to open the dry cleaning business I mentioned earlier. I remember their evening conversations, laying out the floor plan and making decisions about which equipment to buy. I was naturally curious about the process of starting a new business and tried to hang around the conversations as much as I could before being told to scram. Even as a 12-year-old boy, I could tell my parents were betting everything on this new business venture.

My parents worked long, hard hours for many years. My mother was relentless in her efforts to be the best and do the best for the customers. Over the years, my parents did pretty well.

During those years working with my parents, I became hooked on being an entrepreneur. Sooner or later, the urge to build my own company and create something uniquely special was going to become a reality. I wanted the opportunity to define my personal success — on my own terms.

I was 23 when I opened my first business in 1973. It was a hair salon. That's right, I went from cleaning and pressing clothes to cutting and styling hair. I worked hard and truly cherished every minute and experience. That salon was a success from day one. So much so, that two years later, I opened a second salon. Now, as the owner of two locations, I moved away from providing services and devoted all my efforts to leadership and growing my little company. Then something unexpected and very interesting happened. The results I was getting in my business came to the attention of a major product company. They asked me to share my success story as a speaker at their national business conference. I was 27 years old.

> **Neilism**
> Success is not a gift that can be bestowed upon you. It must be earned.

All it took was one keynote presentation, and I was hooked. My passion for business was forever bound to my passion for the teaching and coaching business.

Do I feel successful? You bet I do. I have a great company and an amazing team. We work hard, and we all feel the pride of helping other business owners and leaders work to discover their own success. There is a shared passion for our work that drives us all. Am I satisfied? Not even close. Success is like a foundation that just keeps getting stronger, so that it supports bigger ideas and a more focused vision.

> There is a shared passion for our work that drives us all. Am I satisfied? Not even close.

As I said at the beginning of this lesson, success is something deeply personal. For me, it's simply a measurement of how far I've come and how much this inquisitive 12-year-old kid has grown.

One thing is certain: The success that I feel today is something I've proudly earned, and the passion for the work I do has never been greater.

My success lessons

The road to success can get pretty bumpy, offering up some interesting life lessons along the way. Like me, you might encounter some failures that can throw you off course. All in all, the quest for success is a life journey of discovery. Take in every bit of it, and savor every morsel of progress. I hope these lessons make your own journey a little smoother.

- **Balance personal and business life.** If your life is all about business and being a workaholic, you're asking for trouble. Marriage and family must come first. There is a reason I've been happily married for over 38 years.
- **Success means taking risks.** Remember, I bought a printing company in 1991 and almost lost everything. I started Strategies in 1993 with a credit card and have never looked back.
- **Stay on the offensive.** If you want to rest on your laurels, sell your company. Business is about being innovative and aggressive.

- **Do what you do best.** The work you do should fuel your passions and capitalize on your natural strengths. Leave what you're not good at for those who do it best.
- **Be proud of your financials.** Pay attention to your balance sheet, profit-and-loss statement and statement of cash flows. If you're not proud of your financials, you're not paying attention to your business scorecard.
- **Know when to let go.** You can't do it all. Surround yourself with talented and passionate people who share your vision and values. Success will come, and it will be bigger than you ever envisioned.
- **Keep learning.** You can never learn enough about business and what makes it work. New ideas, thinking and strategies just keep coming, and you need to stay on top.
- **Find a way.** Never allow obstacles or problems to slow you down. Find solutions.
- **No compromise.** It's been my battle cry for years. I try to live it every day.

Lesson 3: Teamwork — Hard to get, easy to lose

Business leaders toss the word "teamwork" around like some boundless, renewable resource. Well, it's not. In fact, teamwork is a precious commodity revered by those who have achieved it and envied by those who want it. You can refer to employees as "team members," use scoreboards and huddle every day, but those exercises bring no guarantee that teamwork will follow.

Teamwork is an outcome. It is the culmination of a multitude of complex forces, systems and accountabilities that merge into one truly dynamic *state of being* called teamwork. *In this teamwork state of being, the energies of many individuals harmoniously synchronize to achieve the extraordinary.*

It's much like achieving a true meditative state. You must learn to quiet the mind until a oneness with the world is achieved. This meditative state is difficult enough for individuals to master. Consider the added complexity of groups of individuals, all possessing unique personalities, ambitions and job functions, coming together to achieve that state of being we call teamwork. Simply put, teamwork is more work than most leaders and employees realize.

By repositioning teamwork as a state of being, leaders gain a new appreciation for this much ballyhooed term. Suddenly, all claims of teamwork are put into question.

The test is simple. Is there a unified, shared vision in your company? If so, is it evident in the actions and performance of all employees in all departments? Is everyone pulling the company in the same direction?

Yes, even the best sports teams drop the ball and bungle plays every now and then. But those who possess that true teamwork state of being have the highest degree of execution. In business, their scorecards show high customer retention, fierce employee loyalty with low turnover and financial performance that make leaders proud.

In business, change is relentless. And change is the ever-present nemesis of teamwork.

Companies have fantastic stories of how everyone pulled together to overcome and achieve the impossible. In the heat of those quests, there existed a teamwork state of being. Such is the power of working together.

Given that teamwork is a state of being, it's easier to comprehend its fragility. In business, change is relentless. And change is the ever-present nemesis of teamwork. For change to occur, new systems and behaviors need to be learned. It's like a sports team learning new, more challenging plays. *Change exerts pressure on teamwork. It disrupts its state of being.*

Unforeseen changes, such as the loss of a key leader, team member or major customer, or a cash crisis forcing challenging cutbacks, can snap a business out of its teamwork state of being. A by-product of change, planned or not, is the toxic drama that can follow in its wake. Drama is a teamwork killer. Leaders who don't have their finger on the pulse of the business can quickly find teamwork deteriorating into chaos.

All teams have leaders, but few leaders do the work necessary to elevate individuals into a cohesive teamwork state. Inspiring, demanding, tenacious, compassionate, tough decision making and pure no compromise describe leaders who create high-achievement, teamwork environments.

What to do to prevent teamwork fizzle

Teamwork fizzle can happen in an instant. Follow these tried-and-true strategies to maintain team focus, energy and momentum:

+ **Teamwork is fueled by vision, mission and objectives.** Don't expect teamwork if the challenge is vague or undefined. A neat idea might get teamwork out of the gate, but it won't keep it going. Be specific.

+ **Communicate your vision, mission and objectives.** Too many leaders stop communicating and wonder why teamwork deteriorates. Lack of communication can signal that the mission is over.

+ **Keep score.** When the answer to "How are we doing?" is "Not good enough," you're inviting fizzle. Scoreboards show progress and opportunities for improvement.

+ **Celebrate progress and wins along the way.** Doing so fuels teamwork energy and maintains momentum. Achieving incremental milestones is like climbing a ladder; each step brings you closer to the top.

+ **Coach teams and individuals.** They will encounter those inevitable obstacles. That might require additional resources or mini-teams to brainstorm solutions. The key is getting back up to speed before fizzle sets in.

+ **Make tough decisions.** If you have to pull a weed or two from your team, do it. If coaching efforts fail, you must act to protect the integrity of the team.

+ **Teams love rewards.** There's nothing like that surprise lunch or bonus celebration to power up teamwork. Sometimes simpler is better. Learn what motivates your team.

+ **Make it fun.** Teamwork, games, winning and celebrating should have fun built in. Sure, there will be tough moments, but fun should be waiting when breakthroughs occur. Fun is contagious. Fun is empowering. Have fun.

Lesson 4: All forward progress begins with a sale

It always amazes me how such a simple word like "sales" can instantly manifest myriad emotional responses. For some, selling is a totally gut-wrenching task and they do whatever they can to avoid it at all cost.

Imagine actually having to approach or call strangers, invade their privacy and "sell" them something. What if they say no? What if they hang up? What if they're annoyed that I intruded into their personal space? For some reason, fear and anxiety block the most important question of all: What if they buy what I'm selling?

In contrast to the "I hate to sell" contingent are those who simply love — even live — to sell. For these naturally motivated super-salespeople, selling is viewed as everything from a competitive game to discovering and filling the needs of others. Selling is in their blood, and they couldn't imagine doing anything else.

Fact: All forward progress begins with a sale. Want to start a business? You'll need to sell your business plan to the bank or investors. Have a great idea that will save or make tons of money for the company you work for? You'll have to sell your idea. Participating in a planning meeting? You'll have to sell others on your opinion, sales plan, budget, project or point of view. Want to run for public office? You'll have to sell not only your platform and agenda, you'll have to sell people on you as a person with values and integrity. As kids, we sold our parents on getting us that new bike or letting us do our first solo with the family car.

Let's face it, everyone possesses the selling gene. And with the desire to learn, understand and refine your selling abilities, extraordinary results can be achieved. For example, more innovative ideas, concepts, plans and solutions can become reality with the added benefit of selling skills. Change initiatives that live or die based on employee buy-in will directly benefit, when those communicating the initiatives hone their selling skills. Think of all the great ideas, services, products and procedures that never see the light of day or go down in flames simply because you or someone in your company can't "sell" others on them.

Now we get to the real selling issues that make or break companies. I have a rather straightforward Neilism on selling responsibilities: "Everyone plays a sales role. No compromise."

Companies and organizations have a natural tendency to become highly compartmentalized. Those in administration, finance, personnel, marketing, customer service, production and shipping can unknowingly become afflicted with tunnel vision and leave the selling to the sales team. But teamwork and company growth mean that everyone is moving the company toward its goals and growth objectives.

> **Neilism**
> Everyone plays a sales role.
> No compromise.

Selling is the process of communication, discovery, listening and, finally, filling needs. Whether a sale is closed or not, every point of contact with your company is a selling opportunity. An error on an invoice, indifferent customer service or shipping the wrong product can send a valued customer running to your competitors. *Everyone sells.*

Celebrate the selling process through your company as a reminder that without selling, there can be no progress.

Never be held hostage by those who produce sales

It doesn't matter if you're a service business, retailer or manufacturer, you need people who can sell. But what happens when your super-sellers get out of control and hold your business hostage?

Business is all about building relationships with customers. Every salesperson worth his or her salt knows this. And when the bond with the customer is so closely tied to the salesperson, the business is setting itself up to be held hostage. Does this situation sound familiar? Leaders experience a real wake-up call when a top seller says, "I want more commission, or I'm leaving." *They know all too well how easily this person can take "her" customers to the competition.*

Notice that I said "her" customers. Since when does a company hand over ownership of a customer simply because a company representative took care of him or her? Well, it happens every day.

If building relationships is the key to business, then a company must design its business around creating customer relationships with the company — not just the individual who services them. The company should be keeping the database of customer preferences, not the salesperson.

This is one of the reasons I have never been a proponent of sales commissions. By design, it's an "I/me" pay system that encourages the "It's my customer" mentality. And that mentality will always do damage to an otherwise fine business culture. There are many ways to motivate people to sell without commission. Examine your pay system for sales. Design it to reward team performance for creating growth. It works.

> Examine your pay system for sales. Design it to reward team performance for creating growth. It works.

Finally, how about suggesting that salespeople give a round of applause to those "non-selling" people who, by their attention to detail, make the sales staff look great. That's no-compromise leadership in action.

Lesson 5: A business in balance is a measure of success

I was boarding a 20-seat commuter plane with six other passengers. We took our assigned seats, most of which were toward the front of the plane. Just before the captain started up the engines, he came into the cabin and asked a few of us to take seats toward the rear. "We need to balance out the plane," he explained.

Given the explanation, I was happy to move to an aft seat. In the process, I found it interesting how immune we frequent flyers on commercial jets have become to flight dynamics. I know I never give it a thought.

But on that tiny plane, I was reminded how performance and safety depend on the proper balance. That captain knew that had he not balanced the weight, he would have had to overcompensate on the controls to keep the plane flying straight and true — especially on takeoff and landing. As captain of your business, how often do you find yourself trying to overcompensate when things are out of balance? You know exactly what I'm talking about.

It's trying to lead when sales take a dive, because the sense of urgency has dissipated. It's when you take your eyes off the financial controls, and expenses get out of hand. It's when team morale and motivation turn into a toxic stew that contaminates a once-vibrant culture. *Simply put, when the symptoms indicating that a business is even slightly out of balance begin to appear, it's imperative for the leader to engage and restore balance.*

But before you can do that, you must look at your own life. Do you have a sense of balance in your life? Are you calm? Happy? Have a clear sense of priorities? You need to have your personal house in order. If not, your staff will sense a "do as I say, not as I do" attitude, and that will affect your business culture.

Everyone has an interpretation of what a great culture is. A balanced business has a culture that fuels a sense of energy and momentum. The different departments synchronize, with everyone coming together for a common purpose.

So what does balance look like in business? That's an interesting question, as balance can't be seen. However, you can experience it and measure it. Consider these points:

- **It's capable, confident and aggressive:** The staff of a balanced business enjoys pushing the envelope. They do so because when there's a state of balance, the natural tendency is to compete and drive forward. An unbalanced business gets bogged down in its own internal issues.

- **The pace is fast and steady:** If you exercise regularly and take care of your body, you know what balance feels like: You feel energized and have the endurance to go the distance — whatever goal you've set for yourself. A business that can consistently function at a fast and steady pace is balanced. An unbalanced business always seems to be running out of gas and having engine problems.

- **Execution at its best:** Balance is like a football team that makes it to the Super Bowl. Every player and every coach is there to work together and win. A balanced business is disciplined, yet flexible enough to be self-correcting when things go awry.

+ **The results are measurable:** When a business is in balance, it's evident in the numbers, from sales and profits to customer and employee retention.

If you want your business to fly high and fast, it's your job to get and keep it in balance. Flying any other way is dangerous.

Business balance basics

If you want to achieve a state of balance for your company, you'll have to commit to what is essentially a no-compromise health and fitness program for your business. And just like any health and fitness program, some of this is common sense. It's going to take discipline. So, just commit and begin.

+ **Know your purpose:** Why does your business exist? People work for many more reasons than money. The most empowering reason is for a high and worthy sense of purpose. A bricklayer who thinks he's just laying bricks is a lot different from a bricklayer whose purpose is to build a cathedral. Purpose pulls everything and everyone into balance. Purpose is the prime objective.

+ **Be persistent:** You exercise for life. You get up every day and work out. It's no different in business. Without persistence, your purpose will elude you. Just like people who jump from diet to diet, losing and gaining the same 10 pounds, it's easy for leaders to jump from business fad to business fad. Funny, all those diets work; it's the persistence that's missing. Persistence is the energy of purpose.

+ **Stretch to grow:** Complacency quietly and methodically destroys balance. Like exercise, a business must stretch to grow. Keep stretching for incremental growth. Each year, strive for one or two big business gains. Status quo is an invitation for complacency. Stretch.

+ **Measure it, and share it:** Every goal has a starting point, which means that everything in between can and must be measured and communicated daily, weekly and monthly to everyone. A business stays in balance by charting its progress.
+ **Celebrate:** All wins, large and small, must be celebrated in some fashion. Why do the all the work if there's no opportunity to celebrate and be rewarded? Celebrate to reinforce and maintain balance.

Lesson 6: Finding the "it" factor

The most coveted quest in business is to reach and surpass the tipping point that separates the ordinary from the extraordinary. The further you reside on the side of extraordinary, the brighter your "it" — what makes your business special — will shine, setting you apart from the competition.

Achieving your "it" signifies the successful pursuit of something special. Achieving "it" pushes that entrepreneurial button that ignites passion, innovation and determination. "It" is cool and exciting. "It" is financially and emotionally rewarding. *But beware: Your "it" can evaporate in a heartbeat.*

When we examine the journey to achieving "it," the first thing we see is a simple sign with the words "Pass no farther if you're not disciplined and willing to take risks." You can't achieve success without both.

You can have the greatest product or service, yet still never achieve your "it" if you can't lead, manage, control and deliver "it" with superb execution. And if you're not willing to take risks, your great product or service might never move beyond concept; if it does, it won't go far.

> And if you're not willing to take risks, your great product or service may never move beyond concept; if it does, it won't go far.

Because each "it" is extraordinary and unlike any other, "it" only occurs in certain situations. In their book, *Blue Ocean Strategy*, W. Chan Kim and Renée Mauborgne contend that "it" can only be achieved in a blue ocean, a place of uncontested market space where the competition is irrelevant. This is a space where demand is created rather than fought over. (To order *Blue Ocean Strategy*, go to www.strategies.com.)

Starbucks, Apple, FedEx and Cirque du Soleil are examples of companies that created their own blue oceans. By the way, Kim and Mauborgne consider a "red ocean" to be where ordinary companies, with similar products and services, fight over the same customers. Red oceans are crowded. Blue oceans are not. Which ocean are you in?

The disciplines of "it"

Though you might start with a great idea, for your "it" to enter the blue ocean, you must do the work. If you don't, then you shouldn't complain that you're swimming in an overcrowded, shark-infested red ocean. Here are some disciplines involved in achieving "it."

No-compromise leadership: You can't demand, command, dictate or fake your way to "it." "It" cannot exist in an environment of compromising leadership behavior. Making the tough decisions, integrity, trust and instilling a "we are the best" belief throughout the company is the work of the leader. "It" flourishes in cultures that are compromise-free.

Leaders push, inspire and nurture the creation and continued vitality and evolution of the company's "it." Your precious "it" must be protected at all cost.

Do what others dare not: It's so easy to get stuck in the same thinking and behavior as your competition. Even the time-honored practice of benchmarking against others in your industry is, by design, a game of outplaying your competitors, while you're all swimming around in the same red ocean.

You must do what others dare not. As explained in *Blue Ocean Strategy*, Cirque du Soleil reinvented the circus. They eliminated the animal acts (and therefore the huge expense of transporting, feeding and caring), the three rings and costly star performers. Cirque du Soleil combines the fun and thrill of the circus with the intellectual sophistication and artistic richness of the theatre. Cirque du Soleil kept the clowns, the tent and the acrobats, but changed the look and feel.

The tent, more than any other feature, makes a circus special. By glamorizing the tent — giving it a grand external finish and comfortable seating — Cirque du Soleil put a unique spin on a familiar form of entertainment.

Redefine price and value: Because you are redefining your offerings, the price and value of your "it" is no longer relevant to that of the competition. Rather than going after the family market, Cirque du Soleil created a new market among adults seeking more intellectually unique entertainment — adults who are willing to pay for the Cirque du Soleil experience.

This is not to say that the "it" always commands a higher price; it simply means that your business stands out from the crowd. A salesperson can demonstrate this in the way he or she caters to the needs of customers. Starbucks reinvented the coffee experience. Rendezvous Ribs in Memphis, Tennessee, built an empire not only around its ribs, but also around its service and location down an alley.

Apple did it with the iPod and again with the iPhone. FedEx did it with overnight delivery. Aveda did it with all-natural products. Seattle's Pike Place Fish Market did it with entertaining antics to attract attention.

> "It" can be as basic as delivering on the promise to be the very best you can be.

Discover your "it." Find your own piece of uncontested market space. "It" can be as simple as adding value to what you already do. "It" can be as basic as delivering on the promise to be the very best you can be.

Lesson 7: Money — Are you "managing" to make it or lose it?

Money has to be the most mysterious, alluring and necessary pain in the butt for all humankind. You spend your life in pursuit of it, because without it, the lights won't turn on, the phone won't work, you can't pay the mortgage, you can't put gas in your car, and, most importantly, you can't put food on the table. Of course, that's for those of us lucky enough to live in a place where those things are a given.

Want to live in a nice house, drive a cool car and travel to exciting and exotic places? Gotta make money. Want to retire in comfort and style? Gotta manage your money!

Money in business is where the action gets interesting. A business exists to make money. That requires making sales. Once you have the money, what are you going to do with it?

To start, you owe product and material costs for those sales you just made, or labor cost for those of us who sell services by the hour. You have payroll and payroll taxes to pay, not to mention employee benefits. You have all those operating expenses, such as rent, advertising, insurance and utilities, to pay.

Hey, remember those discounts you gave to close those sales? Bet you wish you thought those deals through. As those sales drop through your profit-and-loss statement like a side of beef through a river of piranhas, it's time for a heart-thumping drum roll to see what money survived to become net profit. *Woo hoo! Now you see some profit.* A Neilism: "Profit is not cash; profit is just a measurement."

Leading, inspiring and managing employees, and creating super-happy customers — that's where the action is in business. But it can all come crashing down if you run out of cash. No cash, and everything stops; everyone can go home to lick their wounds.

I take you through this little tirade to help you view the complexity of managing and making money in business. Large or small doesn't matter. You've seen countless examples of little guys going out of business just as often as the big guys. And they go out of business because they run out of money.

Making money is an outcome. It is the end result of a collection of disciplines. Please allow the word discipline to resonate a bit. If you are dis-ciplined about money, your thinking will be embedded into your company culture. If you're an uncontrolled spender, don't expect those you lead to practice otherwise. In fact, they don't stand a chance to be fiscally accountable, because it will be you who violates every budget and spending rule. Making money in business begins with a leader who is disciplined about money.

Neilism
Profit is not cash; profit is just a measurement.

Being disciplined means determining how much money you want to make, and using all of your resources, energies, systems, drivers and accountabilities to achieve that financial outcome. If you are determined to achieve that money goal, you must create and adhere to your plan until it is reached. That's how profitable companies do it. There is no magic, only discipline and determination.

In the daily battle to grow a business, it's common for leaders to detach themselves from the financial reality of what's really happening to their money. It's identical to how you would feel flying in a plane and discovering that the pilot had no idea where the plane was headed. It's that scary. You make money by design, not by chance.

> **Making money in business begins with a leader who is disciplined about money.**

If the "cost piranhas" are chomping away at your money, only you can stop them.

Lesson 8: Navigating through conflict

Are you a leader who gets anxious working in or around conflict? If so, is the thought of resolving that conflict unsettling enough that you put it off as long as possible? Those are two very interesting questions. If you don't like conflict, it makes sense to engage in the resolution of it. But if engaging in the resolution of the conflict is so unsettling that you disengage, the conflict will continue. It's a classic chicken-and-egg scenario.

In contrast, there are the mighty leaders who bravely enter the conflict like invincible knights in shining armor. They slay the culprits' hidden agendas and bludgeon the issues until the conflicting parties surrender. But is the conflict resolved or just hiding, waiting to conflict another day?

Be it a wimpy Homer Simpson or a confronting General George Patton, there isn't one ideal personality or leadership style capable of banishing conflict from the workplace. Conflict resolution requires a more specialized set of leadership skills.

Conflict is a natural occurrence. Want to avoid conflict entirely? Live in a protective bubble! As long as you're content being isolated and cut off from all human contact, it could work for you. But, you might experience the conflict of being trapped.

Simply put, conflict is part of life. There will always be lightning strikes that transform tranquil forests into blazing infernos of conflict. It's going to occur in your life, in the workplace and in the world around you.

Change brings conflict. Change stirs the pot of emotions. Conflict is the natural chaos that exists between the status quo and the desired outcome. It's the temporary disruption in what has become unacceptable normalcy, as behaviors, thinking, processes and environments evolve into the new desired state of normalcy. Companies, systems, cultures and behaviors must change in order to grow. Conflict, be it a ripple or a tidal wave, is a companion of change.

Leaders lead through conflict. If leading your team or company to dominate your market or industry doesn't get your adrenaline flowing, whatever compelled you to become a leader? It's impossible to lead without encountering adversity or setbacks.

Striving to achieve a vision, or even just to hit this month's sales or production goal, is the essence of leadership. *If you think about it, business is much like war: full of conflict.* You fight competitors for control of territories or markets. You plot strategies. You even have divisions and "general" managers. You lead your company through adversity to victory. That's no-compromise leadership. That's business.

The tough stuff defines you. To be a leader is to accept responsibility for growing and protecting the company, its people and its customers — to create a sustainable and enduring enterprise. You cannot lead without being accountable to the tough stuff. That means dealing with conflict.

You will cut costs and take away jobs. You meet with your biggest customer to apologize for a mistake. You will discipline, or even fire, a subordinate whom you consider a friend. You enter the fray of conflict between clashing personalities, differing opinions and the dreaded change-resisters. It's what you do as a leader. How well you do the tough stuff will define your effectiveness and success as a leader. No compromise.

Are you creating conflict?

As a leader, I must confess that I sometimes create conflict in my own company. However, there is conflict that is good and conflict that is bad.

Good conflict:

+ The very best conflict a leader can create is conflict centered on a worthy, really big goal. Taking your company to that next level means shaking things up and getting the company's collective creative juices flowing. This is conflict focused on positive change. Differing opinions and ideas might conflict, but what emerges from resolution is a unified and powerful force.

+ So, something didn't go right, and it needs to get fixed fast. The conflict of finger-pointing and blame gets you nowhere, but containing and focusing the conflict on a solution does. Leaders shine when they shift the energy of conflict to finding and executing the solution.

Bad conflict:

+ Left unchecked, conflict between individuals spreads toxic waste all over everyone. Dialogue can lead to resolution. It's the leader's role to be the catalyst for that dialogue, before the situation escalates. Leaders cannot ignore interpersonal conflict.

+ Leaders who get caught up in or create internal drama are self-destructive and the worst igniters of conflict.

> **You cannot lead without being accountable to the tough stuff. That means dealing with conflict.**

+ Double standards create conflict and destroy trust and loyalty.

+ Leaders must live, breathe and model the behavior and culture of the company. Leaders who break their own rules fuel conflict.

+ Breaking promises is the most serious way to breach trust. Trust is everything.

+ Leaders who do not follow through on the projects that they initiate are major sources of conflict in their companies.

+ And the number-one way leaders create bad conflict is through poor communication.

Lesson 9: Everyone's a negotiator in your company

There's an old saying that nothing happens until something gets sold. That's not completely accurate. In fact, it only addresses that euphoric moment when someone utters the words, "I'll take it." Ta da! You made a sale! But what about all the delicate steps that preceded that sale? The sale is simply the outcome. The negotiation leading up to the sale is what really counts. That's where all the emotion and magic happen.

"Hey, I'm not even in sales, so why should I bother to read this?" The answer is simple. What happens when the customer says, "I'd like to return this?" There goes the sale, or maybe not with a little more negotiation. What if a customer is having a problem with your product or service, or believes there is an error on the invoice? *The customer is seeking a satisfactory resolution.*

The company wants a satisfied customer who will buy again. The process between the problem and the solution is all about negotiation. Blow the negotiation, and the customer might be lost forever.

"All right, this is all about keeping the customer happy, but I don't deal directly with the customer. What does this negotiation stuff have to do with my job?" Oh, this one's easy. Have you ever asked your boss for a raise? Remember how you rehearsed your lines, but the words came out like mush when the big moment arrived? You guessed it; you were in the thick of a negotiation.

"Of course, I want a better paycheck, but I still don't see how this negotiation stuff plays into my daily work life. Why should I invest the time to be a better negotiator?" Most people naturally equate negotiation with selling and closing a deal, or with "getting" something. But negotiation is really about interactions between people for the purpose of achieving a specific outcome. A Neilism: "There is nothing to negotiate until a need, problem or conflict is put on the table."

How many needs, problems or conflicts did you encounter today? Consider how each of those situations required you to influence others to achieve an agreed-upon outcome? It's likely that not everyone got exactly what he or she wanted, but agreement was reached. You talked about things. You influenced the thinking of others. You closed the deal. That's negotiation. Time to break out the champagne!

But before you sip that bubbly, remember that this win assumes that you have polished negotiation skills and that you're comfortable in your role as negotiator. If not, the outcomes may be unpleasant, even costly. For example, you are put in charge of an important new project that requires you to create an implementation plan. This is a big career opportunity for you. Finally, after weeks of work and lots of all-nighters, it's time to present what you believe is a breakthrough plan. Your mission is to influence the powers that be that your plan is the way to go. You start out strong, but your confidence begins to wane, as elements of your plan are challenged. In the end, your plan gets shot down, along with an opportunity for advancement. Your plan was the best; you just lacked the negotiating skills to "sell" it.

"I thought negotiating was for the sales guys and big decision makers. Now I realize everyone in business is a negotiator." Congratulations. You've got it. Begin polishing your negotiation skills by seeking out situations that call on you to create win/win situations. This is not negotiable.

> The process between the problem and the solution is all about negotiation.

Negotiating all day long

There is something dynamic about the word "negotiation." It heightens your senses and gets your juices flowing, much like getting ready for the big game. But negotiation isn't the exclusive domain of the sales department or executive offices. In business, negotiations are taking place throughout the company all day long. So much so, you may even be quite a negotiator yourself. Consider these often-overlooked negotiating situations:

+ **Placing orders:** You're going to place a bigger-than-usual product order. You ask the vendor if there is a price break for a quantity order. You negotiate back and forth to arrive at an attractive price — as long as the order is paid for net 10. Everyone wins.
+ **The furious customer:** You answer the phone and find yourself on the receiving end of a customer tirade. You listen and ask

questions, so you can understand the problem. You offer a solution; it doesn't fly. You modify your solution; the customer settles down. You controlled the situation, agreed on a solution and retained a valuable customer.

+ **Performance problems:** Your department is way off target.

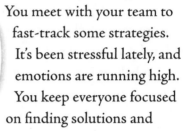

Neilism
There is nothing to negotiate until a need, problem or conflict is put on the table.

You meet with your team to fast-track some strategies. It's been stressful lately, and emotions are running high. You keep everyone focused on finding solutions and away from the finger-pointing. The ideas start to flow, and robust debate whittles it down to one strategy that everyone agrees to support. You are a master negotiator.

+ **Work schedules:** An employee asks for a significant change in her work schedule. Being already short-handed, you know you can't agree to the request. You and the employee explore some options and discover that a little flexibility on both sides produces an acceptable schedule. It's not exactly what the employee wanted, but it works.

In a no-compromise culture, it's just another day of negotiating.

Lesson 10: Protect the environment — No compromise

The debate is over. Global climate changes have grabbed the attention of almost every human being on planet Earth. Smog-filled air, polluted rivers, contaminated soil and landfills at capacity send an undeniable message that we all must do our part to protect and save our environment.

Consider this thought from author Upton Sinclair: "It is difficult to get a man to understand something when his job depends on not understanding it." This quote illustrates the conflict between doing what's right for business and being responsible for the environment. Sure, an individual might be environmentally responsible at home. But at work, that same individual might create harmful products, waste and pollutants, and inefficiently use energy and resources. When it comes to business, environmental account-ability begins with a no-compromise leader.

I believe that individuals can do their part to help save the environment. And they should. But real progress occurs when groups of individuals with shared values join together for a vital cause.

When business leaders talk about culture, teamwork, systems and values, it's usually directed at business goals, performance, employees, customers and community responsibility. But that one word — values — is what defines and binds individuals and companies.

What does it reveal about a company's values when it says, "We honor and respect our employees and customers," but the product packaging is more waste than product? Values define what and who you are. The same goes for a company. There's no in-between: You either live your values or you don't. No compromise.

If you personally care about the environment, are you bringing that same level of caring and commitment to your company and those you lead? It's a case of actions speaking louder than words. For instance, if you throw an empty bottle in the trash rather than in the recycle bin, expect others to do the same.

You care, or you don't. Worthy causes abound to which you can donate time and money. But the environment is certainly one of the worthiest of causes. And it's the one cause that requires the leadership and commit-ment of a values-based company to truly make a difference. Saving energy, reducing waste, recycling and avoiding the use of contaminants is a cause you can rally your troops behind. But it takes work. It might even increase costs, although it may save them in certain areas, as well.

To be an environmentally responsible company is no longer optional. Need more convincing? Think about the melting glaciers every time you turn on a light.

If you are not engaged already, this is your opportunity to harness the resolve of your company to do what's right. This is putting your company's values at the forefront of everything you do. Such a commitment will enrich and protect lives.

Earth first

Make no mistake, a company's values and behaviors change lives — not just those of employees, but their families, vendors, customers and community. Take some first steps, and stand out from the crowd.

+ **Be a learning organization.** Companies have the power to instill positive life behaviors by the way they conduct business. Given that, a company that has protecting the environment as a core value will instill that value in others.

+ **Think bigger than your company.** It's easy to get bogged down in chasing goals and deadlines. Focusing on doing what's right for the environment creates a worthy non-business goal that touches and engages everyone. Pride

When it comes to business, environmental accountability begins with a no-compromise leader.

and sense of purpose are the perfect companions to chasing goals and meeting deadlines. And if that trims expenses, all the better.

+ **Make "green" vividly visible.** Worthy causes should stand out. If a visitor to your company can't observe and experience your environmental behaviors, you're not doing enough. If you're serious, it's obvious.

+ **Choose with whom to do business.** Your values should guide your business decisions. Will you buy products, materials or services from companies that are environmentally responsible, or those that are not? Living your values makes the choice simple — even if it costs more.

+ **Keep searching for new ways.** A company commitment to the environment must be driven by one simple question: What else can we do? Once you begin, the ideas will flow, not just from leaders, but from everyone in the company. Collect, evaluate and implement a couple of new ideas at least once a quarter.

+ **Be bold.** There are going to be some ideas that will challenge the resolve of the company. Let your values dictate the decision.

Lesson 11: Will your company live on without you?

If you're like most entrepreneurs, succession planning is the last thing on your mind. You're busy dealing with sales, employee challenges, making sure the bills are paid and that screw-up that has your best customer in an uproar.

Let's face it, when things go right, you love being a business owner and a leader. But, when things go wrong, the entrepreneurial knee-jerk reaction is, "I don't need this stuff — when I get through this, I'll sell the business." Ah, if only life were that simple.

As a business evolves beyond the exhilarating start-up phase and matures, it's natural for business owners to stay in control and lead the company they built. Heck, isn't that living the entrepreneurial dream?

However, there are two fundamental flaws in this thinking. First, when the leader and the business become indistinguishable from one another, the viability and value of the business are compromised. The business can die, because of the owner's actions and/or its acquisition appeal and value are diminished because the owner is the business.

The second flaw is a simple fact that you might forget: The lifespan of a business can far exceed the working life of the owner.

Every four years, the citizens of the United States vote for a candidate to be president and lead the country. This planned leadership succession has worked for more than 200 years. We've had some great presidents and some clunkers, but the system works.

For a business to thrive and endure beyond its current leader, it too must have a succession plan in place. One basic reason to do so is because the livelihoods and security of employees and their families must be protected. In addition to that, after all the work of building a successful company, the last thing owners want to see is their companies in distress, because they are no longer in charge.

Here are some reasons to create a succession plan:

+ **Sudden death of the owner:** Instantly, the company leader is gone. It's like dying without leaving a will that communicates your last wishes and instructions.

- **Illness and health issues:** Preparing a succession plan under the pressure of the pending long-term or permanent absence of the leader hinders the thorough evaluation of options and invites conflicts.
- **Assuming a family member is the right one to take over:** Your successor should be the best person to lead the company. Family and blood relations hold no guarantee of effective leadership. Moreover, they might not even want your job. Better to plan than be surprised.
- **The Peter Principle:** Congratulations! You grew your company to the limits of your leadership capabilities. Now, it's time for someone with the right leadership skills to take over before the company starts springing leaks.
- **Falling out of love with your job:** Hey, it happens. And why should your company suffer because of it? Get over it. Your succession plan will allow you to redefine your role and allow new leadership to continue to grow the business. You still own the company, but now you're having fun again.
- **Time to retire:** Retirement doesn't translate into "sell the company." Why sell the business if it's successful and continuing to create wealth for you?
- **Preparation for a future sale:** A succession plan creates a personal exit strategy from your company. Even if selling is a distant thought, it begins and defines the process that will allow new leaders or a new owner to take over the company in a smooth and orderly fashion. The search for a buyer willing to pay a premium for your company can be enhanced when a succession plan is already in play.

The lifespan of a business can far exceed the working life of the owner.

I was recently a guest on a local television show for entrepreneurs. The host ends every show with this question: "What is your definition of an entrepreneur?"

Here's my response: *"An entrepreneur is someone with the vision, the determination and the willingness to take risks to create a business, have fun growing it into something spectacular, and, when they're ready to do so, sell it for an amazing profit."*

It's not about you, it's about the business you create. When the line that separates you from your business becomes indistinguishable, it's unlikely that you will find value in creating a succession plan. Simply put, if this describes your situation, you are your business. It doesn't work without you. You will hold on to control until you or something else breaks. Then it's too late. Get over yourself. This is not about you, it's about the enduring success of your business. The no-compromise leader gets this.

Celebrate, honor, respect and protect what you have worked so hard to build. Create your succession plan to give your business life after you. You create a business plan to start a company. You create a succession plan to ensure its future. Both are non-negotiables. No compromise.

Lesson 12: You, your business and the path to greatness

There is a huge difference between having the desire for success and actually achieving your definition of it. Desire is a longing for something; success is an outcome.

Greatness is something else entirely. Success, based on your interpretation, is earned, while greatness is bestowed. Greatness is how your peers and the world around you define your success and that of your company.

For a company to enter the coveted realm of greatness, its values, thinking and actions must synchronize to create an unyielding gravitational pull that draws it through levels of success to greatness. The only thing that can disrupt this gravitational pull is a compromise in the company's values, thinking and/or actions.

Let's explore what this gravitational pull looks like in a successful company versus a great no-compromise company. *Yes, there is a huge gap between success and greatness.*

A successful company does many things right. It has a leader (or leaders) capable of inspiring performance and consistency. It demonstrates steady sales, financial discipline and profitability. It has functional levels of authority. It delivers on its brand promise, giving it impressive customer loyalty.

Employees have opportunities for growth, giving the company a reputation as an attractive place to work. The company is regarded by its peers as a worthy competitor in its marketplace or industry.

A company that lives in the greatness realm certainly does all of the above, but there are distinct differences. More than any other single factor, great companies are both values- and purpose-driven. This instills the highest degree of trust throughout the company, because intentions are clear. Values, purpose and trust create a rock-solid foundation to support a dynamic and empowering culture. The company culture is transparent — no hidden agendas exist.

Even in the most competitive of industries and marketplaces, a great company stands out, not only as a brand leader but in the manner in which it conducts business internally with its employees and externally with its customers. It innovates faster than the competition. It does things so differently and consistently well that it wows its customers and leaves the competition asking, "How do they do that?"

Neilism
In a great company, average anything stands out like a flashing warning light.

Another mark of a great company is its ability to adapt, respond and change as the world it functions in evolves. Call it optimal leadership, innovation or a superbly accurate ability to predict the future, but great companies always seem to already be where the competition wants to be. Again, competitors ask, "How do they do that?"

A company can be successful, even though its leadership is a bit inconsistent, some of its systems are weak, follow-through is sometimes spotty and performance is average. It will work through challenges and find a way to grow and prosper. But a successful company will never rise to greatness as long as it continues to ignore or tolerate its propensity to be average.

A Neilism: "In a great company, average anything stands out like a flashing warning light." In fact, average anything barely stands a chance of gaining a foothold. Why is that? A great company's values, beliefs and standards simply won't allow it. Average anything is quickly identified and cut out. It's no different from the values, beliefs and commitment of a world-class athlete to do everything it takes to win, including relentless training, to do it better than anyone else.

Successful companies come and go; great companies have the capacity to endure. But to endure, great companies can never falter, even for a moment. **Compromise of values, beliefs or trust is the beginning of a fall from greatness unless resolutely and completely restored.** Yes, many great companies will fall from greatness and remain successful, but the magic will be gone and is unlikely to return. For greatness to endure, no-compromise leadership is not optional. It is an ongoing process. The leader of a great company must continually review the practices of the company. Companies that coast along will not achieve greatness.

In his book *Small Giants: Companies that Chose to be Great Rather than Big*, Bo Burlingham profiled

> More than any other single factor, great companies are both values- and purpose-driven.

10 diverse companies, from a document storage and retrieval company to a delicatessen. Burlingham sought out successful companies that had the opportunity to go big but chose greatness instead. They resisted the temptation to expand beyond what the owners felt was right for their companies. Simply put, they chose to nourish and protect their greatness.

The path to greatness begins by answering one question: *How good do you want to be?* If your answer was to be the best, you chose a road less traveled, a road that will test your determination to create something worthy of admiration. Only a few go the distance; as a no-compromise leader, you can be one of them. Small giant or big giant, it doesn't matter. Go for greatness. Go *no compromise.*

Those 12 lessons demonstrate the varied applications of no-compromise leadership thinking and behavior in daily life. Discuss and role play them at training meetings during your culture shift to no compromise. Refer to and use them as you make your personal shift and incorporate no compromise into your company culture.

CHAPTER **10** LIVING NO-COMPROMISE LEADERSHIP

You've come a long way in your no-compromise leadership training. Now it's time to begin living no-compromise leadership.

No-compromise leadership = consistency across all four business outcomes. It's such a simple equation. Yet, within its simplicity is a profound message to all who lead, or seek to lead others. The word that speaks to me is *consistency*. Consistency is perhaps the most challenging aspect of no-compromise leadership to comprehend and live. That's because how you lead is influenced by your collective abilities, beliefs, behavior styles, perceptions and life experiences.

How long your voyage to no-compromise leadership will take depends on current behavior patterns. Some people are natural achievers, while others are procrastinators. Yet, there are those who obsess over every minor detail in their quest for perfection. In leadership positions, they can bog things down by micro-managing everything. At

> **For a company's performance and culture to be consistent, its leader must be a model of consistency.**

the other end of the spectrum are those who hate the details and do all they can to avoid them. In leadership positions, they can wreak havoc by communicating in such broad brush stokes that the outcomes they desire are vague and open to broad interpretation, if those outcomes can be achieved at all. For a company's performance and culture to be consistent, its leader must be a model of consistency. That is non-negotiable. *It is your commitment and ability to be consistent that defines the no-compromise leader.*

No-compromise thinking is like an internal compass that guides your leadership behavior in the right direction. No matter which direction you face, it points toward leadership consistency.

When you connect *consistency* **to The Four Business Outcomes, the result is a leadership mission of the highest order.** Consider this equation as the first line of your job description. Now, take it a step farther and consider it the first line of any job description in your company. What would the performance of your company look like if everyone were held accountable for creating and maintaining consistency across The Four Business Outcomes? *Needless to say, the performance would be nothing short of world class.*

So what does living no-compromise leadership look and feel like? I would have to say it's a sum total of all no-compromise moments, choices, actions, behaviors, communications and decisions. Given that, how does a person seeking to practice no-compromise leadership behave? No-compromise leadership is more than just a philosophy or cool business battle cry. It's stepping outside your comfort zone, looking within for possible motivators and blind spots, and analyzing why a certain decision, course of action or behavior is chosen. Consider something as simple as how you conduct your day-to-day time management. What you intend to do versus what you actually get done encompasses a host of no-compromise moments and chosen behaviors, ranging from high achievement to total procrastination.

> No-compromise leadership is more than just a philosophy or cool business battle cry.

Consider the following situations

A manager is in her office working on a project with a deadline that impacts the entire department. A team member enters with a pressing issue he wants to discuss. How does this manager determine the right no-compromise leadership choice in this situation? How does this manager process the situation to make the best no-compromise decision? Is it a compromise if she stops working on that critical project to address another seemingly pressing issue? Is it a compromise to turn the team member away? The no-compromise leadership way would be to say, "I want to give my undivided attention to your issue. Can we meet at 8:00 am tomorrow morning?"

A sales manager learns that his top salesperson has been fudging her daily activity reports while still growing sales. It's the 26th of the month and the department needs to hit goal. A serious bonus payout is on the line for meeting sales and performance standards. What would the no-compromise leader do in this situation? A decision to compromise and accept the fudged numbers opens up serious issues of integrity and trust. The consequences of upper management discovering the fudging was identified but not addressed. The no-compromise decision to expose the fudged reports is the right decision — even if consequences are unpleasant.

> **A decision to compromise and accept the fudged numbers opens up serious issues of integrity and trust.**

A high school principal witnesses a star football player skipping school the day before the big game. Knowing that any disciplinary action would have tremendous impact on the team, the school and the popularity of this leader, what would the no-compromise leader do? He must do as Coach Carter did at Richmond High School when his basketball players failed to uphold their signed contracts to attend class and maintain grades. Carter banned all basketball activities. The no-compromise principal must take disciplinary action, even if it means losing the big game.

A doctor makes a decision to write a prescription for a patient influenced heavily by the kickback from the drug company — not the needs of the patient. Was the doctor following his internal no-compromise compass? Clearly not. The doctor had the opportunity to make the right choice, but decision to compromise was made instead. If this doctor is the leader of the medical practice, his decision to compromise for a monetary kickback set a new acceptable behavior pattern for all he leads to follow. He contaminated the culture of his medical practice.

A waitress in a restaurant that pools tips decides to pocket a $10 bill from a customer because the customer was very demanding and difficult. The waitress felt "entitled" to take the money, but her entitlement thinking guided her into making a decision that compromised one of the core teamwork policies of the restaurant. Her chosen behavior shifted from "we, us, the team, the company," to, "I/me." The decision took no more than a nanosecond to make, but the contamination done to the team culture created a breech of trust that will linger for a very long time.

The antonym of consistency is inconsistency. From a leadership standpoint, the quest for either begins with a choice. If you made it this far in the book, you are clearly intrigued by the philosophy of no-compromise leadership. However, to incorporate what you've learned in this book into your daily leadership life, you will have to make a choice between no compromise and compromise — between striving for consistency or allowing and accepting inconsistency.

A higher calling

Being accountable to yourself means living your life according to your personal values. It's that self-discipline to listen and really hear that little voice inside you that always seems to speak the truth. To become a no-compromise leader, you must connect with and govern your actions in accordance with your values. Yes, you can and will slip, fall and experience setbacks, but no compromise means that you will stand up again and continue on your voyage. You will learn and regard every slip and setback as a lesson and a reminder that compromise is an easy behavior to allow back into your life. For an alcoholic, it's the absolute understanding that taking just one harmless drink will most certainly lead to another and another. It's about the choices we make in our lives. Being a no-compromise leader is a choice to follow a specific path of disciplined leadership behavior. It is truly a higher leadership calling.

It's a mode of thinking and an internal operating system that will lead you on the path to achieving your full potential.

In my own company, I can see and feel the power of no-compromise leadership and the no-compromise culture it created at Strategies. What's more important, every team member at Strategies can see and feel it. And yes, we can all measure the performance of our no-compromise culture in our financials and client retention rates.

> **I kept my shields down and allowed myself to create an internal balance sheet on what I liked and what I didn't.**

When I began writing this book three years ago, I was very comfortable with the topic of no-compromise leadership. For years, I taught it in seminars and keynote presentations. I coached my clients on it. I always considered myself a no-compromise leader, but immersing myself in writing a book on this topic touched me in a deeply profound way.

I couldn't write this book without looking inward at who and what I am as a person and a leader. I discovered behaviors that bothered me. I began to focus on and change them. I kept my shields down and allowed myself to create an internal balance sheet on what I liked and what I didn't. I began to change. I'm not talking Jekyll and Hyde change. I'm talking about changing my personal accountability and consistency in my actions and behaviors to myself and to those I lead. Simply put, I raised my personal no-compromise leadership bar to the highest rung. I knew it was always set fairly high, but writing this book made me realize that I was compromising by not setting it at the highest level. No, it wasn't a walk in the park. I'll explain why in the next chapter.

That simple decision to set the bar at the highest rung opened my mind to consider new opportunities for my company and myself. Honestly, as I continued to write this book, I could feel a new excitement for my company and my professional career. New ideas began to flow. I let go of those last few controls that I felt I needed to hold on to in order for Strategies to stay a vibrant and growing company. As founder and CEO,

I'm now free to focus on promoting this book, as well as other new projects that are exciting and add value to my company. Yes, I'm still in a leadership role, but it's more focused on pointing the company in the right direction, maintaining its sense of urgency and doing the work that I love.

I took a giant step toward reaching my full potential by allowing myself to commit fully to no-compromise leadership thinking in a way I couldn't do before writing this book. In the process, my company took a giant step toward reaching its full potential. Our four business outcomes are in balance and our future is predictable. We're positioned for quantum leap growth in a way we never were before. You can do the same for the company you lead. *Everything you need to change your thinking is in this book.*

A bookmark in time

You cannot change the past. What's done is done. Consider this a bookmark in your life as a leader. You can write your future as a no-compromise leader, because all the pages are blank. You can raise your no-compromise leadership bar high enough to make you stretch and grow. (Remember, small wins add up to big wins.) Then raise it some more. Learn and grow from the compromises that will creep into your leadership behaviors. Consider these lessons growing pains and move on with new resolve. The no-compromise leader within you will begin to emerge. You'll know it and feel it. Those around you will know it and feel it. In the process, your no-compromise culture will become focused and resilient. Balance will come to your four business outcomes wheel. It's all there if you chose to take the no-compromise path of leadership.

The only question that remains is when you will make the decision to become a no-compromise leader? To complete this book and tuck it away on a shelf with no decision for or against is, in my opinion, a compromise.

CHAPTER **11** MY JOURNEY TO NO-COMPROMISE LEADERSHIP

You've come this far with me. Now let me tell you the story behind this book and about my personal journey to no-compromise leadership.

In the introduction to this book, I told the story of the origin of the "no-compromise" mantra. No compromise empowers the action and decisive thinking that yields breakthroughs, excellence and greatness. It also sets the highest standards that form the foundation of interpersonal relationships; trust, respect, integrity and values. Since the early 1990s, I challenged my audiences and clients to allow no compromise to guide their thinking, action and behaviors. From the very instant I completed a statement with "no compromise," it was clear how deeply it resonated in one's thinking — that it made a profound and lasting impression.

Over time, I found the words *no compromise* fitting well into my writing for articles and training programs. No compromise communicated the importance of an issue I was tackling or a lesson I was trying to teach. It just felt right and became part of my writing and speaking identity.

I had the idea of writing a book that somehow incorporated no-compromise leadership spinning around in my head for quite some time. Then, in December 2004 at Strategies' annual planning session, the book idea was put on the table for discussion. By the end of that planning session, we decided it was time for me to get the book I had inside me on paper.

I was inspired by my team's confidence in me and not at all fazed by the daunting task of writing a book. My team even freed up my schedule for most of 2005 to give me the focused time I needed for writing.

Like any writer, I employed the trusted art of procrastination for a few months to ponder exactly what this book was going to be. After almost three months of wracking my brain, finally in March 2005, I decided that if I was going to write a meaningful business book, the title had to be *No-Compromise Leadership: A Higher Standard of Leadership Thinking and Behavior.*

From the very beginning, my intention was to write a book that would be worthy of sitting on a shelf alongside my favorite business books, like Jack Stack's *The Great Game of Business*, Larry Bossidy's *Execution* and Verne Harnish's *Mastering the Rockefeller Habits*. Simply put, I wanted to write a book that could go toe-to-toe with the best business books and writers out there. My book had to not only inspire no-compromise leadership, but provide the tools necessary for both an individual and a company to make the transition.

> I was writing a leadership manifesto not only for the reader — but for me as well.

On March 29, 2005, I wrote the chapter outline that divided the book into three parts. Part I focused on the individual and how to become a no-compromise leader. Part II introduced The Four Business Outcomes and gave the tools, systems and steps required for a leader to transition a company to no compromise. Part III was all about the culture shift and making it stick. I liked the flow. I was ready to begin.

For the next five months, I worked from home. Slowly but surely the words began to flow. As I completed each chapter, I would print it out and add it to the manuscript pile. That pile represented progress and, as it grew, I'd glance at it every now and then for motivation.

The 61,078-word wall

As the writing slowly progressed, I found myself getting deeper into the true essence of no-compromise leadership. What was once an *exclamation mark* that I used to emphasize a point became something profoundly personal. Where I had once thought of myself as a no-compromise leader, my writing proved otherwise. My writing lifted my personal leadership bar to a place it had never been. In the process, the writing became more labored and difficult. I was writing a leadership manifesto not only for the reader — but for me, as well.

It was as if my writing was doing the ultimate gap analysis on my own leadership thinking and behavior. I kept thinking about my own company and if "the author" of No-Compromise Leadership was, in fact, a no-compromise leader himself. It's difficult to express just how deep my own words and self analysis pushed and questioned my own value as a leader.

I had just completed chapter nine on making the culture shift to no compromise when I hit the wall. *I was at 61,078 words when I stopped writing.* I was unsettled and frustrated. Where I once wrote with vigor and confidence, at 61,078 words I felt self doubt — I felt like an imposter. How could I continue to write a book on no-compromise leadership, when I was questioning my own validity as a no-compromise leader?

My company was doing fine but it wasn't without its challenges. There were lingering issues that, while writing the book, I realized I had been avoiding. Why? Because I knew addressing those issues in a no-compromise manner could cause a major

> **Where I once wrote with vigor and confidence, at 61,078 words I felt self doubt — I felt like an imposter.**

upheaval. Simply put, the team I had come to love and enjoy working with would have to change. *I compromised and my company paid the price.*

Depression hurts

Writing the book set something in motion within me. I became angry at myself for not seeing my own compromise. And then there was the unfinished book manuscript sitting on the corner of my desk to remind me that the guy who wrote those words wasn't worthy of the title of his book. And the fact that it sat unfinished for two years was a testament to my own compromise. I just couldn't bring myself to write another word. Something needed to change first. I knew that change had to be me.

From the summer of 2005 until May 2007, I literally drove myself into a state of depression. For the first time in my business life, I blew up in the office and yelled at an employee. Not in private but at a leadership team meeting. It was ugly. I felt sick to my stomach. I didn't recognize this person I had become. I'll never forget the looks of despair on the faces of my team. This was not me. This certainly was not Strategies. Yet, it was real. I needed help.

The last thing I ever thought I would be doing is sitting on a nice leather sofa in a therapist's office getting my head shrunk. But I was a wreck and needed to find answers. We talked about all sorts of stuff, like family and upbringing. There were some enlightenments, but it just felt good to be able to talk freely and to have someone explain that depression is something you just can't snap out of.

> **I didn't know this person I had become. I'll never forget the looks of despair on the faces of my team. This was not me.**

The sabbatical

It was the middle of May 2007 when I hit bottom. I wasn't happy. I was questioning my abilities. Most of all, I knew I was creating a funk in the office. I decided to make some serious changes in order to get better and get back to "being Neil" — the torch carrier for no-compromise leadership. I had to do it for my wife, Joanne, my family, my company... and myself.

A few months earlier, I was speaking at Jack Stack's National Gathering of Games in St. Louis, and decided to sit in on Verne Harnish's pre-conference workshop. There was one statement he made that really resonated with me. Verne said, "Every six or seven years, a leader should take six or seven weeks off to recharge." I had been thinking about what it would be like to take a month or so off, but each time my entrepreneurial voice would say, "Hey, are you nuts? You can't take a month off. Get back to work."

So, with the support of my team, I decided to take some extended time off. Not just six or seven weeks, I decided to take a three-month sabbatical from Memorial Day until just after Labor Day. I must admit that when I was leaving the office to begin the sabbatical, I felt like I would never return to Strategies... the company I founded and loved. It was quite unsettling.

The very first thing I did was read a book called *Younger Next Year* by Chris Crowley and Henry S. Lodge, MD. Following the book's recommendations,

I committed to going to the gym every day rather than my usual every other day. Wow, within a week I could feel a difference.

After a few weeks, I decided to kick it up a notch and started doing spin class in addition to weight training. I thought I was going to die at that first spin class — but kept going back. Since I live in the beautiful Connecticut River Valley and Long Island Sound area, I decided to buy a road bike to enjoy my workouts outside. I did 10 miles, then 20, finally working up to 30 to 50 miles per ride. Six months later on New Year's Eve, I had racked up 901 miles on that bike. During the winter, I did spin class four to five times a week. On weekends, I worked out on my bike mounted on a trainer. And if the temperature went over 40 degrees, I went for a 30-mile ride.

I was hooked. In April 2008, I bought a carbon fiber road bike. Three weeks later, I did my first 75-mile ride. On June 27-28, I did a 150-mile ride for MS from Boston Harbor to Provincetown at the tip of Cape Cod. (*In the process, I raised $5,600 for MS — 15th highest individual fund raiser out of 1,700 riders.*) I did my first century ride (100 miles) that August and second century in the Berkshires of Massachusetts that September.

So what's the point of all this? At 58 years old, I'm in the best shape of my life. I'm more productive and more on top of my game than at any other time in my career. My thinking is clear and I have the energy to do whatever comes my way. My attitude

> On June 27-28, I did a 150-mile ride for MS from Boston Harbor to Provincetown at the tip of Cape Cod.

is purely positive. Strategies is having our best year in its 15-year history. Problems don't wreck me — I wreck them with action.

It all began with a commitment to take care of me, so I can take care of everyone and everything else. For me, working out was the key to managing stress. (A fine wine or a Bombay Sapphire doesn't hurt either.) If you say that you don't have the time to work out, my response is simple, "Stop compromising. You'll have the time if you make time." No compromise.

And here's what makes it all worth the effort. In the past year, more people have said to me, "You look great, you look younger." Younger next year — that was my goal. *This no-compromise stuff works.*

My return to no-compromise

I have to admit that during my sabbatical, I thought about selling Strategies. I just wasn't sure I wanted to go back. I even had a few conversations, but they did more to convince me that selling Strategies now would be akin to that unfinished book manuscript sitting on my desk. If I truly believed in myself, I had to go back. I had to finish what I started. There was no way I was going to go out a depressed pile of compromise. No way.

I returned to work on September 10, 2007. It was really strange walking back into the office after three months at home — but I was ready. I already knew the changes that had to be made and all that started falling into place the next day. Two employees who had been with the company for eight years resigned. All three of us knew it was coming to an end and that it was time for them to move on.

> There was no way I was going to go out a depressed pile of compromise. No way.

My next challenge was to decide the future of *Strategies* magazine. We had been publishing our 16-page business newsletter for almost fourteen years. When the first issue was printed in January 1994, there was no Internet. In time, selling a subscription for $89 for 12 issues became increasingly difficult. We hired circulation consultants who designed some pretty cool mailers, but the response rates were consistently less than inspiring. When I took a hard look at the numbers in October 2007, the publication was a mere 7.4 percent of the company's revenue. Our strength and reputation were built upon our business training, seminars and coaching business. The problem was, I loved my skinny publication and for too long, refused to confront the reality that it was a pure cash drain. My other concern was what to do with the 2,500 paid subscribers. We had an obligation to fulfill their subscriptions.

We did explore some interesting options to publish *Strategies* in an on-line format. However, that would still have us in the subscription business. I also didn't feel our current subscribers would see the value in pixels over print.

I finally confronted the reality of *Strategies* magazine and decided that the December 2007 issue would be its last. That would represent 14 complete years of publishing. Not too shabby, considering the short life span of many publications. And I came up with the perfect solution to fulfill our obligation to our paid subscribers. We created a fine-looking CD that contained PDFs of all 14 years of *Strategies* — 168 issues in all. We even included a $200 gift coupon that could be applied to the registration fee for any Strategies seminars.

That final issue went out in a poly bag, along with a letter from me explaining exactly why we were ending the publication, as well as the gift CD. How did it all turn out? A few months later, while attending an awards banquet in Chicago, an executive from a global technical training company approached me, shook my hand, and said, "The way you ended *Strategies* magazine was pure class."

I finally confronted the reality of *Strategies* magazine and decided that the December 2007 issue would be its last.

With the publication behind us, I turned my attention to our education and coaching businesses. First, I wanted to rebuild our education offering and get it back to delivering the solid and aggressive business content *Strategies* was founded on and away from the softer motivational stuff. The coaching business definitely needed retooling and some kind of automation to control and manage it. We especially needed a central database that our coaches around the country could access remotely.

Just before Thanksgiving, I took a ride to New Jersey to see a respected business owner and friend, John Harms, president of Harms Software. Harms Millennium software is the premier point-of-sale system for salons, spas and medical spas.

As a featured speaker at the Harms User Group Conferences for many years, as well as an avid supporter of Millennium, I would sit in awe, as John Harms previewed Millennium's new features and capabilities. So much so that I began to crave having all those capabilities at Strategies. From scheduling coaching calls and seminars to processing sales, coaching packages and business training products, I wanted to have all that vital data in one company database. Every time John finished his presentation on new features, I would say, "I wish we could do all that at Strategies." He would always answer, "We run Harms Software on Millennium. You can, too."

I had an awesome meeting with John and I learned exactly how Millennium, with barely any tweaking, could run not only our coaching business, but our seminars and mail order businesses, as well.

Strategies went live on Millennium in January 2008. Our national network of Certified Strategies Coaches (CSC) now has access to their coaching and training schedules, not to mention a convenient system to record coaching client notes, progress, assignments and next steps. And as long as there is Internet access, CSCs and Strategies corporate office can access Millennium from anywhere in the world.

> **I will answer any and all questions. When I finish, we close the book on yesterday and start building the future of Strategies.**

The high accountability Millennium brought to our coaching business can only be described as no compromise at its best. Nothing, absolutely nothing, falls through the cracks.

In December 2007, I brought our team of coaches together for our annual planning session. It was the first time everyone came together since my return and the personnel changes in the office. When the meeting started, they all had one question that needed to be answered. Is Neil really back and functioning in no-compromise mode? I started the meeting off with a full explanation of what transpired in my personal life and at the company. I completed that segment by saying, "I will answer any and all questions. When I finish, we close the book on yesterday and start building the future of Strategies." *We never looked back.*

That four-day planning session was truly empowering. We divided up into groups and rebuilt our education offerings piece by piece. Actually, I clarified the mission and let them loose to build *their* futures. I wanted them to have ownership — for Strategies education to be their creation, not something built in the office. They were on fire and innovation flowed.

I also made more significant changes. I put five of our coaches on payroll and gave three of them key positions in the company. We had tried paying piece work and that just created a commission mentality that no one on either side of the relationship cared for.

Here's the power of no compromise. Within four months of returning from my sabbatical, I completely reengineered my company. The funk that had permeated the office was gone. Yes, I take ownership for that funk because I created it. I was the one responsible. I was the one who had to clean it up.

In the first four months of 2008, Strategies' revenues were running 40 percent over the same period last year. Profit was running at over 35 percent. It was the company's best four-month start ever.

That unfinished manuscript

It was March 17, 2008. I was on a flight from Edmonton, Alberta, to Chicago. I was flying home after completing a speech at a conference. On that flight was another presenter, my old friend and author, Dr. Lew Losoncy. As Lew passed me on the way to the restroom, I remembered him saying how he helped a couple of women pitch their book idea to his publisher. I decided it was time to do something about that unfinished manuscript.

I opened my computer to the cover design for *No-Compromise Leadership* and lay in wait for his return. I stopped Lew in the aisle and said, "This is the cover of a book I've been writing. I have 61,078 words done. Can you help me get this book published?" I gave him an overview of the book. Lew flipped over what he saw and heard. He spent the

> Within four months of returning from my sabbatical, I completely reengineered my company.

next 30 minutes standing in the aisle as we talked about the book. He told me he would call his publisher about my book as soon as we landed in Chicago before catching his connection to Florida.

It was great to feel that excitement return to a project that had become my nemesis for over two years. Before I even walked off that plane, I made the decision that it was time to complete the book — that I finally had what I needed to write the ending. It didn't matter if Lew was going to make that call to his publisher or not, I was going to finish the book. At 6:30 that night, Lew called me with instructions to call his publisher,

Dennis McClellan at DC Press. "He's anxious to talk to you about your book." I called Dennis the following day and sent him the cover page, spread designs and, of course, the manuscript. Needless to say, I was nervous, as only a few had seen all that I had written. Was it worthy? Could my book compete with the best-of-the-best business books out there? Those were my burning questions.

About two weeks passed without a word. I was on pins and needles. Then, on April 10, I received an e-mail from the publisher that said, "I read your book cover-to-cover. *This book needs to be published.*"

My personal journey to re-discovering the no-compromise leader took me down some strange and emotional paths. For me, the journey was worth it. I sincerely hope your journey to no compromise brings wondrous accomplishments and fulfillment to you and all those you lead.

NEIL DUCOFF is the founder and CEO of Strategies, which provides business education and coaching to small- and mid-sized companies. Based in Centerbrook, Conn., Strategies' cutting-edge curriculum of business courses is offered throughout the U.S. and Canada, taught by a national network of certified coaches who have completed a rigorous training program. For 13 years Strategies published a monthly business magazine that provided real-world solutions to entrepreneurs.

Neil has gained international respect as the guru of team-based compensation. Neil is the author of the award-winning No-Compromise Leadership: A Higher Standard of Leadership Thinking and Behavior, and is co-author of Fast Forward, the salon and spa industry's only business reference manual.

Neil Ducoff has taught countless businesses how to achieve the highest levels of success and profitability, while creating a positive, rewarding workplace. He has led seminars in the U.S., Canada, United Kingdom, Taiwan, Spain and Mexico – and has served as a presenter at healthcare, computer, manufacturing and franchise conferences, including Jack Stack's National Gathering of Games, the 2011 Quality Conference and the inaugural Esthetics China Exhibition and Congress.

He has been honored with the 2005 Art of Business Award, named one of 12 business "Legends and Icons" by the 2006 Serious Business Conference, and invited by the B.E.S.T Foundation and the Anderson School of Business at UCLA to serve as a judge for both the 2006 and 2008 Global Salon Business Awards.

He lives in Old Saybrook, Conn., with his wife, Joanne, and their spoiled Lhasa Apso named Rocky.

"As the premier resort in the Sacramento Region, Arden Hills Resort Club & Spa's management and staff have all benefited from Neil Ducoff's systems, books and business philosophies. Ducoff's unique no-compromise leadership approach consistently enables our management team to work through interpersonal roadblocks and difficult personnel decisions, and create departmental systems to maximize productivity and collaboration. His books and business values are paramount for any business leader looking to achieve success within their organization."

Scott Sharrow, general manager
Arden Hills Resort Club & Spa
Sacramento, California

INDEX